Scenarios and Indicators for Sustainable Development—Towards A Critical Assessment of Achievements and Challenges

Scenarios and Indicators for Sustainable Development—Towards A Critical Assessment of Achievements and Challenges

Special Issue Editor

Joachim H. Spangenberg

MDPI • Basel • Beijing • Wuhan • Barcelona • Belgrade

MDPI

Special Issue Editor
Joachim H. Spangenberg
Helmholtz Centre for Environment Research UFZ
Germany
Sustainable Europe Research Institute SERI Germany
Germany

Editorial Office
MDPI
St. Alban-Anlage 66
4052 Basel, Switzerland

This is a reprint of articles from the Special Issue published online in the open access journal *Sustainability* (ISSN 2071-1050) from 2018 to 2019 (available at: https://www.mdpi.com/journal/sustainability/special_issues/scenarios_indicators_sustainable_development)

For citation purposes, cite each article independently as indicated on the article page online and as indicated below:

LastName, A.A.; LastName, B.B.; LastName, C.C. Article Title. *Journal Name* **Year**, *Article Number*, Page Range.

ISBN 978-3-03897-672-1 (Pbk)
ISBN 978-3-03897-673-8 (PDF)

Cover image courtesy of Joachim Spangenberg.

Contents

About the Special Issue Editor

Joachim H. Spangenberg is research coordinator at the Sustainable Europe Research Institute SERI Germany in Cologne. With a PhD in economics, but an academic background in biology and ecology, he is an inter- and transdisciplinary researcher by education and dedication. He works on sustainable development strategies, scenarios, and indicators, sustainable consumption, biodiversity conservation by pressure reduction, ecosystem services, and their valuation—with a focus on the limits of economic measurement. Joachim is a member of the Scientific Committee of the European Environment Agency, and a former member of the OECD Green Growth and Sustainable Development Task Force and the European Commis-sion High Level Economists Expert Group on Resource Efficiency. Currently, he serves on the **executive committees** of the International Society for Sustainable Development Research ISDRS, the **executive committee** International Network of Engineers and Scientists for Global Responsibility INES, and the Steering Committee of the Ecosystem Services Partnership ESP. His publication record includes more than 550 publications, including more than 90 in international peer reviewed journals, and 15 books. In Google Scholar (of Feb 6th, 2019), his most cited article has been quoted 450 times, contributing to 8098 citations in total, and a h-index of 43. In academia.edu (60 million mem-bers) he is ranked amongst the top 2% of scholars. For more information, publications, presentations and a CV please visit http://seri.academia.edu/JoachimHSpangenberg or https://www.researchgate.net/profile/Joachim_Spangenberg

Preface to "Scenarios and Indicators for Sustainable Development—Towards A Critical Assessment of Achievements and Challenges"

The global ecosphere is a complex, evolving system, and the anthroposphere is another, more rapidly evolving one. Globaliza-tion and telecoupling are enhancing their complexity, and even more that of coupled socio-ecological systems. Sustainable development as a global normative development concept, as defined by the UN Agenda 2030 and its Sustainable Develop-ment Goals SDGs, adds another level of complexity. As a result, the demand for tools to identify transformative innovations, assess future risks, and support precautionary decision making for sustainability is growing by the day in business and poli-tics.

Scenarios and indicators are such means for simplification, reducing the real-world complexity to a potentially high but lim-ited number of factors, analyzing and monitoring their interaction, and supporting policy formulation. However, there are no 'objective' representations of reality as they will inevitably reflect the orientations and norms held by their authors (and inter-preted by readers based on their values and understanding).

While political or management demands can emerge rather spontaneously, the development of new models and scenarios takes time. In particular, responding to such demands by running new scenarios with updated data and parameter setting while the models' structures remain largely the same is the standard reaction, as the integrated assessment models (IAMs) used all over the world for sustainable development strategy development are complex, combine sub-models from different disciplines and require time, work, and funding to be structurally modified. However, these models themselves are criticized (and, in particular, the economic computable global equilibrium CGE sub-models most of them incorporate) for a lack of transparency, veiled implicit assumptions, inability to capture stark and structural changes of effect driving mechanisms, technical insufficiencies, and political bias. For instance, the IPCC's model-based warnings are ever more severe with every new report—is this due to a worsening situation (i.e. so far unrecognised dynamics), or can one of the reasons be the implicit habit of scientists of avoiding type 2 errors (claiming a relationship when it does not exist) at the expense of making type 1 errors (not finding a relationship when it exists)? What roles do other habits and routines, and the world views of scholars, play in the assumptions made and the interpretations given? The latest IPCC scenarios, assuming continuous economic growth in affluent countries at the price of running into a greenhouse gas overshoot indicate that scholarly beliefs can trump physical insights—the economists involved refused to test any scenario analyzing how a no-growth, steady-state, or even degrowth economy would work out on social structures, economic prospects, and community flourishing.

To fully grasp the ongoing environmental decay (biodiversity loss and nutrient cycle overload being those where planetary boundaries have long been crossed, with climate change a rapidly upcoming third), a biophysical perspective must be the basis of scenario development. While in current modeling many (but far from all) social and economic impacts on the depend-ent trajectory of the environment are calculated, the opposite effect, direct and indirect impacts on the economic and social dimension from developments in the environmental one are hardly ever spelled out explicitly. It would require accepting posi-tive or negative feedback loops, with social and economic variables becoming dependent variables, significantly influenced by environmental development, and with a need to be managed politically to adapt societies to new external conditions. In par-ticular, 'the social' as one of the core dimensions of sustainable development is often neglected or reduced to a few measura-ble phenomena like income or employment quota. However, it includes much more than that, in particular, a society's institu-tions: The effects and dynamics of public orientations including values and preferences, decision-making mechanisms includ-ing equity, gender issues, power statures and democracy, and implementing organizations, their role and functions. All fac-tors often lend themselves better to qualitative description (at best ordinal scale, semi-quantitative measurement as used by IPCC and IPBES) rather than to quantification. That is why good scenarios consist of a narrative which is able to incorporate these qualitative arguments, and which can be illustrated with model calculations falling short of doing so. As a consequence, the 'hard data' from modeling are not the definitive result of scenario work, but they have to be interpreted in the context of the scenario narrative, which may lead to significant corrections.

Similar questions apply to indicators, one of the main tools to communicate scenario results, help to monitor selected real-world trends recognized as decisive, support communication about them, and, ultimately, decision making. However, which parameters are chosen for monitoring and which yardsticks (indicators) are applied in doing so has often more to do with established measurement methods and data availability—in particular, time series—and data consistency than with which problems are currently of the highest importance, politically, ecologically, socially, or economically. If newly emerging trends do not become an issue of reporting due to missing data time series, this implies that no phenomenon recognized as a prob-lem worth monitoring less than a quarter century ago can make it into the monitoring and reporting mechanisms. Similarly, if the data collection focusses on parameters which have been considered relevant under past theoretical assumptions, there is a risk that if such theories are falsified or recognized as outdated, the indicator reports will point in the wrong direction. This is a particular risk if only inputs, pressures, and the like are being monitored (as they are often easier to observe and quantify), and—assuming a largely linear correlation—are considered to provide evidence about a system's performance.

Reflecting these considerations, the authors of this book test established methods against new challenges, assess the weak-nesses of prevailing innovation theories and the political-ideological embedment of archetypical scenarios, highlight deficits in taking the physical basics into account, and the need to understand global interactions and the stepwise process of energy transitions. However, they not highlight the weaknesses but also possible ways to escape these dilemmas.

In a similar vein, they discuss the conceptual challenges of indicator development in a time of "fake news" and "alternative truths", point out technical as well as basic weaknesses in data collection, harmonization, and indicator generation, always with a view to solving problems. As both the rigorous analysis of weaknesses and the positive attitude to solving the prob-lems are rare in the scenario and indicators scholarly community, we sincerely hope that this volume will stimulate discus-sions and reflections, supporting colleagues in addressing those weaknesses and overcoming them. The importance of scenari-os and indicators for effective sustainability policies makes this attempt so important.

Joachim H. Spangenberg
Special Issue Editor

![sustainability logo] *sustainability*

MDPI

Article

The Politics of Selection: Towards a Transformative Model of Environmental Innovation

Daniel Hausknost [1,*] and Willi Haas [2]

[1]   Institute for Social Change and Sustainability, Vienna University of Economics and Business,
     1020 Vienna, Austria
[2]   Institute of Social Ecology, University of Natural Resources and Life Sciences (BOKU), 1070 Vienna, Austria;
     willi.haas@boku.ac.at
*   Correspondence: daniel.hausknost@wu.ac.at; Tel.: +43-1-31336-6045

Received: 8 November 2018; Accepted: 15 January 2019; Published: 18 January 2019

Abstract: As a purposive sustainability transition requires environmental innovation and innovation policy, we discuss potentials and limitations of three dominant strands of literature in this field, namely the multi-level perspective on socio-technical transitions (MLP), the innovation systems approach (IS), and the long-wave theory of techno-economic paradigm shifts (LWT). All three are epistemologically rooted in an evolutionary understanding of socio-technical change. While these approaches are appropriate to understand market-driven processes of change, they may be deficient as analytical tools for exploring and designing processes of purposive societal transformation. In particular, we argue that the evolutionary mechanism of selection is the key to introducing the strong directionality required for purposive transformative change. In all three innovation theories, we find that the prime selection environment is constituted by the market and, thus, normative societal goals like sustainability are sidelined. Consequently, selection is depoliticised and neither strong directionality nor incumbent regime destabilisation are societally steered. Finally, we offer an analytical framework that builds upon a more political conception of selection and retention and calls for new political institutions to make normatively guided selections. Institutions for transformative innovation need to improve the capacities of complex societies to make binding decisions in politically contested fields.

Keywords: environmental innovation; sustainability transition; transformation; evolutionary economics; multi-level perspective; innovation systems; long-wave theory; agency; decision-making; institutions

---

1. Introduction

The world is in the process of a two-fold 'socio-ecological transition' [1,2]. On the one hand, large parts of the world, including the 'emerging economies', are enmeshed in a transition from an agrarian, biomass-based economy to an industrial, fossil-energy-driven one. On the other hand, there are increasing global efforts to initiate a so-called 'sustainability transition' [3–5] away from a fossil-energy based economy to a post-fossil, sustainable one. While the industrial transition is by far the dominant phenomenon to date [2], there are signs that the per-capita energy and resource use has started to level off in the most advanced industrial countries [6]. There is a clear danger, however, that if the societal project of a transition to sustainability fails, there will be another type of transition: one that results from a combination of resource depletion and the violation of vital biophysical boundaries and that may end in socio-economic collapse [7–9].

Innovation policy has played an important role in both the on-going industrial transition and the incipient sustainability transition. However, while the industrial transition is driven by the inherent dynamics of socio-technical evolution in a globalising world economy and by the universal quest for economic growth and material prosperity, the incipient *sustainability transition* is driven by *normatively* and *scientifically* defined goals that are, to some extent, countervailing these dynamics. Innovation has traditionally been at the service of the project of economic expansion, thereby contributing "massively to the current resource-intensive, wasteful and fossil fuel-based paradigm of mass production and mass consumption" [10], but has now to be put at the service of a transformation toward sustainability [11,12]. Innovation policy thus needs to become instrumental to transformation policy [10]. The *normative* nature of the sustainability transition, however, makes it an irreducibly *political* project, whose goals and objectives will always remain contested as they challenge vested interests, established values and deep-rooted social practices [13]. Until today, "transition and innovation policies [have] only [been] aligned when they stimulate innovations that contribute to both economic growth and sustainable development", as Alkemade et al. [11] put it. But as long as further growth continues to stimulate further resource consumption and as long as the leakage and rebound effects inherent to efficiency-driven innovations remain unresolved, this might not be good enough [14,15]. In this paper, therefore, we undertake a re-examination of dominant conceptions of environmental innovation with a view to their capacities to propel a comprehensive sustainability transition. We are particularly interested to find out if theories of innovation and socio-technical change in the environmental domain are adequately addressing the *directionality* of change required for a purposive societal transition [12]. In any truly transformative model of innovation theory and policy, directionality expresses the fact that the socially or politically willed direction of change might differ significantly from the patterns of change that typically drive innovation processes. Thus, the crucial question a transformative model of innovation needs to answer is how such externally (as in: extra-economically) defined directionality can be implemented and secured against the dominant dynamics of socio-technical progress in case both turn out to diverge significantly. More concretely, how can a purposively defined transformative trajectory be empowered and retained, even if the unsustainable alternatives were to promise more growth, higher consumer utility and higher profits?

In addition, we argue that a transformative theory of innovation needs to be able to address the problem of incumbent regime *destabilisation* [16] and thus of *creative destruction* [17] in a proactive, effective and purposive manner. Put another way, a transformative model of innovation fit for the purpose of a time-bound and radical transformation of industrial society toward sustainability may not content itself with the innocent role of fostering novelty, diversity and market choice; it will most likely have to be of a more determined, conflictive and 'creatively destructive' nature than its growth-oriented predecessors.

Theories of innovation (including the three dominant strands we analyse in this article) typically rely on evolutionary conceptions of socio-technical change. In evolutionary economic theory, change is emerging as a pattern of interactions between processes of variation, selection and retention of novel traits. While innovation is frequently reduced to its function of generating 'diversity' (variation), the crucial functions of selection and retention in turning diversity into purposive directional change are frequently undertheorised or left to the 'micro-processes' of individual choice which are conceptualised as aggregating into 'meso-trajectories' of change [18,19]. While convincing as descriptive-analytical accounts of socio-technical change in a market-mediated society under conditions of universal economic expansion, these evolutionary models, we argue, are lacking the conceptual instruments to capture fully the *political* nature of directionality and thus the *political* dimension of the selection and retention functions, in particular. In analogy to its epistemic roots in biology, socio-technical evolution is frequently portrayed as a *natural* and *apolitical* process that can be steered only by influencing the 'selection environment' within which populations of consumers and entrepreneurs make their respective choices. The idea that variation, selection and retention all can be (and usually are) subject to political (that is, binding collective) decision-making and will-formation has not yet been sufficiently applied to these theories of change. We argue that a theory of transformative innovation has analytically to embrace the political dimension of selection as well as of retention and variation and propose institutional and procedural answers to the crucial question of how to implement transformative directionality, regime destabilisation and creative destruction.

Against this backdrop, we discuss the contributions of three influential strands of literature in the field of environmental innovation and transition studies. These are the multi-level perspective on socio-technical transitions (MLP), the innovation systems approach (IS), and the long-wave theory of techno-economic paradigm shifts (LWT). We then propose an analytical framework, based on the distinction of so-called 'agentic operators', which proposes a more political conception of selection and retention. We conclude with some concrete proposals for the conception of transformative innovation policy and with suggestions for further research.

2. The Multi-Level Perspective (MLP)

In recent years, the multi-level perspective on socio-technical transitions has become perhaps the most influential theoretical framework in the field of environmental innovation [20]. Combining concepts from evolutionary economics, science and technology studies, structuration theory and neo-institutional theory, the MLP builds on an analytical distinction of niches, regimes and landscapes as functionally distinct but interrelated levels that shape the process of socio-technical transitions. Niches are the locus of radical innovation; they are 'protected spaces' such as "R&D (research and development) laboratories, subsidised demonstration projects or small market niches where users have special demands and are willing to support emerging innovations". In this perspective, "niches are crucial for transitions, because they provide the seeds for systemic change" [21].

Such systemic change can only occur, however, when and if radical innovations manage to pervade and restructure the level of the socio-technical regime. Since transitions are defined in the literature as shifts from one regime to another, this is the crucial analytical level for transition research [21]. The socio-technical regime forms the 'deep structure' that accounts for the stability of an existing socio-technical system. It "refers to the semi-coherent set of rules that orient and coordinate the activities of the social groups that reproduce the various elements of socio-technical systems" [21], such as "cognitive routines and shared beliefs, capabilities and competences, lifestyles and user practices, favourable institutional arrangements and regulations, and legally binding contracts" [21].The rules of a regime account for the stability and lock-in of a concrete socio-technical system [22].

The landscape level, finally, "highlights not only the technical and material backdrop that sustains society, but also includes demographic trends, political ideologies, societal values, and macro-economic patterns" [22]. What defines the landscape level analytically is that it presents "an external context that actors at niche and regime levels cannot influence in the short run" [22].

A typical pattern of a socio-technical regime transition would be that (a) niche-innovations build up internal momentum, (b) changes at the landscape level create pressures on the regime, and (c) destabilisation of the regime creates windows of opportunity for niche innovations [22]. Historical examples of radical innovations like the automobile show an impressive journey from their start in a niche, through the domination of entire regimes to their structuring of the global socio-technical landscape.

The main transformative task from the multi-level perspective is to *manage* the all-important interaction between niches and regimes in a purposive and goal-oriented way. To support a sustainability transition means to help radical environmental innovations get off the ground in niches and pervade the socio-technical regimes. In order to do so these innovations must break established rules and structures in the regimes, which lock them into their current state. The purposive management of the interaction of niches and regimes has become a central concern within the MLP literature, and led to the development of specific sub-strands like transition management (TM) [23] and strategic niche management (SNM) [24].

Drawing on evolutionary economics, the MLP and its transition management variants apply the Darwinian concepts of variation, selection and retention to the socio-technical evolution of modern societies. Regimes are conceived both as *retention* structures and *selection* environments for innovations (*variation*) [22,25]. In their capacity as selection environments for innovative variants regimes comprise a number of structural features that work as selection mechanisms, including market mechanisms and dominant user practices, established industry structures, dominant technologies and infrastructures, and public policies [25]. The aim of transition (and strategic niche) management now is to introduce a certain measure of agency into these processes. Whereas variation in capitalist market environments is usually driven by the profit motive (i.e., by firms' interest to survive in the market and, ideally, to grow; see [26]), the aim is now to introduce 'directed variation' that is not only driven by market interests but also by other (sustainability-related and thus normative) intentions [22].

What the evolutionary perspective tends to neglect, however, is the fact that the evolutionary dynamics of modern industrialism, which serve as the epistemological foundation of the MLP, could only unfold in an environment that was characterised by an expansive (fossil) energy system. The evolution of modern economy has been based on the availability of ever increasing quantities of cheap, concentrated and abundant energy [27–29]. The selection mechanisms at work were and are geared towards further expansion and growth of the system. When left to the evolutionary dynamics that were unleashed some 250 years ago, it appears likely that the system will use up all the available energy it can find until it runs into the landscape pressures of resource shortages, price increases and severe environmental constraints. The MLP and its variants aim at overcoming the evolutionary selection trap either through protecting and nurturing niches for sustainable innovations (SNM) [25] or through designing complex governance models that try to influence both variation and selection (TM) [30]. Both strategies tend to naturalise evolutionary selection pressures, however, by taking markets as given selection environments. Geels [31] argues that "most transition-scholars focus on 'green' niche-innovations, they pay less attention to existing regimes and incumbent actors, or conceptualize regimes as monolithic 'barriers to be overcome', which runs counter to the initial MLP-formulations and the emphasis on multi-level alignments". A literature review covering 386 journal articles concludes that a reason for new ideas not diffusing rapidly through companies may be due to "overarching structures of markets, patterns of final consumer demand, institutional and regulatory systems and inadequate infrastructures for change" [32]. This suggests that—despite its focus on governing the interface between niches and regime—the MLP literature tends to regard the selection mechanisms as naturally given, unquestionable and subject only to modification and management. Thus, TM, for example, "understands the relation transition initiatives adopt towards existing regimes not in political, but in market terms" [33]. According to Kemp and Loorbach [34] TM is about 'context control', so as "to orient market dynamics towards societal goals". While this may involve regulation and economic instruments, change itself emerges in an evolutionary manner as the aggregate of consumer choices. In that way, Kenis et al. [33] admonish, "transitions stay locked in a liberal market model that does not acknowledge the need of its own transition". In a word, MLP scholars try to insert some directionality into the governance of selection mechanisms they consider to be naturally given, instead of challenging the very nature of the selection mechanisms themselves. Recent attempts to unravel the political in MLP-based transition literature [35] tend to overstate the complexity of political processes involved when trying to give directionality to markets, thereby creating an endless field of future research that allows the more pressing task of designing transition mechanisms beyond the market to be evaded. We argue instead that the evolutionary selection trap may be effectively overcome only through the purposive construction of selection mechanisms that negotiate and ultimately express societal goals. It might, thus, be more important to focus on innovating the selection mechanisms of industrial societies and to equip them with purposefully designed (and democratically controlled) selection criteria than to focus on getting sustainable innovations selected by *unsustainable selection environments*.

A managerial approach toward the relationship between niches and the regime on the basis of market mechanisms also raises questions about the power of the niches to ever escape the normative force of the regime. As Bulkeley et al. [36] aptly put it, the "key role ascribed to government actors in creating 'protected' spaces for niche development [also] raises questions as to whether niches are established in order to maintain regimes rather than as a means of fostering change". As long as niches are at the mercy of the regime to protect their space from the forces of the market until they are ready to compete, they remain subjected to the dominant logic of the regime and the market, which defines what successful competition means.

Thus, we suggest focusing on 'selection' instead of 'variation' and on regimes instead of niches. This is not because variation or niches are unimportant, but because the limiting factor is the purposive selection, upscaling and mainstreaming of innovations—if necessary against the regime—in order to transform the regime. Niches may be nested within regimes, but transformative innovation requires acknowledgement that their relationship may (or perhaps even must) at some point become antagonistic and thus requires institutions that are not managerial but political.

3. Innovation Systems

Another influential strand of innovation research is the innovation system (IS) approach. Rooted in evolutionary economic theorizing, it was developed as a policy concept in the mid-1980s [37–39]. In contradistinction to the MLP, the IS approach does not focus on the interaction between different levels of socio-technical emergence, but on the interaction of actors, networks and institutions in steering and influencing innovation dynamics. Its original aim was to make national economies more competitive and resilient under conditions of increasing global competition and receding growth rates after the oil crises of the 1970s [10]. According to Jacobsson and Bergek [40], innovation systems are composed of a set of structural elements: actors in the whole supply chain, networks, institutions, and, in some approaches, technology. While actors can be individuals or organisations, institutions are conceived along the lines of neo-institutional theory as formal and informal rules, "comprising laws and regulations, socio-cultural as well as technical norms, shared expectations, etc." [41]. Over the years, different types of innovation systems were analytically distinguished and conceptualised, including national innovation systems (NIS), sectoral innovation systems (SIS), regional innovation systems (RIS) and technological innovation systems (TIS).

With respect to sustainability transitions, the most productive approach within the innovation systems literature so far has been the TIS approach, which focuses on the development and diffusion of *specific* technologies, rather than on the general conditions of innovation in nations, regions or industry sectors. The purpose of TIS analysis is to identify possible system weaknesses that often result from the misalignment of system components in the sense that certain structures of the system hinder actors at cooperating or that the institutional preconditions for entrepreneurial experimentation are lacking. Institutional frame conditions such as funding schemes or research frameworks heavily influence the direction of search for new technological solutions and can potentially lead a TIS into a dead end. Similarly, there is a range of institutional and organisational preconditions for successful (human and financial) resource mobilisation and market formation. In the absence of a specific regulatory framework, for example, a new technology will have severe difficulties developing a market or attracting capital. In addition, a range of institutional conditions has to be met in order for a new technology to gain the political and cultural legitimacy to be diffused successfully [40].

In sum, the IS approach looks at the actors and institutions of specific innovation systems with the goal of identifying points of policy intervention that would help enhance the overall performance of the system or stimulate certain types of innovation. The focus of the IS approach is thus on the politics (the socio-institutional setting) of innovation rather than on the economics of innovation in a strict sense. This makes it an interesting approach in terms of addressing the purposive, normative and goal-oriented nature of a sustainability transition. Since the prospect of such a transition is widely believed to depend on the development, diffusion and comprehensive use of radical environmental innovations, the IS approach can help identify the points of intervention necessary to stimulate and support the success of such technologies. A clear focus in this literature is on the role the state plays in the creation and transfer of knowledge within innovation systems [42,43]. The assumption is that knowledge does not build up linearly but has to be mediated between different actors and organisations in order to become productive in an entrepreneurial way. Particular importance is attributed to the role of state-funded research and universities in connection with private R&D activities, implying that "universities should become more entrepreneurial, fostering new company formation through spin-offs and licensing technology produced through university research" [10]. Recently, Mariana Mazzucato has emphasised the role states have (and have always had) in providing the direction towards "new 'techno-economic paradigms', which do not come about spontaneously out of market forces"[44]. Past socio-technical revolutions were decisively enabled and shaped by direct investments and funding decisions of states, who took on the role of venture capitalists [45]. However, the approach arguably suffers from constraints similar to those of the MLP as it grounds its ontology in an evolutionary process that it assumes as 'given'. Despite its acknowledgement of the state's role in "shaping and creating markets" [44], it considers market diffusion as the natural goal and (venture) capital attraction as the natural condition of innovation [44,45]. For the IS approach, "technological change and other kinds of innovations are the most important sources of productivity growth and increased material welfare" [46]. That way, fostering innovation appears as a naturally beneficial goal. In subjecting its concept of social utility to market forces, however, the IS literature risks paying insufficient attention to the question if and how selection can be controlled by societal goals other than productivity growth and material welfare. Put differently, the state in IS may be instrumental in strategically creating the conditions for new markets (and thus technologies) to emerge and, therefore, has the power to insert a certain measure of directionality into the innovation process (like promoting energy efficiency or raising the prices of fossil energy), but success or failure of the new technologies are decided under the 'normal' conditions of market take-up by consuming individuals and other market participants. As in past socio-technical revolutions, the strategically supported direction of innovation has to offer higher (or new) consumer utility, higher profits and new growth opportunities to prevail in the market, which remains the ultimate selection environment. To the extent that a sustainability transition requires the primacy of societal goals that might be incompatible with the above naturalised 'selectors' of the market, however, the IS approach in its current state may be ill equipped to lead societies beyond the established trajectory of socio-technological evolution.

4. Long Wave Theory—A Sustainable 6th Kondratiev?

The theory of long waves or techno-economic paradigms (TEPs) is the third approach to innovation thinking we want to discuss here. It combines the theory of long waves of economic development put forward most prominently by Nikolai Kondratiev (1935) with the evolutionary economic theory of Joseph Schumpeter that posits radical technological innovation as the "single root cause of the cyclical behaviour of the capitalist economy" [26]. Thus, Kondratiev waves are conceptualised as a succession of TEPs, each based on a decisive technological innovation (like the steam engine, the automobile or microelectronics), a core input (e.g., coal, oil or silicon microchips) and a carrier branch that drives the development (like railways, automobiles or the computer industry). Five such long waves or TEPs have shaped capitalist development since the Industrial Revolution at the end of the 18th century. The first was based on the water-powered mechanisation of industry and on the iron industry and started in the 1770s. The second was relying on the steam-powered mechanisation of industry and transport, dating back to the 1830s. The third was based on the electrification of industry, transport and the home and started in the 1870s. The fourth TEP was constituted by the motorisation of society, with the key innovation being Ford's Model-T automobile from 1914. The fifth and current TEP, finally, is based on microelectronics and started in the 1970s [26,47].

The succession of TEPs transforms societies economically and technologically in that it leads to extended phases of economic growth but also to socio-economic crises of 'creative destruction'. Typically, the new wave emerges out of the crisis of the old: as profit rates decline in the application of the incumbent paradigm, more and more 'idle' capital is invested in new technologies that promise greater potential for future profits. In socio-economic terms, however, the greatest disruptions occur when a new TEP is in its explosive growth phase competing fiercely with the established paradigm. It is the phase where investment bubbles in the new TEP occur, leading to great financial crises, and where societies have to adapt institutionally and organisationally to the new paradigm (reacting to new forms of employment, new industries, the destruction of old industries and infrastructures and concomitant political changes). After this turbulent phase, the new TEP will continue to grow, promising a short period of sustained growth that Perez calls the 'Golden Age' of a TEP [48].

The study of TEPs is interesting for scholars of socio-ecological transitions for several reasons: Firstly, if the theory is a valid interpretation of capitalist development, it offers opportunities for ex-ante analyses of long-term socio-technical change in that "the recurring features of Kondratiev waves can be used to extrapolate forward to possible future waves" [49]. An interesting question, from a SET perspective is, then, which new technologies might qualify for constituting the next TEP and what contribution to a sustainability transition they could offer. Secondly, if a transition towards sustainability is our normative goal, the role of purposive agency in steering a TEP or in deciding which technology will dominate the next half century or so is decisive: can long waves be influenced or even purposively steered? Or are modern societies exposed to an evolutionary dynamic that is, more or less, beyond their control? A third issue regards the energetic basis of the long waves and the question whether a 'post-fossil' energy regime could sustain a sixth wave of capitalist development at all [50].

With regard to the forecasting of the next long wave, most literature regards biotechnology and nanotechnology to be the 'hottest' candidates for the role of key technologies and sees further potential in the development of information technologies [51–53]. To what extent these technologies have the potential to carry the burden of a sustainability transition is, for obvious reasons, difficult to establish. However, the more important question might be whether a future low-carbon Kondratiev wave is a plausible scenario at all. While Kondratiev waves or TEPs represent cyclical patterns of innovation, economic growth and socio-economic crisis, the historical metabolic profile of the five historic waves so far shows the pattern of an upwards spiral. Thus, these waves have shown cumulative metabolic rates, which means that each wave added further energy and material consumption to the previous one. As Köhler points out, "the first four waves were based around intensified use of energy resources, which increased pollution through new industrial activity" [49]. Similarly, Pearson and Foxon ([54] p. 125) point to the fact that previous industrial revolutions were "*high carbon* industrial revolutions: […] their success was built on the exploitation, largely unconstrained by environmental or other regulatory concerns, of fossil fuel stocks that freed the economy from constraints it would otherwise have faced". Two important questions follow from these observations:

First, can a new TEP be envisaged that de-carbonises (by virtue of its technology-inherent properties) not only the new segment of growth industries that it adds to the inherited structure but the *entire* economy? The energy consumption in the Fifth Kondratiev, at least, does not suggest as much, since all it has achieved so far in this respect is a stabilisation but not an effective reduction in per capita energy consumption [6]. Related to this, can such a new, sustainable TEP be expected to not only decarbonise the legacy of its predecessors but also *add* a further wave of capitalist *growth and expansion*? It is of course difficult to make predictions about these questions but with the metabolic profiles of the hitherto Kondratievs in mind, which were all based mainly on cheap fossil energy, it is difficult to imagine that any technological innovation within reach today could help decarbonise the entire economy *and* add further growth to the system [50].

These considerations are important when contemplating the possibility of a *low-carbon industrial revolution*, as would be necessary for a sustainable next Kondratiev wave. As Pearson and Foxon point out, such a prospect faces a range of serious challenges [54]. Firstly, while the low-carbon technologies within reach today are good at helping decarbonise the existing economy in that they substitute 'green' alternatives for unsustainable ones, "they do not offer significant private benefits to users beyond the social benefits of lower carbon emissions" [54]. *Green* electricity, for example, is not *better* at powering our gadgets and appliances than *grey* (fossil) electricity—it is just environmentally more sustainable. What is worse, it is up to now often more expensive and, therefore, even less attractive from the perspective of private utility. Similarly, the electric car so far is not a utility-improving innovation but has some practical drawbacks like reduced range and long charging procedures; this might change, however, with the development of autonomous driving, which may add new utility, but which would only add significantly to sustainability if it leads to an overall reduction in ownership and use of cars. Hence, most low-carbon technologies today help save materials and energy but may, by themselves, not contribute to a next long wave, which would require a radical expansion of economic activity and new levels of consumption.

In the face of these challenges, Pearson and Foxon warn that "there has been a tendency to neglect or misunderstand the role that the availability of cheap, high quality, carbon intensive energy sources has played in the co-evolutionary developments in technologies, related institutions and business strategies that have underlain the unprecedented economic growth and creation of wealth in Western countries over the past 250 years" [54]. As a consequence they suggest that "for the low carbon transition to really "work", it may prove necessary to transform our energy and related systems and institutions in more profound ways than we have yet acknowledged" [54]. In other words, a new techno-economic paradigm alone may not do [2,50,55,56].

But it is precisely the question of political agency that the TEP framework is somewhat ill-equipped to address. For the TEP framework, technology is the moving force behind development, and it is difficult to influence or forecast future inventions and discoveries. In TEP, technology drives societal change, whereas in a socio-ecological transition the required societal changes would drive the trajectory of technological development. The ontology of the TEP framework grants explanatory priority to the 'landscape level', to use the MLP terminology, whereas 'niches' and even 'regimes' are of secondary importance. Consequently, Geels and Schot admonish that long-wave theory is "too much focused on the macro-environment of socio-technical systems [...] and does not provide many insights into how these transitions happen" [22]. Similarly, Köhler contends that "[t]here is no explicit treatment of agency and this means that there is no theoretical basis for proposing ways in which society can influence the development of a Kondratiev wave" [49]. Although some proponents of the TEP framework seem to be aware of this shortcoming and propose to put the question of agency centre-stage on the research agenda [57], the resulting challenge of subjecting socio-technical evolution to societal goals rather than to the 'natural' forces of capitalism appears colossal.

The discussion of the three dominant paradigms in innovation studies so far has revealed severe limitations of evolutionary economic thinking to adequately capturing and responding to the challenges of a transition to sustainability. These limitations, however, are not inherent to evolutionary theory as such, we argue, but result from its reified application to economic theory. While the past socio-technical development of modern societies can be fruitfully described using evolutionary concepts as a heuristic, it would be a mistake to conclude that future change must necessarily be subjected to the same evolutionary patterns, that is, to grant evolutionary patterns of change ontological status. The problem is the level at which the selection environment for processes of innovation is conceptually defined. In economics, the market obviously constitutes a 'natural' selection environment for product innovation. This is all well as long as the only thing that interests the analyst is the economy itself (as an abstract model based on monetary values) and not its relation to the *biophysical* environment. As soon as we are talking about a socio-ecological transition, however, we have to include the biophysical world and its limitations into the analysis, which constitutes the ultimately much more relevant selection environment. Put differently, if economic development is to be constrained by and re-embedded within *scientifically* defined 'planetary boundaries' [58], then the mode of selection has to be different to the normal workings of a market economy, for which the market is the *natural* selection environment. In evolutionary approaches technology is the independent and socio-ecological outcomes the dependent variable, while for a socio-ecological transition the desired outcomes are the independent and technology a dependent variable. Thus, the nature of the market needs to be accommodated within biophysical nature in a way that can only be defined and decided *politically*. The consequence of this is that a transition to sustainability requires a socially constructed, purposively designed set of selection mechanisms that is geared to steering that transition if necessary *against* the lure of consumer utility, profitability and the requirements of capital accumulation. This implies that a transition to sustainability is primarily about the *politics of selection* and only in the second instance about technological innovation and consumer choice. A transformative politics of socio-technical selection, however, needs to be based on robust political institutions and requires deep democratic legitimation. In the next section, we present an analytical framework that may help to better understand the challenge ahead and may become beneficial for the design of the institutions required for a seriously transformative innovation policy.

5. 'Agentic Operators' and Transformative Innovation

The framework developed in Hausknost [59] analytically distinguishes three modes of agency or 'agentic operators'. We call them 'operators' because they do different things to reality, just like mathematical operators do different things to numbers. The idea is that just like *addition, subtraction, division* and *multiplication*, so *decision, choice,* and *solution* do different things to the realities they are applied to. The concept of agentic operators offers an analytical framework to explore patterns and strategies of change, as operators are frequently combined in certain ways that result in particular trajectories of change. By applying the framework to evolutionary theorising we aim to show that the latter tends to construct an agentic regime based on the recursive interaction between 'choice' and 'solution', while largely neglecting the potential of 'decision'. There are two distinctive criteria which define the characteristics of agentic operators and which separate them from each other. One is the question whether or not the operator *eliminates the options* that are not selected in the operation. The other is the question whether the operator *selects between incommensurable options* or not, that is, whether or not it involves the need for political decision-making. Each operator combines different answers to these two questions and, therefore, constitutes a unique way of 'processing' reality. Table 1 summarises the resulting typology.

Table 1. Typology of agentic operators.

Operator	Elimination of Options	Incommensurability
decision	✓	✓
choice	-	✓
solution	✓	-

There are three logically distinct operators: decision, choice and solution. According to the two selection criteria identified, they cover all possible modes of agency. Decisions create path dependency in that they eliminate the discarded options: if I decide for X, then Y and Z are eliminated as options. Any future development will have X as its point of departure. Importantly, however, a decision always selects between options that are *incommensurable*, that is, between options that differ at least in one aspect for which there does not exist common rational ground. For example, a government of a coal-rich country might decide to ban the use and export of coal, despite negative economic consequences and some social disruption this might cause. In doing so, it would *eliminate* coal as an option instead of just promoting sustainable alternatives in the energy market and hoping for change to emerge. The decision could be based on the rationality of climate science but might make little sense in the rationality of (mainstream) economics. The act of privileging one rationality over the other—and thus of *deciding*—would ultimately have to be based on values, world views and what is sometimes called ideology. It cannot, by itself, resort to an overarching, neutral rationality that would allow for *only* this particular option.

Decisions, then, are selections between different ways to frame reality, which cannot be compared in objective terms of measurement or calculation. That is why Jacques Derrida defined decisions paradoxically as having to *pass the field of undecidability* [60]. A decision that is *decidable* would not decide anything but reveal the *solution* to a calculable problem [61].

Solutions, therefore, are defined as selections between *commensurable* options, that is, between options that can be assessed and compared within the same rational framework or paradigm. One of the options will be the *best* solution, others will be *less* ideal or even *wrong*—this ranking can be established unambiguously by applying a common unit of measurement or rationality. The selection a solution executes also eliminates the discarded options, just like in a decision: the wrong or second-best options will no longer play a role as soon as the best option is established. A more energy efficient engine, for example, will (ceteris paribus) supplant a less energy efficient one, if energy inefficiency is the problem for which a solution was sought. The ability of solutions to create path dependency, however, is severely restricted, since the path is implicitly pre-selected by the common frame of rationality. The path is calculable on the basis of the common rationality. Solutions only constitute different stages or steps of following the same path.

Choices, finally, are marked by the peculiar trait that they do *not* eliminate the options between which they select. Hence, while the options are incommensurable like in decisions, the ones a choice discards remain in the pool for further selections. A choice can be repeated at will: this time, I select X, next time Y, and another time Z. This feature makes choice the genuine agentic operator of the marketplace: Today I select a Mars chocolate bar, tomorrow a muesli bar, and the next day an organic and fair-trade chocolate bar. The options are incommensurable in that they cannot be ordered according to a one-dimensional rational framework: one day, my preference for the taste of Mars will prevail over my ambition to lead a healthy life and my desire to contribute to the creation of a 'better world'. Another day, the ranking may be reversed on the basis of different moods, cravings or manipulations by adverts [62,63].

While choice is the genuine operator of the market place, solution can be attributed to science and technology. Decision, finally, is the operator of politics proper, by virtue of politics being the name of the *undecidability* of the social: if society were a *decidable* structure, there would be no need for politics in the first place [64]. The typology, it should be mentioned, presents *ideal types* in a sociological sense rather than clear-cut phenomena of social life. In reality, the boundaries are often somewhat blurry in that large investments in a market may take the form of decisions as they actually eliminate other options for an investor, or in that 'solutions' are sometimes highly political when their actual undecidability is (deliberately) disguised under the veil of scientific rationality. But this is precisely the messy terrain we enter when talking about the steering of a purposive transition of society toward sustainability. Such a transition will inevitably require changes in all three variants-solutions to technological problems, choices for individuals and collective decisions to introduce and maintain the required directionality of change. We argue, however, that the transition to sustainability so far has largely been conceptualised as a co-evolutionary process of solutions and choices with little need for conflictual political decision-making. We challenge this naïve conception of transformation and argue that decision is perhaps the most important agentic operator for a societally steered transition process, as it sets the bounds within which solutions and choices need to take place.

5.1. Socio-Technical Evolution as a Matter of Solutions and Choices Only?

As shown above, the evolutionary economics approach to socio-technical change might be ill-equipped to design and prepare an exit strategy *out of* the fossil energy regime. The reason for this is that evolution does not pursue any *normative* goals—it simply evolves on the basis of existing conditions. However, once *normative* objectives for societal development are defined, the mechanisms driving evolution will need to be actively designed according to the *normative* requirements of change.

The mechanisms driving evolutionary change are those of variation, selection and retention. In evolutionary economics, variation is conceptualised as diversity generated through innovation. Selection reduces diversity through acts of choice by boundedly rational individuals and groups [65]. Although selection is considered to be driven by "competition, regulation and institutions" [19], the act of selection itself is understood as the cumulative result of choices that restructure the field of options. Retention, finally, is conceived as the selective replication of technologies and practices (mainly) through imitation. Here, too, retention is the result of an eventual sedimentation of patterns of choice, which may be stimulated by policies, but has little to do with collective decision-making.

Overall, socio-technical evolution is depicted as a co-evolutionary process of demand and supply, which is organised through the complex interaction of solutions (technological change) and choices (consumer preferences) [66]. When conceptualising sustainability transitions, evolutionary economics rely on the micro-meso-macro framework that has also been adopted by the MLP. The micro-level is constituted by individuals and their interactions. Individuals are conceived as carriers of rules, which, in turn, are called 'meso-units' [18]. Rules are acquired problem-solving mechanisms. They always originate from micro-processes on the level of individuals. The macro-level is where rule dynamics are governed and where rules congeal to collective routines and formal regulations. The interplay between dynamics on the micro-level (rule-generation) and macro-level (rule-coordination) creates processes of change that play out at the decisive meso-level, where new configurations of rules may stabilise.

The upshot of all this is that change is the result of myriad individuals solving problems and making choices. The recursive interrelation of all these solutions and choices generate patterns and configurations of stabilised rules, routines and institutions, which, in turn, act selectively on the option space of new choices and solutions. Directionality is thus an effect of aggregate choice. This co-evolutionary coupling of solutions and choices may be *influenced* by policies aiming at individuals and organisations, like tradeable permits and environmental taxes [19] or "ethical consumption and healthy habits" [67], but change remains the cumulative effect of individual action. This perspective seems largely to neglect the idea that democratically constituted societies have the ability, in principle, through institutionally coordinated processes of contestation, deliberation and collective will-formation to make collectively binding *decisions* that restructure the very terrain on which problems are defined, solutions sought and choices made. Put differently, by fetishizing the 'emergent' character of evolutionary change, which simultaneously mystifies change as an opaque process that cannot be willed and steered but only subtly influenced and stimulated, evolutionary thinking reifies an ontology of the market and delegitimises the power of political decision-making. Polities can in principle (and routinely do!)—through parliamentarian, governmental or direct democratic channels—make decisions that delete entire segments of the option space within which choice takes place or open up new segments; they can make decisions that render certain definitions of problems obsolete and, therefore, discard entire categories of solutions. For example, a polity could decide that the internal combustion engine should no longer be part of its socio-technical option-space (i.e., market) and thus ban it. As a consequence, the entire terrain on which solutions (innovations) are sought and choices made would shift to electric and other alternatives by virtue of a collectively willed decision. Of course, the decision would become possible only based on pre-existing technological solutions—but the point is to *decide* for a solution (or category of solutions), and thus to shift the ground of innovation toward a societally agreed terrain. A polity could further decide that products and ingredients that contribute to deforestation and other detrimental forms of land use change will be eliminated from the option space—for example, palm oil and all forms of fibre and produce that do not adhere to defined standards. Consequently, firms would be forced to search for solutions to replace these ingredients or make sure they are produced according to the politically decided standards—and consumers would be left with a redefined field of choice. The point is that in a *purposive* societal transition *directionality* is necessarily a *political* category and *selection* predominantly a political function. Solution and choice play important parts in socio-technical evolution, but it is a mistake to assign them the responsibility for introducing the directionality of change and its long-term retention. As a coupled regime of variation and selection, solution and choice adhere to the criteria of individual utility and commercial viability, which have guided socio-technical evolution in the past but are the wrong criteria to steer a societal transition toward sustainability. A transformative model of innovation will thus have to focus on the design of political structures and institutions that empower society to make decisions for change.

5.2. Towards a Transformative Model of Innovation

There is of course a reason why decisions in the form we introduced them here are unpopular with evolutionary models of innovation thinking. Collective decisions, some evolutionary thinkers fear, may insert a crude and economically inefficient type of directionality that may run into socio-technical dead-ends. Directionality generated through political decisions rather than through the coevolution of solutions and choices might cut off "alternative development trajectories that may turn out to be promising at a later stage, but which are presently unforeseen" [19]. 'Picking winners' through political decisions has a bad reputation in the innovation literature, as it entails risks of ideological bias, vested interests and corruption to prevail instead of the most rational or efficient solution [68]. The underlying assumption is, of course, that the market-driven co-evolution of demand and supply would produce more worthy and evolutionary 'fit' winners. Searching a way out of the dilemma, Stirling proposes that a transformative model of innovation should not be about 'picking winners', but "about engaging widely across society, in order to build the most fruitful conditions for deciding what 'winning' even means" [69]. While we share the qualms about picking specific winners in specific situations, we see an urgent need to define more concretely what a transformative model of innovation has to achieve and what institutional and political preconditions it requires. For example, what does it mean 'to decide what winning means'? Who is to decide and how? And what does it mean to 'engage widely across society' in this context? What specific mechanism of participation and decision-making are required to arrive at transformative innovation that is both effective in introducing strong directionality and supported by the public?

Strong directionality. Given the 'super-wicked' [70] problem of climate change, which requires a swift and radical correction of the established developmental trajectory, a transformative model of innovation needs to be able not only to "create and shape markets" [44], but to insert directionality that—at least initially—goes against the grain of capital interests and commercial viability. Commercial viability may be an *ex post* effect of a transformative innovation, once the conditions for doing business have been redefined according to societally willed standards; but it need no longer be a precondition for successful innovation. This means that the established pattern of what it means to 'innovate' might need to be broken and replaced by forms of change that prioritise societal objectives over private utility and profit accumulation. We call this the power to introduce 'strong directionality' as it requires the political capacity to bend the curve beyond the scope of 'green growth' [71] and 'ecological modernisation' [72]. This implies that innovation goes beyond questions of technology and must be applied to the more fundamental structures of society including the role and distribution of wage labour and other forms of work [73] and even the ways we define, use and distribute property [74]. Transformative innovation, we argue, must not respect the political-economic taboos that shield the institutional core of contemporary capitalist societies. Without entering that core, innovation will fail to be transformative.

Creative destruction and regime destabilisation. The second critical requirement for a transformative model of innovation is that it needs to be both creative and destructive [16,17]. The doors to a sustainable type of civilisation must be opened, but at the same time, doors leading back to the highly profitable and convenient business model of unsustainability must be closed for good. This means that a transformative model of innovation must come to terms with and have an answer to questions of economic and political power and must be institutionally empowered as a *politics of transformation*. Questions of legitimacy, democracy and inclusiveness arise when unsustainable practices, technologies and structures of society are being negotiated and challenged. Scientific scrutiny, public deliberation and democratic will-formation will have to be joined together in novel institutional settings orchestrating processes of transformative innovation [75,76]. Institutions deliberately designed for that purpose need to be equipped with the democratic *power to decide*, which raises complicated questions of political legitimacy and accountability that growth-seeking industrial societies could manage to evade for a long time. Transformation will create losers, at least in the short term (as well as winners). Unlike in socio-technical revolutions of the past that followed the 'natural' evolutionary trajectories of capitalist expansion, a purposive transformation will have to be politically negotiated to a large extent—and its losers politically accounted for. This is why the *political* nature of transformative innovation needs to be acknowledged and institutionally reflected. This constitutes a novel and unprecedented institutional challenge to modern states and societies. It should be clear that democratic institutions empowered to make transformative decisions by definition cannot guarantee particular outcomes—citizens may indeed decide for convenience and against sustainability in some cases. The point is not to create a naïve conception of unfailing democratic transformation, but to open up windows and mechanisms through which a purposive transformation of industrial societies becomes part of our understanding of what democracy means.

It is beyond the scope of this paper to make concrete proposals for an institutional framework of transformative innovation. However, there are two specific functions that institutions for transformative innovation should fulfil in order to introduce strong directionality and incumbent regime destabilisation: Firstly, institutions on the national or supranational level that define the conditions of what 'winning' means, in the sense expressed above by Stirling [69]. These institutions would combine scientific assessment with public deliberation and democratic decision-making to set the parameters within which societally desirable innovation should take place and is allowed into the field of choice. Such institutions could decide, for example, that technologies, products and socio-technical practices that are likely to further expand the use of fossil fuels, the degradation of natural forests or the further acidification of oceans (even if through rebound or leakage effects) would be severely disadvantaged or even banned by public policy. These decisions would define the bounds of a societally willed trajectory of development without resorting to a politics of picking individual winners.

Secondly, we do believe that in some sectors of transformative innovation, societies need to pick winners after all. This applies, for example, to the field of social and grassroots innovations, where experimentation on the niche level has been going on for many years without much upscaling and mainstream of successful innovations [77,78]. Numerous initiatives around the globe—from low-carbon municipalities and eco-villages to co-operative and solidary models of economy—have proven practicable and sustainable alternatives to the status quo. Most of these alternatives, however, are systematically restrained from breaching the boundaries of their niches and from being normalised and mainstreamed in the heart of modern societies due to institutional and regulatory restrictions or lack of legal and political support. A transformative model of innovation thus needs to entail what Hausknost et al. [79] have called *transmission belt institutions*. These are institutions that are designed to negotiate and decide on the national and sub-national level, by which practicable and sustainable alternatives to the ways "we are doing things" (social practices, economic institutions, work, property, housing, finance) developed in niches around the world should be tested on the *regime* level and then institutionally *implemented* and *mainstreamed*. Far from promoting a planned economy, this model of transformative innovation will require much experimentation, but also the courage to upscale promising social innovations. Here, expert knowledge and democratic procedures of deliberation and collective decision-making will need to be combined in novel and politically powerful ways that enable discourses of social innovation to enter the centre of society and that lead to the implementation of collective decisions that change the very contours of society. *Transmission belt institutions* have the power to overrule market dynamics and incumbent capital interests by redefining bounds to enable the upscaling of innovations by means of democratic deliberation and decision-making. Since the question of demand and supply in social innovations in particular is a political one and cannot be answered by market dynamics, an institutional transmission belt between niches and the regime is required. Otherwise, social innovations remain in their depoliticised state of niche experimentation forever or gradually wither away [80].

As discussed in Sections 2–4, we detect severe limitations of the three dominant paradigms in innovation studies. While we appreciate the underlying theoretical foundations of evolutionary thinking and their analytical capacities regarding past developments, we criticise their market-based selection environments, which ultimately hinder transformative innovation. We think that the two functions of the institutional framework described above could be valuable in strengthening the political dimension of selection in the three paradigms discussed. In the case of the multi-level perspective, the main transformative task is to manage the all-important interaction between niches and regimes in a purposive and goal-oriented way, while regimes play the role of selection environments for innovations. Exactly for this purpose, institutions on a national or supranational level are needed for constructing selection mechanisms that are ultimately guided by societal goals. Transmission belt institutions would then be needed to implement the societally defined selection criteria by normalising and universalising the diffusion of transformative innovation at regime level. As far as technological innovation systems (TIS) are concerned, the state is already instrumental in strategically creating the conditions for new markets but, still, markets act as primary selector. Here such institutions could instead introduce the primacy of societal goals in TIS and transmission belt institutions could guide the diffusion of new preferred technologies and the emergence of new markets, e.g., when energy efficiency gains or even sufficiency strategies become societally favourable to mere utility gains and accumulation interests. Finally, when discussing a sustainable next Kondratiev wave and a low-carbon industrial revolution, we strongly believe that only carefully designed institutions that replace market driven selection by societal selection mechanisms, would create a chance to leave behind the trajectory of utility-guided and resource-blind socio-technical evolution and to enter a trajectory of purposive transformation according to societally negotiated goals and standards.

6. Conclusions

In this paper, we examined three dominant approaches in innovation theory on a conceptual level with regard to their capacities to contribute to a comprehensive sustainability transition. We analysed the multi-level perspective, the innovation systems approach and the neo-Schumpeterian theory of long waves. All three are ontologically based in evolutionary economic theory. While evolutionary theorising can be very helpful to understand processes of socio-technical co-evolution, the approaches we analysed all share a crucial shortcoming in that they accept the apolitical conception of selection mechanisms at the core of evolutionary economic theory, which defines the market as the most important selection environment for technological (and other) innovations. As the market cannot anticipate future external selection pressures, however, it is an improper selection environment for the implementation of purposive changes aiming at the avoidance of future problems.

What is required, then, we argued, is the internal representation of the external pressures in selection systems other than the market. In other words, we need powerful institutional mechanisms of selection that substitute the mechanisms of the market to some extent and insert strong directionality to processes of innovation. The design and implementation of the institutions necessary for a transformative model of innovation might itself become the most important field of innovation in years to come. The main purpose of these institutions would be to secure the main characteristics of a purposive, normatively directed transformation of society that cannot be controlled by the selection mechanisms of demand and supply. Key among these characteristics is the power to insert and sustain a strong directionality of change and to destabilise the incumbent regime of structural unsustainability. These are political characteristics, which need to be enacted through specifically designed political institutions.

Applying the analytical framework of 'agentic operators' our analysis concluded that current innovation policy is dominated by the operators *choice* and *solution* and thus tied to market selection and incremental technological change. What is lacking are *decisions* that shift the entire terrain on which *solutions* are being sought and that make purposive selections between alternative socio-technological trajectories. *Decisions* are rare because they are irreducibly political and face inherent legitimation problems. Nevertheless, they will be needed in the future to provide the level of steering that is necessary to break out of our carbon economy. We propose to acknowledge the inherently political nature of transformation and to design novel institutions that integrate expert knowledge with processes of public deliberation and democratic decision-making. These institutions need to be endowed with the power to make binding decisions. We identified two possible functions of an institutional framework for transformative innovation: to set the bounds within which transformative innovation has to take place and to work as transmission belts for the upscaling of practicable (social) innovations that would otherwise remain stuck in niche experimentation.

Author Contributions: Conceptualization, D.H with contributions from W.H; Writing—original draft preparation, D.H.; Writing—review and editing, D.H. and W.H.; Funding acquisition, D.H.

funding: This research was support by funding through the ESRC Centre for the Understanding of Sustainable Prosperity (CUSP).

Acknowledgments: We would like to thank Joachim Spangenberg as well as the three anonymous reviewers for their valuable comments.

Conflicts of Interest: The authors declare no conflict of interest.

References

1. Fischer-Kowalski, M. Analyzing sustainability transitions as a shift between socio-metabolic regimes. *Environ. Innov. Soc. Transit.* **2011**, *1*, 152–159. [CrossRef]
2. Haberl, H.; Fischer-Kowalski, M.; Krausmann, F.; Martinez-Alier, J.; Winiwarter, V. A socio-metabolic transition towards sustainability? Challenges for another Great Transformation. *Sustain. Dev.* **2011**, *19*, 1–14. [CrossRef]
3. Görg, C.; Brand, U.; Haberl, H.; Hummel, D.; Jahn, T.; Liehr, S. Challenges for Social-Ecological Transformations: Contributions from Social and Political Ecology. *Sustainability* **2017**, *9*, 1045. [CrossRef]
4. Markard, J.; Raven, R.; Truffer, B. Sustainability transitions: An emerging field of research and its prospects. *Res. Policy* **2012**, *41*, 955–967. [CrossRef]
5. Patterson, J.; Schulz, K.; Vervoort, J.; van der Hel, S.; Widerberg, O.; Adler, C.; Hurlbert, M.; Anderton, K.; Sethi, M.; Barau, A. Exploring the governance and politics of transformations towards sustainability. *Environ. Innov. Soc. Transit.* **2017**, *24*, 1–16. [CrossRef]
6. Fischer-Kowalski, M.; Hausknost, D. *Large Scale Societal Transitions in the Past. The Role of Social Revolutions and the 1970s Syndrome*; Working Paper Social Ecology 152; IFF Social Ecology: Wien, Austria, 2014.
7. Tainter, J.A. *The Collapse of Complex Societies*, 23th ed.; Cambridge Univ. Press: Cambridge, UK, 2011.
8. Fischer-Kowalski, M.; Krausmann, F.; Pallua, I. A sociometabolic reading of the Anthropocene: Modes of subsistence, population size and human impact on Earth. *Anthr. Rev.* **2014**, *1*, 8–33. [CrossRef]
9. Krausmann, F.; Lauk, C.; Haas, W.; Wiedenhofer, D. From resource extraction to outflows of wastes and emissions: The socioeconomic metabolism of the global economy, 1900–2015. *Glob. Environ. Chang.* **2018**, *52*, 131–140. [CrossRef]
10. Schot, J.; Steinmueller, W.E. Three frames for innovation policy: R&D, systems of innovation and transformative change. *Res. Policy* **2018**, *47*, 1554–1567. [CrossRef]
11. Alkemade, F.; Hekkert, M.P.; Negro, S.O. Transition policy and innovation policy: Friends or foes? *Environ. Innov. Soc. Transit.* **2011**, *1*, 125–129. [CrossRef]
12. Weber, K.M.; Rohracher, H. Legitimizing research, technology and innovation policies for transformative change. *Res. Policy* **2012**, *41*, 1037–1047. [CrossRef]
13. Meadowcroft, J. Engaging with the politics of sustainability transitions. *Environ. Innov. Soc. Transit.* **2011**, *1*, 70–75. [CrossRef]
14. van den Bergh, J.C.J.M. Effective climate-energy solutions, escape routes and peak oil. *Energy Policy* **2012**, *46*, 530–536. [CrossRef]
15. van den Bergh, J.C.J.M. Environmental and climate innovation: Limitations, policies and prices. *Technol. Forecast. Soc. Chang.* **2013**, *80*, 11–23. [CrossRef]
16. Kuokkanen, A.; Nurmi, A.; Mikkilä, M.; Kuisma, M.; Kahiluoto, H.; Linnanen, L. Agency in regime destabilization through the selection environment: The Finnish food system's sustainability transition. *Res. Policy* **2018**, *47*, 1513–1522. [CrossRef]
17. Kivimaa, P.; Kern, F. Creative destruction or mere niche support? Innovation policy mixes for sustainability transitions. *Res. Policy* **2016**, *45*, 205–217. [CrossRef]
18. Dopfer, K. Evolutionary economics: A theoretical framework. In *The Evolutionary Foundations of Economics*; Dopfer, K., Ed.; Cambridge Univ. Press: Cambridge, UK, 2006; pp. 3–59.

19. Safarzyńska, K.; Frenken, K.; van den Bergh, J.C.J.M. Evolutionary theorizing and modeling of sustainability transitions. *Res. Policy* **2012**, *41*, 1011–1024. [CrossRef]
20. Sovacool, B.K.; Hess, D.J. Ordering theories: Typologies and conceptual frameworks for sociotechnical change. *Soc. Stud. Sci.* **2017**, *47*, 703–750. [CrossRef]
21. Geels, F.W. The multi-level perspective on sustainability transitions: Responses to seven criticisms. *Environ. Innov. Soc. Transit.* **2011**, *1*, 24–40. [CrossRef]
22. Geels, F.W.; Schot, J. The Dynamics of Transitions: A Socio-Technical Perspective. In *Transitions to Sustainable Development: New Directions in the Study of Long Term Transformative Change*; Grin, J., Rotmans, J., Schot, J., Geels, F.W., Eds.; Routledge: New York, NY, USA, 2010; Volume 1, pp. 11–104.
23. Rotmans, J.; Loorbach, D. Towards a Better Understanding of Transitions and their Governance: A Systemic and Reflexive Approach. In *Transitions to Sustainable Development: New Directions in the Study of Long Term Transformative Change*; Grin, J., Rotmans, J., Schot, J., Geels, F.W., Eds.; Routledge: New York, NY, USA, 2010; Volume 1, pp. 105–122.
24. Kemp, R.; Schot, J.; Hoogma, R. Regime shifts to sustainability through processes of niche formation: The approach of strategic niche management. *Technol. Anal. Strateg. Manag.* **1998**, *10*, 175–198. [CrossRef]
25. Smith, A.; Raven, R. What is protective space? Reconsidering niches in transitions to sustainability. *Res. Policy* **2012**, *41*, 1025–1036. [CrossRef]
26. Perez, C. Structural Change and Assimilation of New Technologies in the Economic and Social System. *Futures* **1983**, *15*, 357–375. [CrossRef]
27. Fouquet, R. *Heat, Power and Light: Revolutions in Energy Services*; Elgar: Cheltenham, UK, 2008.
28. Smil, V. *Energy Transitions: Global and National Perspectives*; Praeger an Imprint of ABC-CLIO LLC: Santa Barbara, CA, USA, 2017.
29. Kander, A.; Malanima, P.; Warde, P. *Power to the People: Energy in Europe over the Last Five Centuries*; Princeton University Press: Princeton, NJ, USA, 2014.
30. Kemp, R.; Loorbach, D.; Rotmans, J. Transition management as a model for managing processes of co-evolution towards sustainable development. *Int. J. Sustain. Dev. World Ecol.* **2007**, *14*, 78–91. [CrossRef]
31. Geels, F.W. Regime Resistance against Low-Carbon Transitions: Introducing Politics and Power into the Multi-Level Perspective. *Theory Cult. Soc.* **2014**, *31*, 21–40. [CrossRef]
32. Smith, A.; Stirling, A.; Berkhout, F. The governance of sustainable socio-technical transitions. *Res. Policy* **2005**, *34*, 1491–1510. [CrossRef]
33. Kenis, A.; Bono, F.; Mathijs, E. Unravelling the (post-)political in Transition Management: Interrogating Pathways towards Sustainable Change. *J. Environ. Policy Plan.* **2016**, *18*, 568–584. [CrossRef]
34. Kemp, R.; Loorbach, D. Transition management: A reflexive governance approach. In *Reflexive Governance for Sustainable Development*; Bauknecht, D., Voss, J.-P., Kemp, R., Eds.; Edward Elgar: Cheltenham, UK; Northampton, MA, USA, 2006; pp. 103–130.
35. Avelino, F.; Grin, J.; Pel, B.; Jhagroe, S. The politics of sustainability transitions. *J. Environ. Policy Plan.* **2016**, *18*, 557–567. [CrossRef]
36. Bulkeley, H.; Broto, V.C.; Maassen, A. Governing urban lowcarbon transitions. In *Cities and Low Carbon Transitions*; Bulkeley, H., Castán Broto, V., Eds.; Routledge: London, UK, 2011; Volume 35, pp. 29–41.
37. Freeman, C. *Technology Policy and Economic Performance: Lessons from Japan*; Pinter: London, UK, 1987.
38. Lundvall, B.-Å. *National Systems of Innovation: Toward a Theory of Innovation and Interactive Learning*; Anthem: London, UK; New York, NY, USA, 2010.
39. Edquist, C. Systems of innovation approaches—Their emergence and characteristics. In *Systems of Innovation: Technologies, Institutions and Organizations*; Edquist, C., Ed.; Routledge: London, UK, 2011; pp. 1–35.
40. Jacobsson, S.; Bergek, A. Innovation system analyses and sustainability transitions: Contributions and suggestions for research. *Environ. Innov. Soc. Transit.* **2011**, *1*, 41–57. [CrossRef]
41. Markard, J.; Truffer, B. Technological innovation systems and the multi-level perspective: Towards an integrated framework. *Res. Policy* **2008**, *37*, 596–615. [CrossRef]
42. Gibbons, M.; Limoges, C.; Nowotny, H.; Schwartzman, S.; Scott, P.; Trow, M. (Eds.) *The New Production of Knowledge: The Dynamics of Science and Research in Contemporary Societies*; Sage Publ: Los Angeles, CA, USA, 1994.
43. Etzkowitz, H. *The Triple Helix: University-Industry-Government Innovation in Action*; Routledge: New York, NY, USA, 2008.

44. Mazzucato, M.; Cimoli, M.; Dosi, G.; Stiglitz, J.E.; Landesmann, M.A.; Pianta, M.; Walz, R.; Page, T. Which Industrial Policy Does Europe Need? *Intereconomics* **2015**, *50*, 120–155. [CrossRef]
45. Mazzucato, M. *The Entrepreneurial State: Debunking Public vs. Private Sector Myths*; Allen Lane: London, UK, 2017.
46. Edquist, C. (Ed.) *Systems of Innovation: Technologies, Institutions and Organizations*; Routledge: London, UK, 2011.
47. Freeman, C.; Louçã, F. *As Time Goes by: From the Industrial Revolutions to the Information Revolution*; Oxford University Press: Oxford, NY, USA, 2001.
48. Perez, C. *Technological Revolutions and Financial Capital: The Dynamics of Bubbles and Golden Ages*; Edward Elgar: Cheltenham, UK; Northampton, MA, USA, 2002.
49. Köhler, J. A comparison of the neo-Schumpeterian theory of Kondratiev waves and the multi-level perspective on transitions. *Environ. Innov. Soc. Transit.* **2012**, *3*, 1–15. [CrossRef]
50. Foxon, T. *Energy and Economic Growth: Why We Need a New Pathway to Prosperity*; Routledge is an Imprint of the Taylor & Francis Group, An Informa Business: Abingdon, UK; New York, NY, USA, 2018.
51. Dewick, P.; Green, K.; Fleetwood, T.; Miozzo, M. Modelling creative destruction: Technological diffusion and industrial structure change to 2050. *Technol. Forecast. Soc. Chang.* **2006**, *73*, 1084–1106. [CrossRef]
52. GREEN, K.; SHACKLEY, S.; DEWICK, P.; MIOZZO, M. Long-wave theories of technological change and the global environment. *Glob. Environ. Chang.* **2002**, *12*, 79–81. [CrossRef]
53. Drechsler, W.J.M. Governance In and Of Techno-Economic Paradigm Shifts: Considerations For and From the Nanotechnology Surge. In *Techno-Economic Paradigms: Essays in Honour of Carlota Perez*; Perez, C., Drechsler, W.J.M., Kattel, R., Reinert, E.S., Eds.; Anthem Press: New York, NY, USA, 2009; pp. 95–104.
54. Pearson, P.J.G.; Foxon, T.J. A low carbon industrial revolution? Insights and challenges from past technological and economic transformations. *Energy Policy* **2012**, *50*, 117–127. [CrossRef]
55. Creutzig, F.; Fernandez, B.; Haberl, H.; Khosla, R.; Mulugetta, Y.; Seto, K.C. Beyond Technology: Demand-Side Solutions for Climate Change Mitigation. *Annu. Rev. Environ. Resour.* **2016**, *41*, 173–198. [CrossRef]
56. Hobson, K. 'Weak' or 'Strong' Sustainable Consumption? Efficiency, Degrowth, and the 10 Year Framework of Programmes. *Environ. Plan. C Gov. Policy* **2013**, *31*, 1082–1098. [CrossRef]
57. Kattel, R.; Drechsler, W.J.M.; Reinert, E.S. Introduction: Carlota Perez and Evolutionary Economics. In *Techno-Economic Paradigms: Essays in honour of Carlota Perez*; Perez, C., Drechsler, W.J.M., Kattel, R., Reinert, E.S., Eds.; Anthem Press: New York, NY, USA, 2009; pp. 1–18.
58. Steffen, W.; Richardson, K.; Rockström, J.; Cornell, S.E.; Fetzer, I.; Bennett, E.M.; Biggs, R.; Carpenter, S.R.; Vries, W.; de Wit, C.A.; et al. Planetary boundaries: Guiding human development on a changing planet. *Science* **2015**, *347*, 1259855. [CrossRef] [PubMed]
59. Hauskiost, D. Decision, choice, solution: 'Agentic deadlock' in environmental politics. *Environ. Polit.* **2014**, *23*, 357–375. [CrossRef]
60. Derrida, J. Force of Law: 'The Mystical Foundation of Authority'. *Cardozo Law Rev.* **1990**, *11*, 920–1046.
61. Butler, J.; Laclau, E. Appendix I: The Uses of Equality. In *Laclau: A critical Reader*; Critchley, S., Marchart, O., Eds.; Routledge: London, UK, 2006; pp. 329–344.
62. Baumeister, R.F.; Heatherton, T.F. Self-Regulation Failure: An Overview. *Psychol. Inq.* **1996**, *7*, 1–15. [CrossRef]
63. Shove, E. Beyond the ABC: Climate Change Policy and Theories of Social Change. *Environ. Plan. A* **2010**, *42*, 1273–1285. [CrossRef]
64. Critchley, S. Is there a normative deficit in the theory of hegemony? In *Laclau: A Critical Reader*; Critchley, S., Marchart, O., Eds.; Routledge: London, UK, 2006; pp. 113–122.
65. van den Bergh, J.C.J.M.; Gowdy, J.M. A group selection perspective on economic behavior, institutions and organizations. *J. Econ. Behav. Organ.* **2009**, *72*, 1–20. [CrossRef]
66. Safarzyńska, K. Evolutionary Economics. In *Routledge Handbook of Ecological Economics: Nature and Society*; Spash, C.L., Ed.; Routledge: Abingdon, UK, 2017; pp. 77–85.
67. Safarzyńska, K. Evolutionary-economic policies for sustainable consumption. *Ecol. Econ.* **2013**, *90*, 187–195. [CrossRef]
68. Falck, O.; Gollier, C.; Woessmann, L. Arguments for and against Policies to Promote National Champions. In *Industrial Policy for National Champions*; Falck, O., Gollier, C., Woessmann, L., Eds.; MIT Press: Cambridge, MA, USA, 2011; pp. 3–12.
69. Stirling, A. *Making Choices in the Face of Uncertainty: Themed Annual Report of the Government Chief Scientific Adviser*; Mimeo: New York, NY, USA, 2014.

70. Levin, K.; Cashore, B.; Bernstein, S.; Auld, G. Overcoming the tragedy of super wicked problems: Constraining our future selves to ameliorate global climate change. *Policy Sci.* **2012**, *45*, 123–152. [CrossRef]
71. OECD. *Towards Green Growth*; OECD Publishing: Paris, France, 2011.
72. Mol, A.P.J.; Sonnenfeld, D.A.; Spaargaren, G. (Eds.) *The Ecological Modernisation Reader: Environmental Reform in Theory and Practice*; Routledge: London, UK, 2009.
73. Littig, B. Good work? Sustainable work and sustainable development: A critical gender perspective from the Global North. *Globalizations* **2018**, *15*, 565–579. [CrossRef]
74. Jackson, T. *Prosperity without Growth: Economics for a Finite Planet*; Earthscan from Routledge: London, UK, 2009.
75. Hammond, M.; Smith, G. *Sustainable Prosperity and Democracy: A Research Agenda*; CUSP Working Paper No 8; University of Surrey: Guildford, UK, 2017.
76. Smith, G. *Democratic Innovations: Designing Institutions for Citizen Participation*; Cambridge University Press: Cambridge, UK, 2009.
77. Seyfang, G.; Smith, A. Grassroots innovations for sustainable development: Towards a new research and policy agenda. *Environ. Polit.* **2007**, *16*, 584–603. [CrossRef]
78. Nicholls, A.; Simon, J.; Gabriel, M. *New Frontiers in Social Innovation Research*; Palgrave Macmillan: Basingstoke, UK, 2015.
79. Hausknost, D.; Haas, W.; Hielscher, S.; Schäfer, M.; Leitner, M.; Kunze, I.; Mandl, S. Investigating patterns of local climate governance: How low-carbon municipalities and intentional communities intervene in social practices. *Environ. Pol. Gov.* **2018**, *12*, 249. [CrossRef]
80. Clausen, J.; Fichter, K.; Gandenberger, C.; Braungardt, S. *Umweltinnovationen: Von der Nische in den Mainstream: Policy Paper zum Projekt Umweltinnovationen und ihre Diffusion als Treiber der Green Economy*; Borderstep Institute: Berlin, Germany, 2017.

sustainability

MDPI

Article

Behind the Scenarios: World View, Ideologies, Philosophies. An Analysis of Hidden Determinants and Acceptance Obstacles Illustrated by the ALARM Scenarios

Joachim H. Spangenberg [1,2]

1   Helmholtz Centre for Environment Research, Permoserstr 15, 04318 Leipzig, Germany;
     Joachim.Spangenberg@ufz.de; Tel.: +49-221-216-895
2   Sustainable Europe Research Institute SERI Germany, Vorsterstr 97-99, 51103 Cologne, Germany

Received: 21 May 2018; Accepted: 19 July 2018; Published: 20 July 2018

Abstract: In situations of uncertainty, scenarios serve as input for scientifically informed decision making. However, past experience shows that not all scenarios are treated equally and we hypothesise that only those based on a world view shared by scientists and decision makers are perceived as credible and receive full attention of the respective group of decision makers. While intuitively plausible, this hypothesis has not been analysed by quantitative correlation analyses, so instead of drawing on quantitative data the paper analyses the archetypical scenarios developed in the ALARM project to substantiate the plausibility by a comparative analysis of world views, value systems and policy orientations. Shock scenarios are identified as a means to explore the possibility space of future developments beyond the linear developments models and most scenario storylines suggest. The analysis shows that the typical scenarios are based on mutually exclusive assumptions. In conclusion, a comparison of storylines and empirical data can reveal misperceptions and the need to rethink world views as a necessary step to open up to new challenges. Deeply held beliefs will make this transition unlikely to happen without severe crises, if not dedicated efforts to explicate the role of world views for scenarios and policies are undertaken.

Keywords: scenarios; world views; values; policies; models and modes of science

1. Introduction

Recent forecasts predict that the world economy is set to grow by 238% by the year 2060 and the rich OECD countries by 146%, as compared to 2014 [1]. Air transport will nearly double by 2036 [2]. By 2030, biotechnology could contribute to 50% of primary production, 80% of pharmaceutical production and 35% of industrial production in sectors where biotechnology has potential applications [3]. Peter Johnson, SAP Marketing Strategy and Thought Leadership predicts that in the future digital economy by 2020, the average person will have more conversations with bots than with their spouse, by 2030 organs will be biologically 3D-printed on demand and the 'Internet of Everything' could be worth $19 trillion over the next decade thanks to cost savings and profits for businesses and increased revenues for the public sector. 5G data speeds will be 1000-times faster than today, offering ubiquitous connections across the 'Internet of Things,' engagement across virtual environments with only millisecond latency and whole new Big Data applications and services [3].

At the same time, we know that if the Earth warms by three degrees Celsius (which is the trajectory under the current climate pledges), extreme events could become the normal state in the future, with the drought regions in Europe doubling from 13% to 26% of the total area and the most severe droughts in Europe lasting three to four times longer than in the past, affecting up to 400 million people. In the Mediterranean, with droughts lasting almost half of the year (in Spain up to 7 months), water availability will be reduced by 35,000 m^3 H$_2$O/km^2 of land [4], making large areas virtually uninhabitable. Most European cities will see increases not only in heat and drought but also in river flood risks. Over 100 cities are particularly vulnerable to two or more climate impacts while the predicted magnitude of impacts exceeds earlier expectations [5]. In the last two decades, one-tenth of the earth's total wilderness areas have been lost, an estimated 3.3 million km^2 [6] and today, 28.5% of the species analysed by IUCN have been classified as in risk of extinction.

In the social domain, in the affluent countries GDP per capita has increased roughly 1000% since the 1970s but average worker pay has increased just 11%, essentially stagnating while CEO pay has risen 1000%. Little wonder then that only 13% of employees worldwide are engaged, meaning that the other 87% are not involved in, enthusiastic about and committed to their work and company. This is set to intensify: 75% of Millennials would take a pay cut to work for a socially and environmentally responsible company while in a study of 100 variables, seeing purpose and value in work was the single most important factor that motivated employees, more than compensation. It even makes business sense: organizations in which employees perceive meaning at work are 21% more profitable [3].

All these prognoses are based on scenarios and they are virtually irreconcilable: rather obviously, the rosy economic prognoses, the environmental catastrophe emerging and the social challenges cannot occur simultaneously when taking the economic impacts of the social and environmental developments into account. Deserted countries do not grow economically, starving populations do not consume (and least so consumer electronics) and a bioeconomy without biodiversity is unthinkable. Nonetheless all these scenarios are the basis for decisions being currently taken, spending scarce human, material and financial resources on mutually exclusive visions of the future.

However, there is one big difference between these forecasts: those promising an extended and up-graded status quo where products and consumption patterns change but limits do not exist, receive billions of dollars, euros, yen and yuan in investments, while those calling for damage limitation receive miniscule funding even by governments not known for their problem denial and scientific illiteracy. Most firms fail to take the negative trends into account (except they spot a market niche there). For instance, Renault invests billions of euro to employ virtual reality and immersive simulation technologies to allow its design team, partners and suppliers to experience, interact with and test-drive new car designs without any physical prototypes, while car sharing could reduce the number of cars needed by 90% already in 2035, resulting in only 17% as many cars as there are today (Millennials are keen to share) [3].

Given that global change scenarios represent the best available knowledge of the best informed and educated generation in the history of humankind, how can these discrepancies be explained? Why is the world closely following the most pessimistic of the scenarios presented by the "Limits to Growth" report almost 50 years ago [7,8]? Why always "Late Lessons From Early Warnings" [9,10]? Environmental ignorance of economics, sociology and development theory has been accused but reality is more complex: if a scenario exercise offers a doomsday variant based on incremental change and a transformation based rescue variant, both based on the same disciplines, why is the rescue scenario lauded while the dominating practice of decision making resembles the doomsday scenario? Why is progress measured in metrics which tell us nothing about the emerging catastrophes [11,12]? Why do "modificationists" in science, politics and business not learn from or at least listen to "transformationists" and take the environmental and social facts on board? Economic interests and short-term thinking may explain part of the phenomenon, human inertia and loss aversion another bit (the preference for the "known evil" when facing transaction cost, that is, change is long known, see [13]). The European Environment Agency found that even well-crafted scenarios can fail to have their intended policy impact if they present information considered irrelevant by the recipients, lack support from relevant actors, are poorly embedded into relevant organisations or ignore key institutional context conditions [14]. So, the core question is not what kind of scenarios are needed to underpin a high-quality discourse between scientists and policy makers, considering the different nature of science and politics but how to avoid that some policy explorative (but not prescriptive) gain superiority while others of the same quality are neglected. Our hypothesis is that the joint world views held by groups of scholars and decision makers are key variable explaining which scenarios are considered relevant. As in the political sphere gradual change is the norm, they are the context conditions which—often unconsciously—make scenarios of deep transformations appear strange, unreal and utopic. While scientifically sound, such scenarios would appear in the political sphere as expressions of illusions or idealism (as was Thomas Morus' "Utopia" in 1517 [15]—but it influenced policies) and not as realistic policy demands. This in turn would deprive them of support from relevant actors however good their scientific backing, the factual relevance of information and the embedment into relevant organisations may be.

In Section 2 we briefly describe the concepts we use in this paper (scenarios, world views, welfare regimes) and introduce the ALARM scenarios we will use to illustrate the link between scenarios and world views in Section 3. Section 4 discusses the results and draws some conclusions.

2. Method and Building Blocks

As so far analyses regarding the impact of underlying world views on the perception and appeal of scenarios are missing, we focus on making the world views underlying scenarios, as well as their social and economic implications explicit, using three archetypical scenarios from the ALARM project [16,17]. As adopting a world view is driven by deeply held beliefs and convictions, for scholars as well as for decision makers, it appears plausible that the implicit basis of scenarios influences their perception, with a similarity of world views enhancing the level of resonance. We will illustrate the plausibility of this hypothesis by explicating the world views and their implications for different scenarios in Section 3 to underpin out hypothesis. As there are no quantitative data regarding the correlation of world views and the acceptance of scenarios, our approach is limited to scenario analysis and common sense based reasoning, illustrating the plausibility of the hypothesis. First, however, we try to clarify what "world views" are in the context of our paper, drawing on philosophical discussions, before turning to scenarios in general and to the ALARM scenarios in particular.

2.1. World Views

World views are comprehensive systems of perceiving reality; which challenges are recognised, issues are emphasised, policies suggested and changes endorsed in order to approach sustainable development depends on the world views held by the respective agents in all walks of life. They have also been described as 'pre-analytic visons,' for example, by Herman Daly et al. [18] and are similar to metaphysics. A worldview can be expressed as the fundamental cognitive, affective and evaluative presuppositions a group of people make about the nature of things and which they use to order their lives. According to Michael Lind, a worldview is a more or less coherent understanding of the nature of reality, which permits its holders to interpret new information in light of their preconceptions [19].

The elements constituting a world view are its ontology including an anthropology, its epistemology and its axiology including a societal vision [20,21]. Ontology is a section of philosophy dealing with questions concerning what entities exist or may be said to exist and how such entities may be grouped, related within a hierarchy and subdivided according to similarities and differences. Epistemology is the branch of philosophy dealing with the theory of knowledge; it studies the nature of knowledge, justification and the rationality of belief. Axiology is another branch of philosophy, encompassing a range of approaches to understanding how, why and to what degree humans should or do value objects, whether the objects are physical (a person, a thing) or abstract (an idea, an action), or anything else. The Dutch World Views Research Group [22] gives a slightly different definition, including as here an ontology (and an explanation of where the world is heading), an epistemology and values (the axiology) but adding a praxeology or theory of action and an aetiology, reflecting on the origins and construction of the respective world view. We leave out the latter (although there are good arguments for including it) as despite the emergence of a 'reflexive modernity' [23] reflecting on world views is a rare case in both scenario development and decision making—the modernity is reflexive but not reflective [24].

Clashes among worldviews cannot be ended by a simple appeal to facts as they permit their holders to interpret new information in light of their preconceptions: even if rival sides agree on the facts, they may disagree on conclusions because of their different premises [19]. For instance, different value systems shape the perception of what is important in reality: from an objective value perspective, there are no instrumental values, only means to things which may be valuable; the means may be valuable in themselves but not by their mean function. From an instrumental perspective, all values can be described in instrumental terms, bequest and existence value included (instrumental for enhancing one's own life satisfaction—a 'feel good' or 'warm glow' effect). According to utilitarian anthropologies, humans try to maximise their well-being in a 'pursuit of happiness' by accumulating as many things as possible. A stoic anthropology holds that a fulfilled and thus good life is not necessarily easy or pleasant but based on virtues and thus material goods can (but need not be) distractions from what makes a life worth living. Utilitarians strive for the greatest good for the greatest number [25], hedonists like the *homo economicus* for a maximum of individual satisfaction [26]. For both, satisfaction can be reached by egoistic or altruistic actions, a distinction which makes no sense for stoics applying deontological criteria to 'do the right thing' [27]. Different world views are associated with different value systems and different political philosophies which are appealing to one audience but can be appalling to another [28]. Accordingly, not only different decision makers but also different scholars (and the scenarios they develop) hold and express different world views, consciously or unconsciously which preform their perception, stance and recommendations.

However, although world views cannot be proven right or wrong, they can be assessed and compared regarding their plausibility, based on their 'fit' with observations. For instance, while a world view denying anthropogenic climate change is immune against the consensus of the scientific community, it may lose supporters due to the contradiction between their own experience, scientific findings and the explanations offered. Similarly, an explicit praxeology as part of a world view, offering a theory of effective action, can be compared with past experience. For example, claims that central planning economies are effective, or that a free market guarantees a just income distribution may be upheld by core believers of the respective world view but will limit their appeal to others as the explanations given for the known facts are of limited persuasive force. Such world views do not simply collapse or disappear (as would be the case if falsification was possible, like in the case of the pre-Copernican ontology) but tend to be gradually replaced by others which offer more convincing explanations for undisputed facts.

2.2. What Are "Scenarios"?

First of all, it appears useful to clarify what are scenarios and how they are distinct from predictions. The latter deal with certainty, requiring at least probabilistic knowledge about all possible outcomes of an event. Prognoses can be exact (A determines B with no ambiguity), or fuzzy (A determining a distribution of B) but are deterministic predictions in both cases. Scenarios are needed when certainty is missing, which is the case for most of the phenomena relevant to economic, social and environmental development. All scenarios are based on (necessarily subjective) assumptions: we assume that an accident may end our ability to work and buy an insurance against the ensuing economic impacts; that is the case of risks. Or we know the impacts of an event (nuclear war causing global winter, greenhouse gas emissions causing climate change) but we cannot say now if the event will be happening (the nuclear war) or if an ongoing process will continue or be terminated (the case of climate change). This is the situation of uncertainty, requiring not insurance but prevention. Then there is ignorance, a situation where we neither know the probability of the event, nor its potential impacts. For instance, we do not know yet if nano-particles from plastic waste will enter the human food chain and accumulate in our bodies and if so, which would be the resulting health impacts—this is the case for precaution. Under both uncertainty and ignorance probabilities of final impacts cannot be quantified, by definition.

Forecasting scenarios are used to both better understand the probability of an event happening, under certain assumptions and to explore the potential impacts, under even more assumptions; backcasting scenarios start from normatively setting a desired or feared result and analyse how it could be achieved or avoided. Thus, scenarios do not predict events and thus cannot be policy prescriptive, they do not claim to outline the future that will be but describe different futures which might become reality. As such they are heuristic explorative tools giving indications how, again under certain assumptions for example, regarding the policies adopted, a system may develop. They can be used to explore what can be done and what should be avoided to redirect the development trajectory, always based on the assumptions made (which is why they should be explicit). Decision makers then have the opportunity to compare different plausible development trajectories, asking "what would happen if A or B was happening and if we did C or D?"

Building a scenario requires simplification to characterise the processes under analysis and support understanding them. Borrowing a phrase from Albert Einstein, scenarios should be as simple as possible but not simpler. This poses the challenge to find a level of complexity simple enough to be comprehensible but complex enough to adequately accommodate the different options to be compared and generate answers which are relevant in a real-world context. For this behalf, a scenario is based on a narrative, a storyline which can accommodate values, subjective motivations and other qualitative elements, which is often supported by computer models to illustrate certain aspects of the scenario quantitatively. However, models are constrained to dealing with the quantifiable parameters and the mostly linear developments their equations can handle. Thus, the quantitative results always have to be interpreted—and sometimes corrected—by embedding them into the narrative context [29–31].

Unfortunately, both academic literature and press releases and media coverage often lack a clear distinction between predictions, projections, probabilistic forecasts and scenarios. Predictions are often referred to as scenarios, while certain scenarios, such as economic growth forecasts, are habitually presented as (probabilistic) predictions. For instance, misinterpreting its scenarios as predictions was one of the main reasons for the economists' profession rejection of the "Limits to Growth" report almost half a century ago. Ironically, some of its worst-case scenarios have turned out to be rather accurate predictions, against the best hopes of their authors [7,8] and in 2014, The Guardian published an article showing that data collected since the report's publication supports the accuracy of the 1972 projections [32]. In the end, of course, as the world consists of different systems with different degrees of predictability, predictions and scenarios will ultimately need to come together to guide decisions.

2.3. The ALARM Scenarios

Developing effective strategies for biodiversity preservation requires analysing all major pressures affecting biodiversity and their interaction. Scenarios developed for this behalf must be broadly based, addressing production, consumption and administration patterns and attitudes alike. This requires scenarios which deal with the effects of quantitative and qualitative physical and social factors in an integrative way. In the ALARM project [16], a number of explorative scenarios was developed; all were based on storylines and included model simulations with a range of different models to assess the impacts of multiple pressures on biodiversity.

The ALARM storylines represent a set of possible development directions, all starting from the status quo but representing different policy orientations based on different world views, leading to diverging policies and results. In doing so, they illustrate that human societies have options to minimise biodiversity loss but that this requires political decisions now and in the future. They also show that the recommendations derived from different scenarios grounded in different world views can be mutually exclusive and thus choices should include opting for a world view—which will probably not be a consensus decision. The three ALARM storylines cover social, economic, environmental, agricultural, foreign and other policies (see Table 1 and the Supplementary Materials):

- "Business As Might Be Usual" (BAMBU) is a policy-driven scenario, that is, a scenario extrapolating the expected trends in EU decision making and assessing their intended sustainability and biodiversity impacts materialise. Policy decisions already made in the EU are implemented and enforced. However, BAMBU is no business as usual scenario, based on trend extrapolation, since recent or upcoming changes in EU policies would have been ignored that way. At the national level as well as in the EU, deregulation and privatisation continue except in "strategic areas." Internationally, there is free trade. Environmental policy is mainly perceived as another technological challenge.
- "GRowth Applied Strategy" (GRAS) is a coherent liberal, growth-focussed policy scenario. It includes deregulation, free trade, growth and globalisation as policy objectives actively pursued by governments. Environmental policies will focus on damage repair and limited prevention based on cost-benefit calculations, with no emphasis on biodiversity beyond the preservation of ecosystem services ESS.
- "Sustainable European Development Goal" (SEDG) is a backcasting (inverse projection) scenario and as such it is necessarily normative, designed to meet specific goals and deriving the necessary policy measures to achieve them, for example, a stabilisation of GHG emissions. It aims at enhancing the sustainability of societal development by integrated social, environmental and economic policy. Policy priorities under SEDG are a competitive economy and a healthy environment, gender equity and international co-operation. SEDG represents a precautionary approach, taking measures under uncertainty to avoid not yet fully known future damages.

Table 1. Selected policies in the ALARM core scenarios. Starting from the same status quo conditions, the diverging policy assumptions drive the results into diverging directions. Source: [16].

Scenario	GRAS	BAMBU	SEDG
Climate envelope	fits to the IPCC SRES-A1FI storyline and its assumptions	SRES A2 (the best fitting available SRES scenario at the time of calculation)	SRES-B1 scenario (lowest SRES scenario available, 450 ppm not in SRES. B1 and SEDG story lines differ significantly)
CAP	Dismantling payments for production and for 2nd pillar (rural development & environment)	Shift 1st to 2nd pillar results in polarisation: intensification of high yielding locations, neglect of low yielding ones	Spatially explicit support structure to maintain (organic) agriculture throughout the landscape (only 2nd pillar transfers)
EU Funds	Phasing out, considered as subsidies	Focussed on infrastructure development and growth in poor regions	Focussed on local green development and opportunities, education and employment
Energy Policy	Efficiency, some renewables based on cost calculations	Efficiency, aiming at 20% reduction of GHG emissions by 2020 and 80% by 2080. Increase nuclear and renewables	Aiming at ¾ reduction of CO_2-emissions by 2050 through savings, changing consumption patterns and renewables
Transport Policy	Increased efficiency due to market pressure, no policy to shift the mode of transport or reduce transport volumes	Technological improvements and changing the share of different modes of mobility (walking, biking, trains, cars, boats, planes: modal split)	Transport reduction priority, plus modal split change (through pricing and infrastructure supply), technical improvements
Chemicals Policy	Focus on innovation and competitiveness. REACH not consequently implemented	REACH implemented	REACH plus; filling gaps for example, for metals, nanomaterials, endocrine disruptors
Trade Policy	Strong support for WTO and free trade	Promoting free trade except in "strategic areas"	Global sourcing reduced due to cost reasons; phytosanitarian controls

Although all ALARM core scenarios represent attempts to reach sustainable development, they diverge regarding how sustainability is operationalised (see Table 2). Whereas GRAS seeks to realise what is known as weak sustainability based on substitutability between capital stocks, BAMBU considers a minimum critical natural capital indispensable and SEDG foregoes the notion of capital stocks altogether. This has immediate implications for the understanding of sustainable development.

Table 2. Diverging concepts of sustainability in the three ALARM scenarios (own compilation). All scenarios are dedicated to reaching sustainability but with divergent definitions and tools, based on different world views, they follow significantly different, partly mutually exclusive trajectories.

GRAS	Three to four capital stocks, non-declining sum, mutually substitutable (weak sustainability), the economy considered as having primacy. Processes including overshoot are reversible. Assumption that once the economy works properly, all other parts of the puzzle will fall in place, that is, social and environmental problems will be solved automatically (the Kuznets- and Environmental Kuznets Curve hypotheses). Focus on adaptation (managing impact), optimal solutions by *maximisation*.
BAMBU	Three to four capital stocks, non-declining sum plus conservation of critical natural capital, mostly comparable and commensurable, attempts to go "beyond GDP," weak to reasonable protection standards. Precautionary principle, safe minimum standards, some ambitious protection standards set but not vigorously enforced, focus on innovation for the market to deliver the desired goods or fully equivalent substitutes. Focus on mitigation (reducing pressures) and restoration (stabilizing the state), optimal solutions by *optimisation*.
SEDG	Co-evolution of four sub-systems, with each having its own reproduction criteria and mechanisms, plus demands to the impacts of each other. Earth is a closed system with limited resources, permanent growth is not possible. Precautionary principle, addressing drivers of environmental and social crises, focus on prevention (redirecting drivers) and mitigation (overcoming pressures) limiting human impact, long term resilient/healthy ecosystems providing ecosystem services. Assessment is only possible by MCA/MCDS, (socially) optimal solutions by *legitimation*.

Developing these three options can be considered archetypical for sustainability-related scenario exercises: comparing a "muddling through" or business as usual scenario and one each representing a primacy of economic or environmental—and sometimes social—criteria, is a frequently used approach. It results in relatively similar, at least comparable scenario sets based on interpretations of two or three 'standard' world views, as Table 3 illustrates. "Tools such as scenario archetypes, that is, grouping scenarios together as classes based on similarities in underlying assumptions, storylines and characteristics, can then be used to integrate visions, thus highlighting conflicts and convergences across scales [33]." Thus, we consider the conclusions we will draw from analysing the ALARM scenarios as not case specific but most probably more generally applicable.

Table 3. Comparison of ALARM scenarios with other structurally similar global scenarios (adapted from an unpublished report for the Millennium Ecosystem Assessment). It illustrates that the typology chosen in ALARM (status quo policies, ambitious sustainability, radicalised neoliberal policies) is indeed archetypical for a wide range of scenario exercises.

ALARM	SRES	GEO-3	Millennium Ecosystem Assessment	Roads from Rio+20
2100	2100	2032	2100	2050
GRAS	A1FI	Markets First	Global Orchestration	Global Technology
BAMBU	A2	Security First	Order from Strength	
	B1	Policy First	TechnoGarden	Decentralized Solutions
SEDG	B2	Sustainability First	Adapting Mosaic	Consumption Change
Settele et al., 2005	IPCC et al., 2000	UNEP 2002	Millennium Ecosystem Assessment 2003	Kok et al., 2018

2.4. The Shocks

In illustrating the ALARM storylines, we combined, for each of them, climate scenarios from the set used by the IPCC, selected to offer the best fit with the expected climate development under the respective scenario [34]; a narrative-specific run of MOLLUSC [35], a spatially explicit land use scenario generator; and a specific set of parameters for runs of GINFORS, a highly endogenised econometric input-output model [36]. In an iterative process, the outputs and inputs to and between the models were harmonised, based on the narratives.

However, assuming a gradual development, that is, no surprises, is probably the most implausible vision of the future. Thus, in ALARM a methodological innovation was introduced by developing scenarios reflecting potential shocks, assuming disturbances with widespread consequences considered extreme at the time of writing. A shock is any event that comes unexpectedly and has the capability to change the development trajectory of a system. In each of the three dimensions used for sustainability concepts, the environmental, the economic and the social one, one shock was defined. The shock scenarios serve to illustrate that there can be a significant divergence of real-world developments from what linear modelling suggests; consequently, the shock scenarios could only partially be simulated in computer model runs.

The three shocks are indicated in Figure 1 together with the core scenarios from which they diverge:

- Cooling Under Thermohaline collapse (GRAS-CUT) is the environmental shock. It describes a collapse of the Atlantic Ocean water circulation (the most familiar part of it being the Gulf Stream) and the resulting relative cooling of Europe; indications observed by now.
- Shock in Energy price Level (BAMBU-SEL) describes the economic shock of a permanent quadrupling of the energy price, as expected when Peak Oil, the global maximum of oil production, occurs or political or other influences limit the supply significantly and permanently. We had a flavour of that in 1972, 1978 and 2008.
- ContAgious Natural Epidemic (BAMBU-CANE) is the social shock, a pandemic out of control. Again, we had a flavour of that, with the Chinese bird flu in 2006 and the Mexican swine flu in 2009 which permitted to observe the political and psychological mechanisms at work, regardless of their relatively limited global health impacts. In 2018, the WHO and Bill Gates, as chairman of the Bill and Melinda Gates Foundation, warn of such a pandemic being unavoidable if not imminent [37].

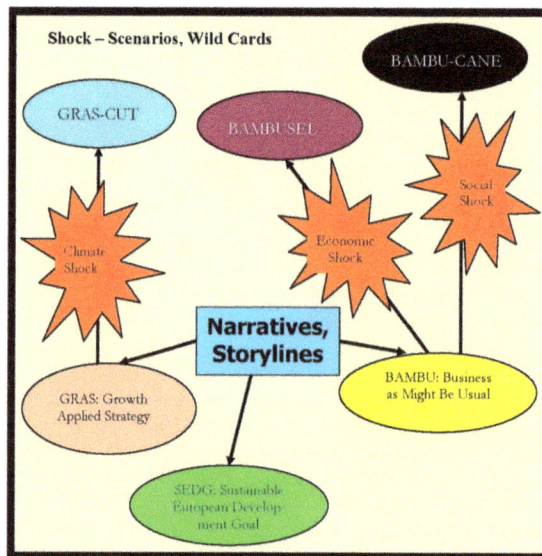

Figure 1. The ALARM core and shock scenarios. As SEDG is designed to avoid shocks, the analysis focusses on shocks under GRAS (as this is the high greenhouse gas emission scenario) and under BAMBU (shocks which are independent of scenario parameters).

As a climate shock is most probable under the scenario generating the highest greenhouse gas emissions, it is assumed to happen under GRAS. The economic shock is attributed to BAMBU as SEDG is assuming a reduction of resource consumption which would make such a shock less plausible. The social shock of a pandemic is essentially possible under all scenarios but probably less so under SEDG which assumes a reduction of global exchange for cost reasons (see Figure 1).

3. Results—Comparing the Scenarios and Their Background Assumptions

The model runs, complemented by biodiversity model analyses [38] and the results from a questionnaire survey addressing ALARM biodiversity experts showed that:

- GRAS consistently provides the least desirable outcome for biodiversity in Europe—across different biomes and for most ecosystems and species.
- "Muddling through" along the BAMBU path, although probably slowing down biodiversity losses, will systematically fail to meet the EU target to end the loss of biodiversity, by 2020 and beyond.
- From a biodiversity point of view, SEDG represents a significant step in the right direction, although not sufficient in every respect (in some biomes some species and ecosystems would still be lost).
- GRAS-CUT would reduce the average European temperatures to the level of the early 20th century. Minor declines in harvest could be compensated by imports or incremental diet changes.
- BAMBU-SEL represents an immediate burden on the economy which however recovers after shrinking significantly. More permanent damage is caused for the environment (by maximising biofuels at the expense of biodiversity) and the levels of disposable income (due to money transfers to oil exporting countries).
- BAMBU-CANE would lead to a collapse of the economy if more than 20% of the population left their occupations to seek shelter in their countryside houses; it does not kick-start again when they return.

3.1. The World Views in the Scenarios: Ontologies, Anthropologies, Axiologies

The reason for the divergences between the three core scenarios can be found in their different ideological orientations (see Table 4). Ideology is here understood in the sense of Söderbaum as praxeology [39], an understanding how means cause results and thus a core element of the respective world views. These orientations are rarely made explicit, in ALARM as in other scenario exercises but they are the result of and representative for the more or less conscious world views held by their authors. The less conscious scholars are regarding their world views and the influences these might have on their work, the more influences will affect the outcomes. This is true for the scenarios presented here and their analysis in this paper as well—although we tried to design all scenarios as we expected representatives of the respective world view would have done, we cannot rule out that the scenario authors' inclination to an ecological or ecological economics world view such as the one underlying SEDG has influenced both.

According to the GRAS *ontology*, nature and society are part of an extended definition of the economy, being described as social and environmental capital and valued as production factors. Those parts of both domains that do not contribute to production are left aside, while those that do deserve protection by policy measures, in particular the ecosystem services ESS. In the SEDG ontology, the environment is not part of the economy but vice versa, the economy is a subsystem of society which itself is embedded in the environment metasystem. One of the direct implications of the differing ontologies is that in the first case, corresponding to the neoliberal approach, the laws of economics apply to society and the environment, while the laws of nature do not necessarily apply to the economy. This assumption allows ignoring the entropy law, the second law of thermodynamics, in neoclassical schools of economics such as those utilised for GRAS.

Table 4. Ideological orientation and institutional arrangements in the scenarios [40–42], modified.

Content	GRAS	BAMBU	SEDG
Ideological orientation	business as usual, sustained growth (macro) and profits (micro), quantitative, monetary criteria (no qualities)	ecological modernisation, qualitative growth, changes of aspects but not system basics, flexible adaptations	precaution, multi-dimensional objectives, limited win-win options, priority for justice, health and environment over net growth
Economic paradigm	Neoclassical	incoherent, neoclassical plus etatism, welfare state, technology, green growth	sustainability economics: ecological, evolutionary, institutional and political economics
Institutional arrangements	Institutions facilitating 'corporate globalisation' like IMF, World Bank, WTO	Focus on regional integration. EU a strong player in international institutions, modifying but not altering rules	Subsidiarity principle. For example, strengthening the UN, evaluating where the EU needs more and where it could have less competences and similarly so on the members state level

On the other hand, if the economy is a subsystem of society which itself is a subsystem of the environment, not only the laws of thermodynamics apply to the economy just like the laws of gravity but this is also true for the laws—or rather the rules—identified by sociology and psychology. Then enterprises can be understood as social constructs, with a lot of processes, far beyond management, shaping their functioning and outcomes, while functions and performance are constrained by the laws of nature [21].

Regarding the *anthropology*, GRAS follows the neoclassical approach of assuming rational decisions of the homo economicus (a necessary assumption in equilibrium models), complemented by a belief in the problem-solving capabilities of technology: the market and human ingenuity, will bring about the right solutions at the right time to permit frictionless development and growth. The humans populating SEDG are different, with reflection, doubt, some selfishness but also concern for others and keen to maintain the public goods and capable of sharing instead of owning.

In terms of values (*axiology*), in SEDG the contributions to citizens' quality of life an enterprise provides is an essential criterion for the 'social license to operate' any business requires [43,44]. However, SEDG inhabitants are open to diverse definitions of what people may consider to be contributing to their respective quality of life. Value pluralism in implementation also characterises the ideas of justice in SEDG, understood as enabling all inhabitants to lead a dignified life, including fair participation in the respective society. This presupposes a needs-based distribution to achieve more social equity (iustitia universalis and iustitia distributiva in the Aristotelian Nicomachean Ethics). Amongst GRAS inhabitants, instrumental values dominate; they identify the value of an object according to its contributions to one's own wealth and well-being. Equity of outcomes is no moral objective—justice is done when people are rewarded based upon what they contribute (meritocratic concept, iustitia communitativa). The three shock scenarios, when motivating demands for more ambitious precaution, philosophically draw on the 'imperative of responsibility' suggested by Hans Jonas: "Never must the existence or essence of man as a whole be made a stake in the hazards of action" [45] (p. 12). He argued: "In order to ascertain the indubitable truth, we should, according to Descartes, equate everything doubtful with the demonstrably wrong. Here on the contrary we are told to treat, for the purposes of decision, the doubtful but possible as if it were certain, when it is of a certain kind," that is, when violating the 'imperative of responsibility' [45] (p. 37), [46].

3.2. The World Views in the Scenarios: Economic Orientations

As a result of the different value orientations, the *economic orientations* listed in Table 5 also differ. GRAS is a market and competition society imaginary representing a typical liberal capitalism approach while SEDG—including markets and competition but embedding them into a social frame—pictures a postmodern, sustainability oriented society. Nonetheless it incorporates many elements of the more traditional model of "Rhenish Capitalism," which is in line with the welfare state to etatistic socio-economic type underlying the scenario. BAMBU is not discussed here as it follows no coherent orientation but, representing EU policies, is a compromise between different approaches (with the balance changing from time to time).

Table 5. The economic orientations result from the values pursued and the ontologies (including praxeologies) prevailing in the respective world views as described in Section 3.1.

Orientation	GRAS	SEDG
Source of profit	Share value, speculation	Dividend, payment to owners
Ownership	Temporary, share-based	Permanent, individual
Level of profit	Fixed management objective, predetermined	Residual, after material, labour and finance costs
Perception of corporate success	Achievement of management and providers of finance (shareholders), at the expense of jobs and salaries	Achievement of partners, sharing of results
Salaries	Residual after material and finance costs, plus profit	Negotiated costs, based on productivity increase plus inflation compensation
Relation management/staff' salaries	Management increasing with profit or more, salaries stagnate or decline to generate profit	Increasing in line
Industrial relation	Exploitation	Partnership
Sustainability ethics	Utilitarism	Fairness, procedural justice

Stakeholders in GRAS rely on the market to deliver environmentally optimal solutions once externalities have been internalised. They trust in solutions to environmental problems and scarcity through better and more efficient technologies necessarily emerging in a competitive and growing market economy. Opposed to that, SEDG citizens call for sufficiency to complement efficiency (and make it effective by skimming off rebound gains), for respecting nature's limits and for fair distribution of access to societal participation including to nature's contributions to people. In SEDG the assumption prevails that economic instruments can offer incentives complementing and dynamising regulations but that the market as such is not a reliable means to achieve environmental sustainability.

Consequently, substituting regulation for green taxation (the Pigouvian approach) and privatisation, definition of unambiguous property rights and deregulation (the Coasean approach) are both part of GRAS. Such instruments play a secondary role in SEDG and are only used on a case by case basis—here no silver bullet exists and each 'bullet' is considered as potentially causing damages to vulnerable groups, target or not [47]. Mobilising private capital is important in both scenarios but the means of doing so differ: while in GRAS public seed money and Public—Private—Partnerships PPP dominate, in SEDG private investment is mobilised by the necessity to comply with legal standards, for example, regarding emissions, waste treatment and product recyclability. As a result, investment in GRAS follows profit maximising criteria, while the obligation driven investment in SEDG can be oriented towards investment into public goods.

3.3. The World Views in the Scenarios: Social Models and Welfare Regimes

As social policies are part of the narratives and where appropriate the modelling, the attitudes towards social justice used in the scenarios have been based on those present in the EU. According to Opielka at the time of developing the scenarios three attitudes were dominant [41]:

- *The liberal model:* if interview partners supported state responsibility for securing individual income levels in at least two of the three cases "illness," "old age" and "unemployment" but not beyond. These preferences were implemented in GRAS.
- *The welfare state model:* if in addition interviewees saw state responsibility for "reduction of income disparities," or "provision of jobs," or both. This corresponds to the BAMBU scenario assumptions.

- *The etatistic model:* if in addition they supported the control of salaries by law (implying a redistributive tax system), or a legally guaranteed general, tax financed basic income. Not all but some elements were included in SEDG.

Table 6 illustrates that the three models indeed represent the attitudes of the vast majority of the European population (which are significantly different from the USA, calling for caution before applying conclusions drawn from US empirical data to Europe).

Table 6. Attitudes towards social justice in Europe. Data source: [41].

	No. State Responsibility	Liberal	Welfare State	Etatistic	Unclassified
Average EU 15 member states	0.5	8.9	29.8	56.5	4.4
Sweden	0.7	20.2	40.9	34.5	3.7
UK	0.2	15.1	32.5	46.7	5.6
France	1.9	8.5	23.9	56.0	9.7
W.-Germany	0.8	13.7	46.8	34.0	4.7
Average CEE EU member states	0.5	4.7	21.8	69.1	3.9
E.-Germany	0.0	2.8	13.9	80.7	2.6
Czech Republic	2.2	12.1	24.2	54.8	6.8
Poland	0.4	3.1	17.2	76.7	2.6
Hungary	0.1	5.1	30.8	61.0	2.9
Bulgaria	0.0	6.7	12.1	76.7	4.6

Despite significant differences between old and new EU member states and within each group, there is still a broad consensus that either the welfare state or the etatistic approach are what citizens want, across the political spectrum. The differences between West and East Germany were rather pronounced in the polls but there were also important commonalities. For instance, the statement "The state must take care that everybody has a good livelihood/a decent life ("ein gutes Auskommen") in cases of illness, need, unemployment and old age" was supported by more than 77 resp. 86% of citizens in West resp. East Germany, across all party preferences, with the liberal party FDP scoring lowest [41]. Today, with more than decade of economic development, neoliberal policy and migration, the data might be different, although the basic patterns probably still prevail. Gerhards and Hölscher, in their analysis of the ISSP (International Social Survey Programme) results identified the same pattern, calling the three models European Commission, social-democratic and socialist [48].

The world views and their values shape the ways societies self-organise themselves, in particular their societal and political institutions, understood in the political sciences sense of being the rules by which political decision-making and implementation is structured (Table 7). Systems of rules shaping behaviour include formal and informal value-based orientations, mechanisms to realise them and including the mechanisms for rule enforcement [49,50]. Political organisations encompass both: they are social entities, appearing as actors in political processes, as well as systems of rules, structuring political behaviour and facilitating societal orientations.

While GRAS and SEDG are characterised by specific institutional settings shaped by the respective world views, BAMBU again exhibits a mix of views due to its character as reflecting the real-world political compromises. When the at least partially mutually exclusive suggestions derived from different world views have to be reconciled in international governance processes, this inevitably leads to either incoherent or vague policy formulations. This was already the case for the Brundtland Report and the Agenda 21 adopted in Rio 1992 and is still true for the 2030 Agenda adopted 2016 [51,52].

Table 7. ALARM Concepts of social justice and its institutional implementation [41], modified.

ALARM Scenario	Concept of Justice (in Aristotelian Nicomachean Ethics)	Institutional Level Involved			Famous Representatives
		Organisations	Mechanisms	Orientations	
		Steering System (Institutional Mechanism)	Social Relation, Typology of Reciprocity	Principle of Justice (Political)	
GRAS	Equity based upon what people contribute (Iustitia Communitativa)	Market	Instrumental association, exchange	Performance	Robert Nozick
BAMBU	Equity of opportunity (no clear relation)	State (often serving business)	Citizenship	Equity	John Rawls
SEDG	Equity based on distribution, needs based (Iustitia Distributiva)	Community	Community Solidarity, Communicative action	Need satisfaction, equality	Amitai Etzoni
	Equity based on enabling participation (Iustitia Universalis)	Legitimation	Political culture, human rights, communication of values	Participation, access, inclusion (N. Luhmann), global justice	Amartya Sen

The attitudes to social justice have also shaped the welfare regimes which emerged in different parts of Europe. Esping-Andersen identified three different political economies of the welfare state (liberal, social-democratic and conservative), with complex patterns of social policy including labour market, community system, family policy and the mode of state regulation itself [53]. We used his systematique to specify the social dimension in the scenario narratives (see Table 8). GRAS was designed to correlate to the liberal regime and SEDG with some—mainly environmental—modifications to the (traditional) social-democratic (the naming chosen by Esping-Andersen pre-dates the New Labour version of social democracy). No scenario is directly related to the conservative regime as traditional conservatism has largely given way to liberal policies. BAMBU as a political compromise is again characterised by a mix of elements from different regimes.

Table 8. Welfare regimes and social justice in Europe and their representation in the ALARM scenarios [41] (p. 330), based on [53], modified. As BAMBU is a mix of several components, the conservative welfare regime is added to make the comparison of sources easier.

Variable	Indicators	Liberal = GRAS	Social = SEDG	BAMBU	Conservative
Decommodification: protection against market forces and income loss	Level of income substitution, % of previous income.	Weak	Strong	Medium	Medium
	Share of individual financing	High	Low	Medium	Medium
Residualism	Share of basic support in total social expenditure	Strong	Limited	Medium to strong	Strong
Privatisation	Share of private expenditure for health and old age as share of total	High	Low to medium	Medium	Low to medium
Corporatism/Etatism	Number of social security systems for specific professions	Weak	Medium	Medium	Strong
	Share of expenditures for life-long employed government staff	Minimised	Increasing	Medium	Medium
Redistribution	Progression in (income) tax structure	Weak	Strong	Medium	Weak
	Equality of transfers received	Weak	Strong	Medium	Weak to medium
Full employment guaranty	Expenditures for active labour market policy	Low	Strong	Medium	Medium
	Unemployment quota, weighted by labour force participation	Medium	Low	Medium	Medium
Role of market in social security provision	Shares of transfers and recipients	Central	Marginal	Medium	Strong

Table 8. *Cont.*

Variable	Indicators	Liberal = GRAS	Social = SEDG	BAMBU	Conservative
Role of state in social security provision	Shares of transfers and recipients	Minimised	Central	Subsidiary to medium	Subsidiary
Role of family/community in social security provision	Shares of transfers and recipients	Subsidiary	Subsidiary	Marginal to subsidiary	Central
Role of human rights	Beyond legal status, respect in social life and employment	Medium	High	Medium to high	Medium
Dominant form of welfare state solidarity	Entitlement basis	Individual	Work focussed (in SEDG incl. unpaid work)	Labour focusses, tax support	Communitarian, etatistic
Dominant means of steering social policy	Agency and organising principle	Market, economic optimisation	State, equity principles for citizens/inhabitants	Mixed market and state, mixed ideas	Moral and economic
Underlying concept of social justice	As realised by institutional mechanisms	Equality of opportunity	Distributional justice	Opportunity & distribution	Fair participation, basic need satisfaction
Archetypical countries	Switzerland	USA	Sweden	EU	Italy, Germany

As one result of all these divergences, some of the most politically relevant factors also diverge, such as the target groups of policy recommendations and the justifications of the recommendations themselves, in particular the assumed resilience resp. vulnerability of the system and the calculation of future costs and benefits (Table 9). The difference in economic valuation mechanisms can be expected to contribute to and legitimate diverging policy priorities. The different ideas about dynamics, that is, whether or not social and environmental developments are reversible, lead to different levels of precaution and thus different policy recommendations. These are expected to appeal to different stakeholder groups—agents with a neoclassical economic background are expected to be more open for recommendations based on a similar world view and the same applies for proponents of other world views which are—other than the GRAS world view—today not hegemonic.

Table 9. Additional policy shaping implications of the world views in GRAS and SEDG, compiled from [54–58].

	GRAS	SEDG
Future value	Exponential discounting, positive discount rates	Object dependent: no, hyperbolic, linear or exponential discounting
Dynamics	Equilibrium with reversible deviations, series of equilibria, largely predictable, high inherent resilience	Nature and society are processes of continuous irreversible change, path dependent but unpredictable, with medium to high vulnerability
Resonance group of policy recommendations	Economic and fiscal policy makers, business	Policy makers, civil society

3.4. The World Views in the Scenarios: Epistemologies and Science Implications

Just like ontologies and axiologies, the epistemologies are different between the archetypical scenarios, with BAMBU an uneasy mixture of elements. Both SEDG and GRAS come with a specific philosophy of science related to the overall philosophical basis of the respective world view and this defines their epistemologies.

While critical realism based assessments searching for answers are dominant in SEDG, in GRAS positivism prevails, allowing scientists to claim knowing a superior truth and communicate that to decision makers ('truth speaks to power'). In SEDG, uncertainty and ignorance are acknowledged, as well as the plurality of legitimate knowledge sources including their potential contradictions, legitimacy plays an important role. Hence the focus on participatory processes, discourses and knowledge co-production (see Table 10).

Table 10. Science and science-society relationships in the scenarios. Mode 1 and mode 2 are terms from the sociology of science, coined by Gibbons et al., referring to the way (scientific) knowledge is produced [59]. Mode 1 is characterised by a co-operation between science and society without any change in working methods of either while mode 2 is defined as a partly descriptive and partly normative way to operationalise sustainability science. Funtowicz and Strand suggested a systematique of science-society relationship distinguishing five models [40]: 1. The initial 'modern' model (perfection/perfectibility), 2. The precautionary model (uncertain and inconclusive information), 3. The model of framing (arbitrariness of choice and possible misuse), 4. The model of science/policy demarcation (possibility of abuse of science), 5. The model of extended participation (working deliberatively within imperfections). Post-normal science is a discursive model developed by Funtowicz and Ravetz [60].

	GRAS	BAMBU	SEDG
Theory of science, mode	Positivism Mode 1	Eclectic mix, positivism dominates, Mode 1 dominates	Social constructivism, subjectivism, hermeneutics, contextualism, Mode 2 dominates
Models of science-society relationship	The initial 'modern' model: perfection/perfectibility	The precautionary model, the model of framing & the model of science/policy demarcation	The model of extended participation: working deliberatively within imperfections
Role of scientists	Outside, truth speaks to power	different attitudes, scepticism about truth and power	Citizen scientist, post-normal science, sustainability science, discourse based. Participatory, multi-criteria and multi-perspective assessments

In science the mode of working, the choice of methods, the composition of teams and the selection of research questions is not an individual free choice of each scholar based on her world views (determining which questions are regarded interesting and relevant), the theories and models of science held by her (of course not independent from the world views but not fully determined by them) and her education, skills and experience (determining the methods and concepts available to each scholar) as the claim of 'independent science' would like to have it. Value free science is even less on the books as already the world views held by each scholar infuse values into the decision making. Instead choices are co-determined by external factors such as the calls and funding conditions, the preferences of journal editors and the reviewers they choose and other institutional settings determining careers in science. Thus, the world views of decision makers in different functions and on different levels—and not only those of the scholars themselves—are crucial for the course the scientific endeavour takes, the information it generates and the advice it offers to inform and support decision making processes.

Besides the implications for our research hypothesis formulated in Section 1, in Section 4 we will point to some additional policy relevant conclusions that can be drawn from the conceptual analysis and its comparison to the empirical data upon which the scenario designs have been based.

4. Discussion and Conclusions

Scenarios are scientific tools to inform political and economic decision making. Consequently, having undertaken a deeper look into their fundamentals than usual, we can draw some conclusions regarding both, the role of science and decision making.

4.1. The Role of Science

That the world views of decision makers in different functions influences the course the scientific endeavour takes has positive and negative effects: on the positive side, according to our hypothesis, an alignment of world views (and thus of relevance criteria) will make it easier for scientific information and advice to be recognised, acknowledged and actively used in decision making. The potentially negative effects result from the character of the political process as interest-driven, which could make it difficult if not impossible for researchers to produce knowledge which may be used in policy processes by opposition parties and counter-hegemonial forces in civil society. The founding of autonomous universities in Spain and other countries in the 1960s and the establishment of ecological research institutes in Germany in the 1970s and the Science Shops ('Wetenschapswinkel') in The Netherlands and elsewhere in the 1980s have been the result of such situations in earlier phases.

Currently however, while civil society complains about the lack of research on sustainability transition processes and other politically relevant issues while criticising the dominant influence of business interests on research spending, it appears to be the outside world, pressure groups and donors beyond the ivory tower, which pressurises the scientific establishment to open up to new thinking and methods developed by heterodox scientists over the last decades [61,62].

4.2. World View Based Science—Policy Resonance: Support for the Research Hypothesis

The GRAS scenario and those similar to it in other scenario exercises is based on a world view related to neoclassical economics, a view shared by many decision makers. While its perception of sustainability as a constant sum of capital stocks ('weak sustainability') has provoked criticism from environmental scientists for the insufficient reflection of complexity and path dependency and the assumption of reversibility of changes, it is considered as a suitable basis for sustainability policies by many decision makers holding a related world view. The result is the wide-spread endorsement of "green growth policies" and their implementation in national policies and international agreements. Not only that, it is also changing environmental science as its terminology (and this its epistemology) are taken up by scholars seeking political attention and scientific bodies in charge of providing information for policy preparation processes such as the European Environment Agency, the IPCC or IPBES which phrase their advice using terms like natural capital and the internalisation of external cost. While the results offered by SEDG-like scenarios are consistently more promising regarding their sustainability effects and endorsed by governance agreements such as the 2030 Agenda, the means to achieve such effects are rejected as unrealistic, resulting in a cognitive dissonance: what is considered realistic is known to be of limited effectiveness (like the EU Biodiversity Strategy assessed by the European Commission itself to be on the brink of failing again) and what is effective is considered to be unrealistic. This is like being between a rock and a hard place—at least one of the two has to give in. In the case assessed here, either the imagination of "realistic instruments" has to be broadened to accommodate more radical measures, or the ambitious targets have to be given up in EU sustainability and climate policy (as it is the trend of the last decade in Germany). Thus, our hypothesis seems to be supported by the findings and offers policy relevant insights.

What is evidence in 'evidence based decision making'? The mechanistic thinking in equilibria inherent in GRAS has been criticised for its low level of complexity which allows for making predictions. This makes it virtually impossible to generate recommendations suitable as the basis for decisions in managing such complex systems as the economy, society or the environment [30]. However, the GRAS world view and the neoclassical economic thinking it supports are widely spread amongst decision makers and the resonance scientific policy proposals based on it find amongst them supports our hypothesis. Such proposals are effective despite the qualified scientific criticism regarding the proposals made, for instance in the cases of geo-engineering or GMO food. World views can be a kind of dangerous Procrustean bed; as Julie "Nelson said "Economists seeking to disguise their value judgements under a veneer of Cartesian objectivity [...] are dangerous" [63]. The reason is not least that deriving policy advice from linear extrapolation of past events in mechanistic systems can be described metaphorically as being like driving a car not looking for the road ahead but trying to determine the course to set by extrapolating from what can be seen in the rear mirror. Unfortunately (for this approach), in evolving systems past evidence is no reliable guide to conclusions regarding future events. Instead of promising evidence, the best available scientific information should be the basis of decision making and as uncertainty and ignorance necessarily remain, science has no "truth" to tell to "power." So, what scholars and decision makers alike can realistically strive for is scientifically informed decision making, not evidence.

Explaining communication failures: While in the ALARM scenarios, every inhabitant in one of them shares her scenario's world view and interacts with other agents on this basis, in the real world of course different groups endorse different world views, or, more precisely, different individuals do, strongly influenced in their decision process by their social environment (family, household, peers, colleagues, friends, role models, ...). Reading the scenarios against this background also illustrates why real-world agents, despite articulating similar goals, cannot agree and sometimes even enter fierce conflicts about the definition of the shared goals (rarely discussed openly) and the way and means to get there—the latter dominating the public debate. The scenarios, read as mental maps of different agents, illustrate that what one agent may consider essential, another may perceive as effective betrayal of the common goal and as utterly obstructive. The UK discussion about the meaning of Brexit provides ample examples of such controversies.

4.3. Policies and World Views—The Probably Most Prominent Example

Limits to growth, the 1972 report of the Club of Rome [7], was perceived differently in the USA, where politicians and the economics profession immediately and fiercely rejected it, while in much of Western Europe it struck a chord with the public opinion and a part of the decision makers. The most prominent endorsement of a new world view, stimulated by the report, was probably the one of the then President of the Commission of the European Communities, Sicco Mansholt, who said in a round table statement on 14 October 1973 [64]:

> "To me, the most important question seems to be: how can we achieve zero growth in this society? It is beyond doubt for me, that this zero growth must be achieved in our industrial societies, in America, Western Europe and Japan. ... Should we not succeed in doing so, then the distance, the tensions between arm and rich nations will become bigger and bigger. ... It would be an illusion and even a lie to pretend there could be no growth for the Third World economies unless we were performing growth as well. I am worried however whether we will manage to get those powers under control, which strive for a permanent growth. Our whole societal system insists on growth—not only single companies, big business, multinational giants." (own translation)

However, in the meantime decision makers holding the SEDG-like world view of Mansholt have become a rare exemption, while the GRAS world view has become hegemonic. To Mansholt, a GRAS scenario, its objectives and policies would have been anathema due to its focus on GDP growth, with a secondary role for environmental concerns and even less dedication to overcome the tensions between the rich and the poor nationally and internationally. Opposed to that, all presidents of the European Commission after Jaques Delors held a GRAS world view, unshakable by environmental failures (biodiversity, climate) and social hardships (Greece, Portugal, ...). To all of them, an etatistic development trajectory, let alone economic degrowth, were a priori unacceptable, even unthinkable. Instead "We need growth" describes the prevailing policy orientation [65], in line with a GRAS world view which expects the solution of social and environmental problems from sufficient economic growth. However, policies based on this world view are confronted with a number of policy failures and public scepticism which are increasingly hard to ignore. For instance:

Social aspiration discrepancy: As far as BAMBU is a realistic reflection of the current EU policies, this comparison demonstrates the divergence of EU policies and EU citizen preferences as they are obvious from table A1. Already this is an important result for European policy making and it underscores the preference of European citizens for a rather BAMBU-to-SEDG kind of policy priorities—which of course has impacts beyond the social domain, for both economic and environmental policies. Current policies tend to follow populist impulses towards a BAMBU-to-GRAS policy with some additional elements like migration controls, an issue dominating political discourses and media but not public concerns. The world views of decision makers and lay people appear to diverge, making communicative processes in decision preparation and mobilising public support for policies based on the GRAS world view ever more challenging; the conflicts around free trade agreements and the unwillingness of the Commission to make substantive concessions are just one point in case.

Biodiversity conservation failure: For EU policies, the ALARM scenario results imply that although certain species and eco-systems may be stabilised under the EU policies as modelled in the BAMBU scenario, current policies will not be able to deliver on the 2020 target, not even with delay. The shock scenarios indicate both the resilience of the socio-environmental system and its vulnerability beyond certain tipping points; currently the EU institutions are not well prepared for such shocks.

Cognitive dissonance: While a reconceptualization of progress is already under way as "targets for human development are increasingly connected with targets for nature, such as in the United Nations' Sustainable Development Goals" [33] (p. 1416), many decision makers suffer from the cognitive dissonance mentioned, an unpleasant and unstable state of mind caused by the political dilemma that while time-tested instruments fail (again), few alternatives exist in the world view held so dear for so long. Bill Rees describes the situation saying that "the ecologically necessary is politically infeasible but what is politically feasible is ecologically irrelevant" (pers. comm). Thus, as mentioned, the current pursuit of Green Growth by the EU but also by the OECD and UNEP can be understood as an attempt to reconcile the incommensurable [66–68]—a political approach which can succeed in conference resolutions and conventions but is bound to fail already in the medium term when the real-world implementation does not allow for the vagueness of paper work anymore [69]. Some of the erratic and inconsistent policy making can be plausibly explained by this constellation.

In a similar fashion, when the Great Recession hit the world's economies in 2008, neoclassical economists—after an initial shock period as the crisis hit them unprepared—modified their stance, endorsing selected elements of the long-condemned Keynesianism but embedding it into their own world view. While reactivating the policy instrument of deficit spending, countercyclical policies were not on the table, let alone the improvement of purchasing power by increasing salaries, both core elements of Keynesian policies. Instead the Keynesian theory was declared to be a valid receipt in times of crisis, justifying the use of heterodox instruments while declaring the own, just failed approach as being the right one for 'normal times.' That following their prescriptions in such normal times had led to the disaster was fiercely denied, saving the world view from critical reflection.

4.4. Conclusions

World views do not manifest themselves as sets of axioms or deep analyses but as the stories which are the means by which we navigate the world. They allow us to interpret its complex and contradictory signals. We all hold a world view and we all possess a narrative instinct: an innate disposition to listen for an account of who we are and where we stand. When we encounter a complex issue and try to understand it, what we look for instantaneously is not consistent and reliable facts but a consistent and comprehensible story. When we ask ourselves whether something "makes sense," the "sense" we seek is not primarily rationality, as scientists and philosophers perceive it but narrative fidelity. Does what we are hearing reflect the way we expect humans and the world to behave? Does it fit together? Does it progress as stories should progress? A string of facts, however well attested, will not correct or dislodge a powerful story and the world view it represents. The response it is likely to provoke is indignation: people often angrily deny facts that clash with the narrative "truth" established in their minds (they reject the epistemology to protect their ontology). The only thing that can displace a story is a story—a world view which is not able to present a comprehensive story is on the losing side of societal battles for influence.

Thus, as their core worldview shapes how they frame their arguments, people chose one scenario not for its outcomes but for the world view it represents and the story told about it. While not being a proof, we have presented a number of analyses of the archetypical scenarios which make it more than plausible that switching the decision basis from one to another world view requires a change against deeply held beliefs and established and time-tested routines, habits and practices—an almost impossible step as long as the world view held does not clash with reality (as is the situation today) and a difficult one even then. This is probably a suitable explanation for the failure of so many sustainability scenarios ever since the "Limits to Growth" to motivate the policy changes the recommended. If even the Great Recession was not a shock significant enough to enforce rethinking (austerity policies were reactivated soon after the first symptoms of crisis began to recede), it is hard to imagine what could cause the shift to a different world view, except a change of leadership to people holding different world views from the outset. Populists have proven that this is possible but so far 'sustainablists' have not achieved similar results—not least as they fail telling a story which has the flavour of being both desirable and realistic (i.e., not ignoring the downsides of a sustainability transition). Scenarios as a combination of narratives and modelling can be a means of developing such stories but have not been exploited to that end sufficiently to make a difference so far. However, while scenarios will most probably not have the power to initiate a real change of course by the incumbents (as they will interpret any new facts in the context of the world views they hold) they may stimulate reflections by the agnostic and empower those critical of the state of policies and searching for better solutions.

As far as a GREEN GRAS scenario is a contradiction in terms (as it is according to the author's world view), unearthing the hidden world views behind different policies and exposing them to the scrutiny of public discourses in the glare facts and figures may be the only chance to enable the public at large to rethink its acceptance of policies not in line with their own world view and support alternative positions differing from the GRAS thinking in more than individual strategies and policy instruments. However, this requires that scientists as well make their world views and the assumptions derived from them explicit, to permit the public to identify those sources of information they consider trustworthy. Telling good stories about scientific findings, beyond the scientific publications, is an art most scientists do not command but which should be part of the curriculum in all disciplines, as step to truly public science for the common good.

Supplementary Materials: A detailed, yet unpublished description of the ALARM scenarios is available online at www.mdpi.com/2071-1050/10/7/2556/s1.

fundin: While this research on values and world views received no external funding, the ALARM project was funded by the European Commission under its Sixth Framework Programme, Grant No. GOCE-CT-2003-506675.

Acknowledgments: The author is indebted to the colleagues of the ALARM project for their contributions to the scenario work described, in particular Joan Martinez-Alier, Martin O'Connor and Josef Settele. The simulation results were produced by different modelling teams, the socio-economic (Joachim H. Spangenberg, Jill Jäger, Ines Omann, Andrea Stocker, Bernd Meyer), land use (Mark Rounsevell, Isabelle Reginster), climate change (Timothy Carter, Kirsti Jylha, Stefan Fronzek), N Deposition (Franz Badeck) and biodiversity teams (Thomas Hickler, Paul Miller, Benjamin Smith, Martin Sykes).

Conflicts of Interest: The author declares no conflict of interest.

References and Notes

1. OECD 2018. GDP Long-Term Forecast. Available online: https://www.oecd-ilibrary.org/economics/gdp-long-term-forecast/indicator/english_d927bc18-en (accessed on 9 May 2018).
2. IATA 2017. 2036 Forecast Reveals Air Passengers Will Nearly Double to 7.8 Billion. IATA Press Release No.: 55, 24 October 2017. Available online: http://www.iata.org/pressroom/pr/Pages/2017-10-24-01.aspx (accessed on 9 May 2018).
3. Johnson, P. 99 Facts on the Future of Business in the Digital Economy 2017. Available online: https://de.slideshare.net/sap/99-facts-on-the-future-of-business-in-the-digital-economy-2017 (accessed on 9 May 2018).
4. Samaniego, L.; Thober, S.; Kumar, R.; Wanders, N.; Rakovec, O.; Pan, M.; Zink, M.; Sheffield, J.; Wood, E.F.; Marx, A. Anthropogenic warming exacerbates European soil moisture droughts. *Nat. Clim. Chang.* **2018**, *8*, 421–426. [CrossRef]
5. Guerreiro, S.B.; Dawson, R.J.; Kilsby, C.; Lewis, E.; Ford, A. Future heat-waves, droughts and floods in 571 European cities. *Environ. Res. Lett.* **2018**, *13*, 034009. [CrossRef]

6. Watson, J.E.M.; Shanahan, D.F.; Di Marco, M.; Allan, J.; Laurance, W.F.; Sanderson, E.W.; Mackey, B.; Venter, O. Catastrophic Declines in Wilderness Areas Undermine Global Environment Targets. *Curr. Biol.* **2016**, *26*, 2929–2934. [CrossRef] [PubMed]

7. Meadows, D.H.; Meadows, D.L.; Randers, J.; Behrens, W.W. *Limits to Growth*; A Report to the Club of Rome; Universe Books: New York, NY, USA, 1972.

8. Meadows, D.H.; Randers, J.; Meadows, D.L. *Limits to Growth*; The 30-Year Update; Chelsea Green Publishing Company: White River Junction, VT, USA, 2004.

9. European Environment Agency (EEA). *Late Lessons from Early Warnings: The Precautionary Principle 1896–2000*; Environmental Issue Report No. 22; Office for the Official Publications of the European Communities: Luxembourg, 2001.

10. European Environment Agency (EEA). *Late LESSONS from Early Warnings: Science, Precaution, Innovation*; Office for Official Publications of the European Communities: Luxembourg, 2013.

11. Spangenberg, J.H. Indicators for Sustainable Development. In *Routledge International Handbook of Sustainable Development*; Redclift, M., Springett, D., Eds.; Routledge, Taylor & Francis Group: Oxford, UK, 2015; pp. 308–322.

12. Spangenberg, J.H. World views, interests and indicator choices. In *Routledge Handbook of Sustainability Indicators and Indices*; Bell, S., Morse, S., Eds.; Routledge, Taylor & Francis Group: Oxford, UK, 2018; pp. 48–65.

13. Machiavelli, N. *Il Principe*; Giunta: Firenze, Italy; Blado: Roma, Italy, 1532. Quoted from the German edition: *Der Fürst*; Insel Verlag: Frankfurt, Germany, 1990.

14. European Environment Agency (EEA). *Looking Back on Looking Forward: A Review of Evaluative Scenario Literature*; EEA: Copenhagen, Denmark, 2009.

15. Morus, T. *Utopia*; De Optimo Rei Publicae Statu: Basel, Switzerland, 1517.

16. Settele, J.; Hammen, V.; Hulme, P.; Karlson, U.; Klotz, S.; Kotarac, M.; Kunin, W.; Marion, G.; O'Connor, M.; Petanidou, T.; et al. ALARM: Assessing LArge-scale environmental Risks for biodiversity with tested Methods. *GAIA* **2005**, *14*, 69–72. [CrossRef]

17. Settele, J.; Penev, L.; Georgiev, T.; Grabaum, R.; Grobelnik, V.; Hammen, V.; Klotz, S.; Kotarac, M.; Kühn, I. *Atlas of Biodiversity Risk*; Pensoft: Sofia, Bulgaria; Moscow, Russia, 2010.

18. Daly, H.E.; Cobb, J.B., Jr.; Cobb, C.W. *For the Common Good: Redirecting the Economy towards Community, the Environment and a Sustainable Future*; Green Print: London, UK, 1990.

19. Lind, M. The Five Worldviews That Define American Politics. *Salon Magazine*, 2011. Available online: https://www.salon.com/2011/01/12/lind_five_worldviews (accessed on 10 May 2018).

20. Hedlund-de Witt, A. Exploring worldviews and their relationships to sustainable lifestyles: Towards a new conceptual and methodological approach. *Ecol. Econ.* **2012**, *84*, 74–83. [CrossRef]

21. Spangenberg, J.H. The world we see shapes the world we create: How the underlying worldviews lead to different recommendations from environmental and ecological economics—The green economy example. *Int. J. Sustain. Dev.* **2016**, *19*, 127–146. [CrossRef]

22. Aerts, D.; Apostel, L.; De Moor, B.; Hellemans, S.; Maex, E.; Van Belle, E.; Van der Veken, J. *World Views: From Fragmentation to Integration*; VUB Press: Brussels, Belgium, 1994.

23. Beck, U.; Giddens, A.; Lash, S. *Reflexive Modernization: Politics, Tradition and Aesthetics in the Modern Social Order*; Stanford University Press: Stanford, CA, USA, 1994.

24. Spangenberg, J.H. Zukunftsfähigkeit als Leitbild? Leitbilder, Zukunftsfähigkeit und die reflexive Moderne. In *Reflexive Lebensführung*; Hildebrandt, E., Linne, G., Eds.; Zu den Sozialökologischen Folgen Flexibler Arbeit; Edition Sigma: Berlin, Germany, 2000; pp. 249–270.

25. Bentham, J. *An Introduction to the Principles of Morals and Legislation*; Reprint of the 1823 edition, with revisions by the author of the 1789 original publication; Clarendon Press: Oxford, UK, 1907.

26. Levine, J.; Chan, K.M.A.; Satterfield, T. From rational actor to efficient complexity manager: Exorcising the ghost of Homo economicus with a unified synthesis of cognition research. *Ecol. Econ.* **2015**, *114*, 22–32. [CrossRef]

27. Whiting, K.; Konstantakos, L.; Carrasco, A.; Carmona, G.L. Sustainable Development, Wellbeing and Material Consumption: A Stoic Perspective. *Sustainability* **2018**, *10*, 474. [CrossRef]

28. Hiebert, P.G. *Transforming Worldviews: An Anthropological Understanding of How People Change*; Baker Academic: Grand Rapids, MI, USA, 2008.

29. Alcamo, J. Scenarios as tools for international environmental assessments. In *EEA European Environment Agency Expert Corner Report 'Prospects and Scenarios' No. 5*; Office for the Official Publications of the European Communities: Luxembourg, 2001.

30. Spangenberg, J.H. Sustainability and the Challenge of Complex Systems. In *Theories of Sustainable Development*; Enders, J.C., Remig, M., Eds.; Routledge, Taylor & Francis Group: Oxford, UK, 2014; pp. 89–111.

31. Spangenberg, J.H. Looking to the Future: Finding Suitable Models and Scenarios. In *Towards the Ethics of a Green Future. The Theory and Practice of Human Rights for Future People*; Düwell, M., Bos, G., Steenbergen, N.V., Eds.; Routledge, Taylor & Francis Group: Oxford, UK, 2018.

32. Limits to Growth Was Right. New Research Shows We're Nearing Collapse. *The Guardian*, 2014. Available online: https://www.theguardian.com/commentisfree/2014/sep/02/limits-to-growth-was-right-new-research-shows-were-nearing-collapse (accessed on 10 May 2018).

33. Rosa, I.M.D.; Pereira, H.M.; Ferrier, S.; Alkemade, R.; Acosta, L.A.; Akcakaya, H.R.; den Belder, E.; Fazel, A.M.; Fujimori, S.; Harfoot, M.; et al. Multiscale scenarios for nature futures. *Nat. Ecol. Evol.* **2017**, *1*, 1416–1419. [CrossRef] [PubMed]

34. Fronzek, S.; Carter, T.R.; Jylhä, K. Representing two centuries of past and future climate for assessing risks to biodiversity in Europe. *Glob. Ecol. Biogeogr.* **2011**, *21*, 19–35. [CrossRef]

35. Reginster, I.; Rounsevell, M.; Butler, A.; Dedoncker, N. Land use change scenarios for Europe. In *Atlas of Biodiversity Risk*; Settele, J., Penev, L., Georgiev, T., Grabaum, R., Grobelnik, V., Hammen, V., Klotz, S., Kotarac, M., Kühn, I., Eds.; Pensoft Publ.: Sofia, Bulgaria; Moscow, Russia, 2010; pp. 100–105.

36. Spangenberg, J.H.; Bondeau, A.; Carter, T.R.; Fronzek, S.; Jaeger, J.; Jylhä, K.; Kühn, I.; Omann, I.; Paul, A.; Reginster, I.; et al. Scenarios for investigating risks to biodiversity. *Glob. Ecol. Biogeogr.* **2012**, *21*, 5–18. [CrossRef]

37. Quick, J. Are We Prepared for the Looming Epidemic Threat? *The Guardian*, 18 March 2018. Available online: https://www.theguardian.com/commentisfree/2018/mar/18/end-epidemics-aids-ebola-sars-sunday-essay (accessed on 18 March 2018).

38. Hickler, T.; Vohland, K.; Feehan, J.; Miller Paul, A.; Smith, B.; Costa, L.; Giesecke, T.; Fronzek, S.; Carter Timothy, R.; Cramer, W.; et al. Projecting the future distribution of European potential natural vegetation zones with a generalized, tree species-based dynamic vegetation model. *Glob. Ecol. Biogeogr.* **2011**, *21*, 50–63. [CrossRef]

39. Söderbaum, P. Issues of paradigm, ideology, and democracy in sustainability assessment. *Ecol. Econ.* **2007**, *60*, 613–626. [CrossRef]

40. Söderbaum, P. Ecological economics in relation to democracy, ideology and politics. *Ecol. Econ.* **2013**, *95*, 221–225. [CrossRef]

41. Funtowicz, S.O.; Strand, R. Models of Science and Policy. In *Biosafety First: Holistic Approaches to Risk and Uncertainty in Genetic Engineering and Genetically Modified Organisms*; Traavik, T., Lim, L.C., Eds.; Tapir Academic Press: Trondheim, Norway, 2007; pp. 263–278.

42. Opielka, M. Gerechtigkeit durch Sozialpolitik? *Utopie Kreativ* **2006**, *186*, 323–332.

43. Thomson, I.; Boutilier, R.G. Social license to operate. In *SME Mining Engineering Handbook*; Darling, P., Ed.; Society for Mining, Metallurgy and Exploration: Littleton, CO, USA, 2011; pp. 1779–1796.

44. Falck, W.E.; Spangenberg, J.H. Selection of Social Demand-Based Indicators: EO-based Indicators for Mining. *J. Clean. Prod.* **2014**, *84*, 193–203. [CrossRef]

45. Jonas, H. The Imperative of Responsibility. In *Search of an Ethics for the Technological Age*; University of Chicago Press: Chicago, IL, USA, 1984.

46. Jensen, T. Moral responsibility and the business and sustainable development assemblage: A Jonasian ethics for the technological age. *Int. J. Innov. Sustain. Dev.* **2007**, *2*, 116–129. [CrossRef]

47. Spangenberg, J.H.; Settele, J. Value pluralism and economic valuation—Defendable if well done. *Ecosyst. Serv.* **2016**, *18*, 100–109. [CrossRef]

48. Gerhards, J.; Hölscher, M. *Kulturelle Unterschiede in der Europäischen Union: Ein Vergleich Zwischen Mitgliedsländern, Beitrittskandidaten und der Türkei*; VS Verlag für Sozialwissenschaften: Wiesbaden, Germany, 2005.

49. Czada, R. Institutionelle Theorien der Politik. In *Lexikon der Politik*; Nohlen, D., Schultze, H.O., Eds.; Droemer-Knaur: Munich, Germany, 1995; pp. 205–213.

50. Göhler, G. Wie verändern sich Institutionen? *Leviathan* **1997**, *Sonderheft*, 21–56.

51. Spangenberg, J.H. Institutional Sustainability Indicators: An Analysis of the Institutions in Agenda 21 and a Draft Set of Indicators for Monitoring their Effectivity. *Sustain. Dev.* **2002**, *10*, 103–115. [CrossRef]

52. Spangenberg, J.H. Hot air or comprehensive progress? A critical assessment of the SDGs. *Sustain. Dev.* **2017**, *25*, 311–321. [CrossRef]
53. Esping-Andersen, G. The Three Political Economies of the Welfare State. *Int. J. Sociol.* **1990**, *20*, 92–123. [CrossRef]
54. Daly, H.E. *Beyond Growth. The Economics of Sustainable Development*; Beacon Press: Boston, MA, USA, 1996.
55. Rink, D.; Wächter, M. Naturverständnisse in der Nachhaltigkeitsforschung. In *Sozial-Ökologische Forschung. Ergebnisse der Sondierungsprojekte aus dem BMBF-Förderschwerpunkt*; Balzer, I., Wächter, M., Eds.; Ökom-Verlag: München, Germany, 2002; pp. 339–360.
56. Spangenberg, J.H. Economic sustainability of the economy: Concepts and indicators. *Int. J. Sustain. Dev.* **2005**, *8*, 47–64. [CrossRef]
57. Renn, O. Sustainability: The need for societal discourse. In *Civil Society for Sustainability. A Guidebook for Connecting Science and Society*; Renn, O., Reichel, A., Bauer, J., Eds.; Europäischer Hochschulverlag: Bremen, Germany, 2012; pp. 18–37.
58. Neugebauer, F. A multidisciplinary sustainability understanding for corporate strategic management. In Proceedings of the 18th ISDRS Conference, Hull, UK, 24–26 June 2012.
59. Gibbons, M.; Limoges, C.; Nowotny, H.; Schwartzman, S.; Scott, P.; Trow, M. *The New Production of Knowledge: The Dynamics of Science and Research in Contemporary Societies*; SAGE Publications: London, UK; Thousand Oaks, CA, USA, 1994.
60. Funtowicz, S.O.; Ravetz, J.R. Science for the post-normal age. *Futures* **1993**, *25*, 739–755. [CrossRef]
61. Strunz, S.; Gawel, E. Transformative Wissenschaft: Eine kritische Bestandsaufnahme der Debatte. *GAIA* **2017**, *26*, 321–325. [CrossRef]
62. Wissel, C.V. Die Eigenlogik der Wissenschaft neu verhandeln: Implikationen einer transformativen Wissenschaft. *GAIA* **2015**, *24*, 152–155. [CrossRef]
63. Nelson, J.A. Economists, value judgements, and climate change: A view from feminist economics. *Ecol. Econ.* **2008**, *65*, 441–447. [CrossRef]
64. Pestel, E. *Jenseits der Grenzen des Wachstums: Bericht an den Club of Rome*; Verlagsanstalt: Stuttgart, Germany, 1988.
65. Juncker, J.-C. G7 Press Conference of EU Commission President Jean-Claude Juncker, 7 June 2015. Available online: https://www.europa-nu.nl/id/vjulg37huam9/nieuws/speech_full_transcript_of_the_g7_press?ctx=vhyzn0sukawp (accessed on 18 May 2018).
66. European Commission. *Europe 2020. A European Strategy for Smart, Sustainable and Inclusive Growth*; European Commission: Brussels, Belgium, 2010.
67. OECD. *Towards Green Growth*; OECD: Paris, France, 2011.
68. United Nations Environment Programme (UNEP). *Towards a GREEN Economy—Pathways to Sustainable Development and Poverty Eradication*; A Synthesis for Policy Makers; United Nations: New York, NY, USA, 2011.
69. Spangenberg, J.H. *Ideology and Practice of the 'Green Economy'—World Views Shaping Science and Politics*; Birnbacher, D., Thorseth, M., Eds.; The Politics of Sustainability: Philosophical Perspectives; Routledge, Taylor & Francis Group: Oxford, UK, 2015; pp. 127–150.

sustainability

MDPI

Article

Deep Decarbonisation from a Biophysical Perspective: GHG Emissions of a Renewable Electricity Transformation in the EU

Louisa Jane Di Felice [1],*, Maddalena Ripa [1] and Mario Giampietro [1,2]

[1]   Institute of Environmental Science and Technology, Universitat Autònoma de Barcelona,
      08193 Bellaterra, Spain; maddalena.ripa@uab.cat (M.R.); mario.giampietro@uab.cat (M.G.)
[2]   Catalan Institution for Research and Advanced Studies (ICREA), Passeig Lluís Companys 23,
      08010 Barcelona, Spain
*   Correspondence: louisajane.difelice@uab.cat

Received: 21 June 2018; Accepted: 26 September 2018; Published: 15 October 2018

Abstract: In light of climate change and security concerns, decarbonisation has become a priority for industrialised countries. In the European Union (EU), decarbonisation scenarios used to support decision-making predict a steady decrease in greenhouse gas (GHG) emissions, mostly driven by changes in production mixes and improvements in efficiency. In the EU's decarbonisation pathways, the power sector plays a large role, reaching zero emissions by 2050. From a biophysical perspective, decarbonisation becomes not just a matter of replacing carbon-intensive with carbon-neutral electricity flows, but also a matter of building and maintaining new infrastructure (funds) which, in turn, is associated with GHG emissions. By not accounting for the emissions associated with funds, particularly those required to increase grid flexibility, scenarios used to inform decarbonisation narratives in the EU are missing a key part of the picture. We show that a rapid and deep decarbonisation of the EU's power sector through a production-side transition between the years 2020 and 2050 leads to cumulative emissions of the order of 21–25 Gt of CO_2 equivalent, within a range of approximately 35–45%. The results are obtained by modelling two decarbonisation pathways where grid flexibility increases either through storage or through curtailment. The analysis suggests that scenarios informing decarbonisation policies in the EU are optimistic and may lead to a narrow focus on sustainable production transformations. This minimises the perceived urgency of reducing overall energy consumption to stay within safe carbon budgets.

Keywords: modelling; science-policy interface; grid flexibility; bio-economics; energy transition; storage; curtailment

---

1. Introduction

The type of primary energy sources (PES) used by societies to generate a given mix of energy carriers (ECs) is central in shaping their organisation, pace and activities [1,2]. Industrial societies have developed through a heavy reliance on fossil fuels, characterised by their high density. In addition, fossil fuels can be stored and transported across borders, bypassing local natural resource limitations. The exploitation of fossil fuels, while shaping industrial societies' activities and allowing for a high living standard and rapid rates of urbanisation [3], has also led to unbearable environmental effects, locally and globally. As a consequence, moving away from fossil-based energy systems has become a priority for industrialised economies. In addition to environmental concerns, in the EU, a renewable transformation of the energy system is also desirable from a security of supply perspective, given the lack of indigenous fossil fuels on local territory [4–6].

Thus, it has become progressively pressing in the EU to shift to alternative (local) energy sources resulting in lower greenhouse gas (GHG) emissions throughout their lifetime [6]. However, the shift itself has not been easy to initiate, model or govern. The Energiewende is an example of this, having led overall to higher electricity prices and higher emissions, despite strong efforts to shift production patterns of energy carriers [7].

Depending on the chosen problem framing, barriers to a renewable energy transition may be conceived as being of a political, economic, social, institutional or biophysical nature. We borrow the term biophysical from the field of bio-economics, where the economic process is viewed not only through the lens of monetary flows, but most importantly through the lens of flows of biological and physical resources that are produced, distributed, consumed and exchanged [8]. In this sense, the amount of water, emissions and labour associated with a certain energy system, for example, may be categorised as biophysical variables, in opposition to economic ones such as energy prices. Within the field of bio-economics, the term energy metabolism is used to describe the way in which societies extract, process and distribute flows of energy in order to carry out tasks that are crucial to the survival of their identity [9].

Taking a biophysical perspective of the energy system, in this paper we focus on the decarbonisation of the EU's power sector. Our aim is to provide an alternative narrative to those underpinning EU decarbonisation pathways, where barriers to energy transformations are mostly relegated to the domain of finance and investments [6]. To do this, we model alternative decarbonisation pathways that include the GHG emissions associated with the lifetime of funds. We borrow the distinction between funds and flows from Georgescu-Roegen [8]. Within Georgescu-Roegen's flow-fund model, given a chosen spatial and temporal scale of analysis, funds are those elements whose identity remains intact, while flows are elements either entering the system without exiting it or exiting it without entering it. From a metabolic perspective, funds are the elements metabolising flows—land, for example, is a fund to be maintained, while the food it grows is a flow. Considering an energy system over a yearly timescale, the electricity and fuels produced and consumed are flows. The infrastructure and human time invested in the production and consumption of flows are the funds of the system.

This distinction is important to study the implications of infrastructural changes in the energy system. The magnitude of infrastructural changes required on the production and consumption side for a decarbonisation of the energy system are not unknown to policymakers [10]. However, there is a tendency within scenarios at the EU's science-policy interface to use biophysical variables to describes changes in flows (e.g., the amount of electricity consumed over a year) and to adopt a monetary perspective to account for changes in infrastructure (e.g., the investments required to build new transmission and distribution lines). When considering changes associated with funds, a biophysical perspective (e.g., the amount of labour, emissions, water and waste associated with infrastructural changes) is often neglected. This is the case, for example, in the EU 2016 Reference Scenario, where capital investments linked to infrastructure are estimated [11].

Building on data available through existing studies, we developed a scenario singling out the EU power sector up to 2050 and hypothesized two different pathways for its decarbonisation. Increasing grid flexibility is central to ensuring that high levels of variable renewable energy (VRE) can be managed by the grid [12]. In the first pathway, grid flexibility was increased through high rates of curtailment of renewable generation and low storage; in the second, lower levels of curtailment were paired with storage technologies. In each pathway, the emissions associated with the cultivation, construction and fabrication (CFC) of funds were calculated at yearly intervals up to the year 2050, in addition to the operational emissions associated with electricity generation (flows). The approach is meta-analytical and adjusts data available in literature, rather than modelling the behaviour of the grid.

The rest of the paper is organised as follows: Section 2 provides an overview of the decarbonisation pathways currently modelled to support EU decision-making and places them within the wider academic discourses of energy and GHG payback time; Section 3 introduces alternative pathways, with an overview of the underpinning assumptions (Section 3.1) and modelling equations (Section 3.2).

The results and discussion are presented in Section 4, split into yearly and cumulative GHG emissions (Section 4.1), variational ranges in results (Section 4.2) and discussion of results (Section 4.3).

2. Background

2.1. Decarbonisation in EU Policy

In the EU, the energy sector accounted for approximately 30% of total emissions in 2016. It was the sector with the highest share of emissions, followed by transport and by manufacturing (accounting for approximately 20% each) [13]. EU decarbonisation policies fall under the 2050 low-carbon economy package [14], as part of the EU's wider climate strategy. The low-carbon economy roadmap calls for GHG emissions to be cut by 80% below the 1990 levels by 2050, with two intermediate milestones of 40% by 2030 and 60% by 2040. The strategy is currently being renewed in order to reflect the Paris Agreement and is expected to be updated by early 2019 [15].

The EU Energy Roadmap 2050, published in 2011, highlights four strategic directions for decarbonisation: energy efficiency, renewable energy sources (RES), nuclear and carbon capture and storage (CCS). The four directions are explored through six scenarios: current policies, high efficiency, high RES, delayed CCS, low nuclear and diversified supply technologies. Since the publication of the Energy Roadmap 2050, significant events such as the Paris Agreement and the release of the Clean Energy for all Europeans package have impacted EU energy discourses. In light of this, new scenarios have been developed to inform the EU's mid-century strategy, to be released by fall this year (2018). The scenarios included in the Clean Energy for all Europeans package model pathways to decarbonisation based on efficiency, integration of renewable energy sources and the functioning of the internal energy market [16]. The main trends, which are an increased share of RES, a linear decrease of GHG and an increased electrification, have persisted across the two generations of scenarios.

In the six decarbonisation scenarios of the Energy Roadmap 2050, RES rise significantly, to a minimum of 55% of gross consumption of energy carriers in 2050 and 60–80% of gross electricity production by the same year. Absolute electricity production increases steadily between 20 and 40% by 2050 across the six scenarios, despite an overall reduction in total energy consumption. This reflects trends in mitigation scenarios, where a gradual electrification of the energy system is seen as a key element for its decarbonisation [17]. Emissions across all sectors decrease steadily and monotonically—that is, there is no increase in emissions associated with infrastructural change and there are no relative peaks of GHG emissions throughout the years. Figure 1 shows an example of projected sectoral emission reduction in the high RES pathway.

The power sector, in particular, is seen to reach zero or almost zero emissions by 2050 for all pathways, as further indicated by the low-carbon strategy: "The power sector has the biggest potential for cutting emissions. It can almost totally eliminate CO_2 emissions by 2050" [14]. Similarly, the Intergovernmental Panel on Climate Change (IPCC) highlights the decarbonisation of the power sector as one of the three main components of mitigation scenario studies, together with a gradual electrification of the energy sector and a reduction in energy demand through technology and other substitutions [17].

The scenarios developed to support the Energy Roadmap 2050 build on the PRIMES (Price-Induced Market Equilibrium System) energy model, "a partial equilibrium modelling system that simulates an energy market equilibrium in the European Union and each of its Member States" [18].

For the accounting of GHG emissions, the model simulates the operational emissions associated with electricity production (a flow) but neglects the emissions associated with the construction of infrastructure (a fund). This omission is linked to the fact that grid flexibility requirements are not modelled. A small but growing body of literature in academia, as highlighted in the next sub-section, points towards the emissions associated with renewable infrastructure and with storage, and to how they may impact future decarbonisation pathways. Additionally, the need to increase grid flexibility at high renewable energy penetrations has been stressed and modelled for specific case studies, including Europe [19], Japan [20], Texas [21] and California [22].

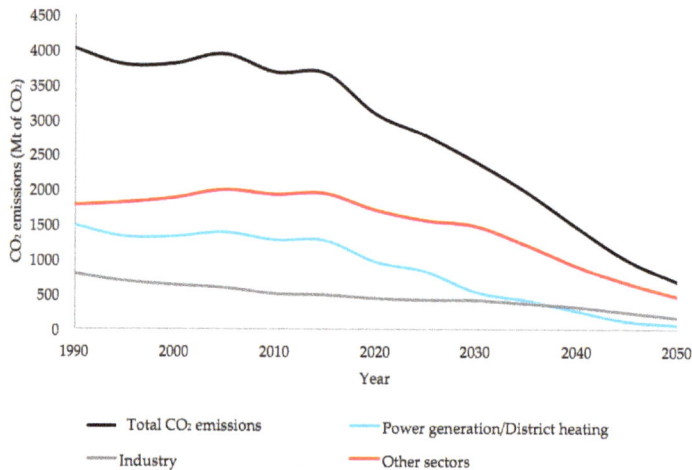

Figure 1. CO_2 emission projections, in megatons (Mt) of CO_2, under the EU high RES decarbonisation pathway. Source: Own elaboration from the EU Energy Roadmap 2050 [10].

However, EU energy policy discourses uphold the narrative that the main barrier to a high integration of RES into the energy system is financial rather than biophysical. The renewable energy package [6], for example, highlights a number of barriers envisioned on the path to a fully renewable energy system, including administrative hurdles, cost-effectiveness, loss of citizen buy-in and uncertainty for investors. Grid stability is also mentioned as an issue, with the electricity system needing to "adapt to an increasingly decentralized and variable production" [6]. Despite this mention, the issue is not framed as being central and no concrete targets for adaptation have been set, nor have the (biophysical) implications of increasing grid flexibility been included in the EU decarbonisation pathways.

2.2. Energy and GHG Payback Time

The biophysical investments (such as energy and land) associated with the construction of energy systems have been the subject of a prolific field of energy analysis. The widely used concept of Energy Returned on Energy Invested (EROI) accounts for the amount of net energy generated by an energy system, when the fixed capital and variable operational energy investments required for its construction and maintenance are discounted [23,24]. EROI is particularly relevant for the assessment of alternative energy carriers, such as biofuels, requiring a high energetic investment throughout their production chain [25]. A parallel concept to EROI is the Energy Payback Time (EPBT), accounting for the amount of time it takes for an energy system to break even in terms of the production of energy carriers (in relation to those consumed in its construction). So far, EPBT has been mostly applied to the analysis of solar panels [26,27]. Similar to EPBT, the emissions associated with the construction and operation of energy systems can be accounted for in what is known as the GHG, carbon or environmental payback time (GHGPBT). The GHGPBT indicates the time it takes for a system to become carbon neutral following an initial emission investment due to material extraction, transport and construction [28,29]. Figure 2 shows a schematic view of the concepts of energy and GHG payback time, central to the biophysical accounting of energy systems.

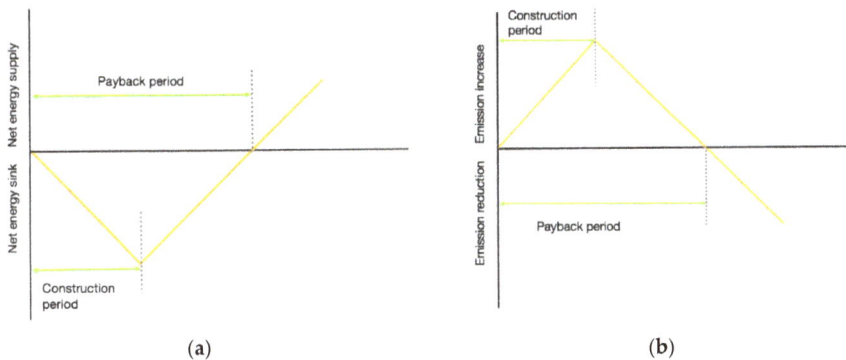

Figure 2. Schematic representation of EPBT (a) and GHGPBT (b).

The concepts of energy and GHG payback time can be applied to storage systems. A high penetration of intermittent energy sources into the electricity grid is likely to require a combination of demand-side management, storage infrastructure and improvement of transmission and distribution lines to ensure that intermittent electricity is dispatchable at all times [12]. Studies on storage estimations for a 100% renewable electricity system present high doses of uncertainty, however, the most thorough reviews point towards storage needs greatly beyond what is currently operational at the global scale [20–22]. Thus, the importance of being able to assess and compare the performance of storage systems has become evident. Building on the idea of EROI, Barnhart and Benson [30] introduced the concept of Energy Stored on Energy Invested (ESOI), accounting for the amount of net energy output provided by storage technologies compared to the energy invested in their construction and operation. Battery technologies show a performance approximately 20 times lower (in terms of ESOI) than compressed air energy storage (CAES) and pumped hydroelectric storage (PHS). However, due to the invasive nature of CAES and PHS and due to the strong limitations to their expansion brought by geographic configurations, batteries have become a popular option in the discussion of storage futures [31].

In a biophysical framing, the GHG emissions of storage technologies throughout their lifetime are a key element in the assessment of future energy scenarios. A thorough review by Denholm [31] showed how PHS is associated with the lowest amount of emissions over its lifetime, while batteries are associated with non-negligible lifetime emissions. In its present form, CAES relies on the use of natural gas and therefore also presents non-negligible lifetime emissions.

Similar to the emissions of storage infrastructure, the GHG emissions associated with the lifecycle of renewable infrastructure have been studied—see Nugent and Sovacool [32] for a thorough review of the topic. The emissions associated with renewable electricity generation over its lifetime are considerably lower than those associated with fossil electricity. As a consequence, not much attention has been placed in exploring the nuances of different pathways and storage options in terms of their associated emissions. Crucial questions regarding the best pathways to decarbonisation in relation to emission curves, thus, remain underexplored [32].

3. Alternative Decarbonisation Pathways

When dealing with complex systems, such as the social-ecological one, modelling may have two purposes: To predict and control future states of the system or to better understand the current one [33]. As the high doses of uncertainty attached to the prediction of future states of the complex social-ecological system become apparent, scenarios used to support decision-making are framed more and more as tools for deliberation, rather than prediction. The EU webpage on energy modelling, for example, states that the EU Reference Scenario, "one of the European Commission's key analysis tools in the areas of energy, transport and climate action", (. . .), "is not designed as a forecast of what is likely to happen in the future but it provides a benchmark against which new policy proposals can be assessed" [34]. In a similar spirit, the aim of the alternative decarbonisation pathways is not to predict the behaviour of future decarbonisation pathways in the EU. Rather, the aim is to flag the need to include emissions associated with the construction of infrastructure in decarbonisation discourses. This is particularly relevant for intermittent sources of energy and their grid flexibility requirements.

We explored two decarbonisation pathways of the EU's power sector for the years 2020–2050, each dealing differently with grid flexibility requirements. Focus was given to the integration of renewable energy into the grid as a means to decrease GHG emissions, in line with the high RES scenario of the EU's Energy Roadmap 2050, on which the two pathways were based. The values of gross electricity consumption up to 2050, in fact, were taken from the high RES scenario, as well as the share of nuclear electricity at each year. Hydropower was assumed to remain unchanged over the years, while solar power and wind power were assumed to increase until producing 90% of electricity, entirely phasing out fossil power plants. Adjusting data from existing studies, we calculated the emissions associated with the construction and operation of funds (renewable and storage infrastructure) with respect to the reduction in emissions due to the substitution of fossil with alternative energy systems (associated with the electricity generated by the systems—flows).

3.1. Modelling Assumptions

Any model informing the future behaviour of energy systems necessarily relies on heavy sets of assumptions regarding technology, consumption and production patterns. Modelling assumptions of the alternative decarbonisation pathways are split into two sections: grid flexibility and GHG emissions.

3.1.1. Grid Flexibility

Integrating high levels of variable renewable energy (VRE), such as the electricity produced by wind turbines or solar photovoltaic (PV) panels, into the grid requires an increase in the flexibility of the grid. Grid flexibility can be achieved in various ways. Kondziella and Bruckner [12] identified seven possible measures on the production and on the consumption side: highly flexible power plants, large-scale energy storage, curtailment of renewable surplus, demand-side management, grid extension, virtual power plants and linkage of energy markets. These measures, either individually or in unison, can ensure that electricity demand is met at all times. Here, focus was given to the production-side measures of large-scale energy storage and of the curtailment of renewable surplus.

Existing studies [12,19–22,35,36] show that increasing grid flexibility becomes essential when the share of VRE fed into the grid reaches levels of 40 to 50%. Grid flexibility can be increased through large-scale energy storage. In this case, surplus electricity generated by VRE when production is higher than demand can be converted into gravitational, thermal or electrochemical energy and fed back into the system when production is lower than demand. Curtailment of renewable surplus, on the other hand, relies on the installation of more renewable infrastructure than what is needed to cover average yearly demand (also known as backup power plants). When the combined electrical output of the renewable infrastructure is higher than the demand at a given point in time, the output of VRE plants is curtailed. As a result, curtailment of renewable surplus as a means to improve grid flexibility has an impact on the utilisation factor (UF) of renewable plants. The review paper by Kondziella and Bruckner [12] provided a thorough overview of existing studies assessing grid flexibility requirements for high renewable integration.

Steinke [19] examined the interplay between storage, curtailment and grid extensions for a 100% renewable electricity system in Europe. Denholm and Hand [21] and Denholm and Margolis [22] modelled, respectively, the electricity grids of Texas and California to provide an assessment of how grid flexibility can be achieved in low and high storage scenarios. The models of US case studies, produced for the National Renewable Energy Laboratory (NREL), have not been replicated in the EU to this level of detail and are the most comprehensive reference points for assessments of grid flexibility. Building on these studies [21,22], we hypothesised two pathways for decarbonisation: a low storage high curtailment (LSHC) pathway and a high storage low curtailment (HSLC) one. In the former, we assumed that no extra storage technologies were added to the EU's electricity system, therefore the only storage services available up to 2050 were those produced by current PHS facilities (at a storage capacity of approximately 600 GWh [37]). To ensure grid flexibility, renewable back up power was added and renewable generation was assumed to be curtailed. In the latter, curtailment was greatly decreased by the addition of storage services. Both scenarios adapted the curtailment and flexibility rates from the comprehensive model of the Texas grid [21]. The relations between curtailment and flexibility in the EU depend on specific geographies and grid configurations. However, for the purpose of these pathways—i.e., to point towards a problem in GHG accounting rather than to provide accurate predictions—this approximation was considered satisfising.

The total amount of storage required by 2050 was calculated following Steinke [19] and Renner and Giampietro [35]. Assuming that grid expansions were limited to the national scale and that no backup generation was provided, Steinke estimated that the EU would require between 7 and 30 days of storage to accommodate shares of 90% or more of VRE. Analysing data for Germany and Spain over an 84 months and 132 months, with a resolution of 60 minutes and 10 minutes respectively, Renner and Giampietro estimated that the two countries would require approximately one week of storage capacity in a 100% intermittent penetration scenario. The study used the comprehensive datasets available for the two countries to check "the extent of the predicted worst annual hypothetical 'failure event' (where the guaranteed level of intermittently sourced electricity is not met)". The results by Renner and Giampietro for Germany are in line with the analysis by Kuhn [36], predicting a requirement of installed storage charging power in Germany of the order of 53 GW by 2050. Similar values apply to the case of Japan [20], where, despite a different energy mix and configuration, it was also found that storage requirements are on the order of a week of average electricity supply.

Thus, storage capacity requirements for 2050, where gross electricity production is assumed to grow to approximately 5140 TWh, were assumed to be on the order of a week of average daily demand. It was then assumed that PHS, the most implemented and mature storage technology in the EU and worldwide, increased up to its viable potential in the EU, following the analysis by Gimeno-Gutiérrez and Lacal-Arántegui [38]. Then, battery energy storage (BES) was introduced to cover the gap between the maximum PHS potential and the total storage capacity needed. The relevant assumptions shared across pathways and those differing for each pathway are collected in Tables 1 and 2 respectively, at ten-year snapshots between 2020 and 2050.

Table 1. Assumptions on the evolution of the energy system shared for the two decarbonisation pathways (low storage high curtailment—LSCH, and high storage low curtailment—HSLC).

Variable	2020	2030	2040	2050
Gross electricity consumption (GWh)	3,665,400	3,666,000	4,357,600	5,140,600
Daily electricity consumption (GWh)	10,042	10,043	11,939	14,084
Hydropower (%)	10	10	9	7
Nuclear (%)	24	16	8	3
Fossil plants (%)	40	27	14	0
Wind power (%)	14	29	46	62
Solar power (%)	6	12	20	27
Other renewables (%)	5	5	5	0

Following the EU high RES pathway, gross electricity consumption increased in both pathways, despite an overall reduction in energy consumption—mirroring the trend of electrification. Hydropower (excluding PHS) was assumed to remain unchanged throughout the years, therefore as electricity generation increased its share in the electricity mix decreased. Nuclear power was assumed to gradually decrease in absolute and relative terms. All other non-renewable power plants were grouped under the umbrella term fossil plants and eliminated by 2050. The share of wind and solar power rose gradually until reaching 90% of the total generation share in 2050. The relative contribution of wind and solar power remained fixed at 70 and 30% respectively, mirroring their 2016 relative contribution in the EU. This was also in line with what was identified by Denholm and Hand [21] as the optimal balance between the two types of generation technologies to ensure minimum curtailment.

Table 2. Relevant characteristics of two decarbonisation pathways: low storage high curtailment (LSHC) and high storage low curtailment (HSLC).

Variable	Alternative Pathway	2020	2030	2040	2050
Gross electricity consumption (GWh)	LSHC	3,665,400	3,666,000	4,357,600	5,140,600
	HSLC	3,665,400	3,666,000	4,357,600	5,140,600
Gross production from wind power (GWh)	LSHC	505,270	1,057,690	2,228,440	5,110,500
	HSLC	505,270	1,057,690	2,049,370	3,194,070
Gross production from solar PV (GWh)	LSHC	216,540	453,300	955,040	2,190,220
	HSLC	216,540	453,300	878,300	1,587,910
Curtailment rate (%)	LSHC	0	0	10	60
	HSLC	0	0	0	20
Storage capacity (GWh)	LSHC	600	600	600	600
	HSLC	600	14,570	51,100	87,630
Wind power UF (%)	LSHC	24	24	21	15
	HSLC	24	24	23	21
Solar PV UF (%)	LSHC	13	13	12	8
	HSLC	13	13	13	11
Wind power capacity (GW)	LSHC	240	500	1060	2430
	HSLC	240	500	980	1760
Solar PV capacity (GW)	LSHC	190	400	840	1920
	HSLC	190	400	770	1390

Given the higher curtailment rate in the LSHC scenario, although the gross electricity consumption was the same as in the HSLC scenario, a higher amount of wind and solar power were assumed to be generated (see the second and third row of Table 2). The surplus generation was not assumed to enter the grid but was curtailed. The curtailment rates, also included in Table 2, were taken from Denholm and Hand [21], by assuming that curtailment rates as a function of VRE penetration can be generalised. Contrary to storage requirements, which tend to increase linearly as VRE integration increases, curtailment increases exponentially, meaning that it becomes less and less favourable to rely on curtailment at higher rates. The amount of storage capacity, in GWh of installed capacity, did not increase throughout the years for the LSHC scenario. Eurostat does not provide statistics on storage capacity, and the value of 600 GWh of PHS in the EU was taken from Kougias and Szabó [37]. In the HSLC scenario, the storage capacity increased up to a week of average demand. The curtailment rates in both scenarios led to a gradual decrease in the utilisation factors (UF) of wind and solar power, calculated as the amount of time throughout the year when electricity generated by wind and solar (GWh$_{used}$) was fed into the grid:

$$\text{UF (\%)} = \frac{\text{GWh}_{used}}{\text{GW}_{installed}} \times \frac{100}{8760} \tag{1}$$

where GW$_{installed}$ is the installed power capacity, and 8760 is the number of hours in a year.

3.1.2. GHG Emissions of Renewable Infrastructure, Storage and Fossil Plants

The values of lifetime GHG emissions of renewable infrastructure, and their associated ranges, were adjusted from the comprehensive meta-review by Nugent and Sovacool [32]. For GHG emissions of storage technologies, values were taken from Denholm and Kulcinski [39]. Table 3 summarises the main technological assumptions of both studies. For renewable infrastructure, Nugent and Sovacool provide intensive data derived from a number of studies, each with different technical specifications. Therefore, the values do not refer to specific technological characteristics. This enlarges the range of the estimated values, but also their robustness. Storage infrastructure values, similarly, refer to a review of various existing plants, with the range of technological characteristics included in Table 3. As the GHG emissions associated with battery energy storage (BES) were an important variable for the results, the values of Denholm and Kulcinski, dating to 2004, were cross-checked against a recent study referring specifically to lithium-ion batteries [40]. and were found to be consistent. Since the scenarios were modelled at the EU level, they did not take into account differences across member states. The values taken from literature, associated with a range of technological characteristics, reflect the heterogeneity of infrastructure required across the EU.

Table 3. Ranges of technological assumptions of infrastructure: (**a**) Renewable infrastructure, adjusted from Nugent and Sovacool [32]; (**b**) storage infrastructure, adjusted from Denholm and Kulcinski [39].

(a)		
Variable	Wind Power	Solar PV
Number of studies	41	23
Hub height (m)	10–108	N/A
Rotor diameter (m)	2–116	N/A
Technology	N/A	Ribbon-Si, Multi-Si, Mono-Si, CdTe
Irradiance (kWh/m^2)	N/A	1600–1800
Mounting	N/A	roof, ground, single axis
Lifetime (years)	20–30	15–30
GHG cultivation and fabrication (mean) (g CO_2 eq./kWh)	42.98	33.67
GHG construction (mean) (g CO_2 eq./kWh)	14.43	8.98
GHG operation (mean) (g CO_2 eq./kWh)	14.36	6.15
(b)		
Variable	PHS	BES
Number of facilities	9	N/A
Completion date	1978–1995	N/A
Power (MW)	31–2100	15
Storage capacity (MWh)	279–184,000	120
Energy/power ratio (hours)	13	8

The GHG emissions from the review studies were adjusted as the renewable share of the electricity mix in the pathways increased, since the electricity mix strongly affects GHG emissions. As we were singling out the power sector, emissions associated with the use of fuels and other forms of thermal energy remained invariant. To adjust the values throughout the years, the carbon intensity of the EU's electricity mix was estimated each year, starting from 320 g/kWh in 2016 [41] and reaching almost zero in 2050. The contribution of the electricity mix to the overall GHG emissions of wind power infrastructure was estimated by comparing existing studies which made a direct link between the carbon intensity of the electricity production system and the GHG emissions associated with infrastructure (see Reference [42] for a comparison of Germany and China, Reference [43] for Brazil and Reference [44] for different values of carbon intensities). The effect of different electricity mixes on the construction on the lifetime of solar panels was assessed directly by Reich [45] in relation to the CO_2 emission factor of electricity supply. Varying GHG emissions for CFC and Operation are included in Table 4.

Table 4. Varying GHG emissions for the cultivation, fabrication and construction (CFC) and operation of renewable and storage infrastructure.

Variable	2020	2030	2040	2050
CFC, wind infrastructure (t CO_2 eq./GW)	906,700	766,020	617,000	470,000
CFC, solar infrastructure (t CO_2 eq./GW)	1,418,000	1,199,000	965,000	735,000
CFC, PHS (t CO_2 eq./GWh.inst *)	33,800	28,500	23,000	17,500
CFC, BES (t CO_2 eq./GWh.inst *)	123,500	104,400	84,000	64,000
Operation, wind turbines (t CO_2 eq./GWh)	5	5	5	5
Operation, solar PV (t CO_2 eq./GWh)	6	6	6	6
Operation, fossil plants (t CO_2 eq./GWh)	450	450	450	450
Operation, PHS (t CO_2 eq./GWh)	1.8	1.8	1.8	1.8
Operation, BES (t CO_2 eq./GWh)	3.5	3.5	3.5	3.5

* GWh.inst: amount of storage capacity installed.

3.2. Modelling Equations

The values of GHG emissions at a given year were calculated from the secondary data, adjusted to the EU's electricity mix for each year, through the following equations:

$$GHG\_st_n = GW_{PV,n} \times GHG\_st_{PV,n} + GW_{wind,n} \times GHG\_st_{wind,n} + GW_{PHS,n} \times GHG\_st_{PHS,n} + GW_{BES,n} \times GHG\_st_{BES} \quad (2)$$

$$GHG\_op_n = GWh_{PV,n} \times GHG\_op_{PV,n} + GWh_{wind,n} \times GHG\_op_{wind,n} + GWh_{PHS,n} \times GHG\_op_{PHS,n} + GWh_{BES,n} \times GHG\_op_{BES} + GWh_{fossil,n} \times GHG\_op_{fossil,n} \quad (3)$$

where:

- GHG_st_n are the GHG emissions, in tons of CO_2 equivalent, emitted at year n due to the cultivation, fabrication and construction (CFC) of infrastructure;
- GW_{PV} and GW_{wind} are the amounts of extra solar PV and wind power capacity installed each year;
- GWh_{PHS} and GWh_{BES} are the amounts of extra storage capacity, PHS and BES, added each year;
- GHG_op_n are the varying infrastructure emissions at each year n, depending, in turn, on the electricity mix and expressed in tons of CO_2 equivalent/GW for renewable infrastructure and tons of CO_2 equivalent/GWh for renewable infrastructure;
- GWh_n is the electricity generation at year n by each technology.

Similarly, the emissions due to the operation of power plants were calculated at each year as the total amount of electricity generated by each type of power plant (including curtailed electricity) times the associated operational emissions. The total GHG emissions at year n, thus ($GHG_{total,n}$) were a combination of multiple factors varying across the years. What we refer to as cumulative emissions, finally, is the sum of the emissions over the 2020–2050 time period:

$$GHG_{total} = \sum_{n=2020}^{2050} GHG_{total,n} \quad (4)$$

4. Results and Discussion

The results and discussion are structured in three sections. Firstly, the yearly and cumulative emissions of the decarbonisation pathways are presented and linked to EU decarbonisation scenarios, and carbon budgets (Section 4.1); then, variational ranges of the results are discussed (Section 4.2). Section 4.3, finally, discusses the role played by biophysical variables at the science-policy interface.

4.1. GHG Emission Curves and Cumulative Emissions

To discuss the results of the two decarbonisation scenarios, emissions can be viewed from three perspectives:

1. Emission curves at a yearly resolution, useful to comment on the temporal behaviour of emissions and their possible non-linear evolution;
2. Cumulative emissions up to the year 2050, i.e., the sum of the yearly emissions, which can be related to carbon budgets;
3. Yearly emissions at the target year 2050, currently the only view used to inform EU decision-making processes (with different targets set for different years).

Starting with the emission curves provided throughout the years, Figures 3 and 4 show the behaviour of the GHG emissions of the EU power sector (including cultivation, fabrication and construction of infrastructure) under the low storage high curtailment (LSHC) scenario. The total emissions are shown in Figure 3, while Figure 4 breaks the emissions down into those linked to the operation of power plants (associated with electricity flows) and those linked to the cultivation, fabrication and construction of renewable infrastructure (associated with funds).

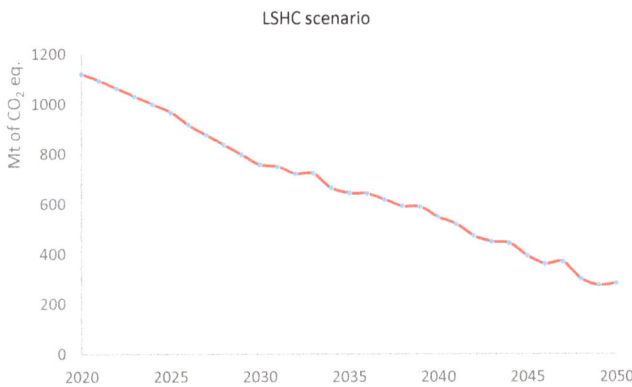

Figure 3. Total GHG emissions in the low storage high curtailment (LSHC) scenario.

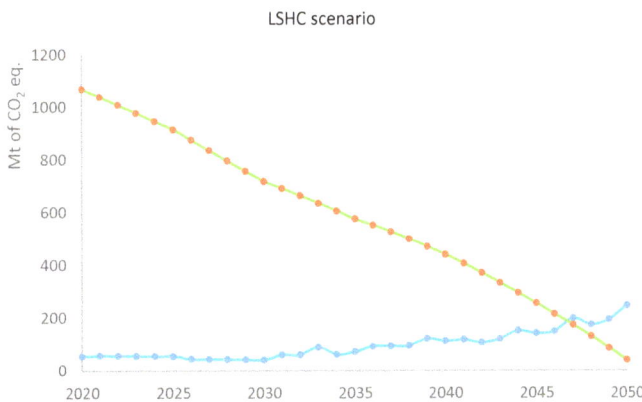

Figure 4. GHG emissions in the LSHC scenario, broken down into operational (flows, green line) and infrastructural (funds, blue line).

In the LSHC scenario, while the amount of wind and solar infrastructure installed each year increased exponentially (see Table 2), the GHG emissions associated with the cultivation, fabrication and construction phases of the infrastructure were mitigated by the steady reduction in operational emissions, which dropped to almost 0 by 2050. The initial steady decrease in emissions became less linear from the year 2030, i.e., when curtailment of renewable electricity started. As curtailment increased, emissions due to an infrastructure rise led to relative peaks in emissions between the years 2030 and 2050, with overall emissions associated with infrastructure increasing despite the increased renewable penetration into the system. The behaviour of the curve depended on the rate that renewable infrastructure was installed.

With high levels of emissions associated with the installation of both PHS and BES storage technologies (see Table 3), the yearly emission curve for the low curtailment high storage (LCHS) scenario displays a behaviour which is less linear, as seen in Figures 5 and 6.

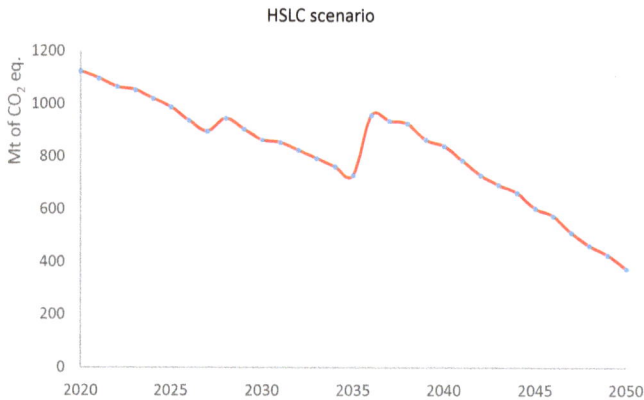

Figure 5. Total GHG emissions in the high storage low curtailment (HSLC) scenario.

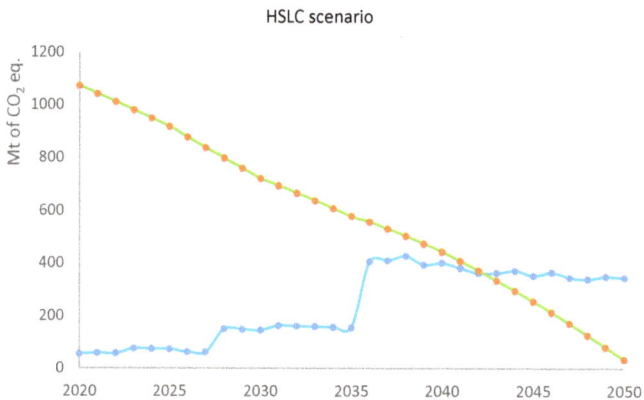

Figure 6. GHG emissions in the HSLC scenario, broken down into operational (flows, green line) and infrastructural (funds, blue line).

Emissions were strongly dependent on the type of storage infrastructure and on when it was integrated into the system. Emissions gradually decreased up to the year 2027, when the amount of installed PHS started to increase considerably. The biggest peak, however, was visible at the year 2035, when BES technologies were introduced, as PHS reached its maximum capacity. The peak can be softened if BES is gradually installed from the start, however, in this case, cumulative emissions would be higher as the manufacturing process would rely more heavily on fossil fuels. Thus, different timing options should be carefully considered from a biophysical perspective.

The behaviour of the curves of Figures 3 and 5, and the presence or absence of relative GHG emission peaks, can be varied by varying assumptions on timings and introduction of technologies. This would also vary cumulative emissions, as the emissions associated with the construction of infrastructure also depend on the yearly electricity mix. Cumulative emissions are a useful indicator as they can give us an idea of how much is being emitted by the EU's power sector during its transitional phase towards deep decarbonisation. It is expected that, on average, the EU has a carbon budget on the order of 90 Gt in order to remain within a 2° temperature range for the period between 2020 and 2100 [46]. Cumulative emissions associated with the power sector and to the manufacturing of infrastructure were of the order of 20,830 Mt of CO_2 eq. and 25,150 Mt of CO_2 eq. respectively, for the HCLS and LCHS scenarios. Thus, under deep decarbonisation pathways, between the years 2020 and 2050 alone the power sector and its associated manufacturing would emit 23–28% of the total budget available to the whole society up to the year 2100. As we discuss in Section 4.3, this suggests that efforts on the production side of the energy system are not enough to stay within safe carbon budgets.

4.2. Analysis of Variational Ranges in the Results

The scenarios presented in this paper build on secondary data collected and adjusted at different levels of the energy system, from individual technologies to systemic production and consumption patterns, expressed in the form of estimate ranges. Table 5 collects the estimate ranges associated with the main variables in the analysis, for the years 2020 and 2050. Table 6 shows how much each variable contributes to the cumulative emissions at the years 2020 and 2050, reflecting the weight that the variable's estimate range holds in the final interval.

The interval associated with the assessments of yearly operational and infrastructural GHG emissions is determined by a combination of estimate ranges associated with GHG emissions in the base year from which the data is taken and the estimate range associated with the adjustment of emissions as renewable penetration increases, using the squaring method for error propagation. At a higher level, the interval associated with the assessment of consumption patterns can be checked by calculating the lowest and highest values of electricity consumption present in the six EU decarbonisation scenarios. The factors playing the largest impact on the final cumulative GHG emission assessments are the GHG emissions associated with storage infrastructure, curtailment rates and the maximum PHS potential in the EU. Combining the various ranges into the final assessment of cumulative emissions leads to intervals on the order of 35% for the high curtailment scenario and 45% for the high storage scenario. This value is high, especially when it comes to storage GHG emissions and estimations of storage requirements, however, it does not weaken the main message of the analysis.

Table 5. Variational ranges of the variables.

Category	Variable	Unit	2020		2050	
			Average	+/−	Average	+/−
Carbon intensity of technologies	CFC wind power	t CO_2 eq./GW	906,700	165,000	470,000	108,100
	CFC solar PV	t CO_2 eq./GW	1,418,000	985,000	735,000	514,500
	CFC PHS	t CO_2 eq./GWh	33,800	4600	17,500	2800
	CFC BES	t CO_2 eq./GWh	123,500	18,000	64,000	11,500
	Operation wind power	t CO_2 eq./GWh	5	1	5	1
	Operation solar PV	t CO_2 eq./GWh	6	1	6	1
	Operation PHS	t CO_2 eq./GWh	2	1	2	1
	Operation BES	t CO_2 eq./GWh	4	1	4	1
Storage	Total storage requirement	GWh	0	0	98,600	32,500
	Efficiency of PHS and BES	%	80	20	80	20
	EU PHS potential	TWh	30	15	30	15
Production and consumption patterns	Total electricity consumption	GWh	3,665,380	146,615	5,140,565	668,273
	Curtailment rate (LSHC)	%	0	0	60	15
	Curtailment rate (HSLC)	%	0	0	20	5

Table 6. Relative contribution of each variable (%) to yearly GHG emissions, 2020 and 2050.

Variable	2020				2050			
	LSHC		HSLC		LSHC		HSLC	
	Mt of CO_2 eq.	%	Mt of CO_2 eq.	%	Mt of CO_2 eq.	%	Mt of CO_2 eq.	%
Solar PV infrastructure	29.5	3	29.5	3	135.6	48	60	16
Wind infrastructure	23.8	2	23.8	2	109.6	39	48.5	13
PHS infrastructure	0	0	0	0	0	0	0	0
BES infrastructure	0	0	0	0	0	0	233.8	63
Fossil operation	1064.7	95	1064.7	95	0	0	0	0
Solar operation	1.3	0	1.3	0	13.1	5	9.5	3
Wind operation	2.5	0	2.5	0	25.6	9	18.5	5
PHS operation	0.1	0	0.1	0	0.1	0	0.7	0
BES operation	0	0	0	0	0	0	2.1	1
Total	1122		1122		284		373	

4.3. Discussion

To inform decision-making, the type of GHG accounting proposed here is incomplete, as it needs to be associated with economic analyses and with the assessment of other biophysical variables such as land and water. While the high curtailment scenario results in overall lower emissions than the high storage one, it would lead to other trade-offs in different domains, including higher electricity prices and large areas of land occupied by renewable infrastructure. On the other hand, the high storage scenario would also be associated with high levels of lithium requirements (to be imported), which may not be desirable from a security perspective. Additionally, increasing PHS to its maximum potential may have important consequences for natural water cycles. Synergies and trade-offs also emerge within and outside EU borders. A part of the emissions derived in the scenarios would necessarily be located outside of EU borders, such as those for the extraction of primary materials. This points towards the need of discussing the impact of EU climate targets at different geographical scales.

When it comes to the integration of renewable energy, differences across countries are also important and should be modelled in relation to grid flexibility and associated GHG emissions. The Netherlands, for example, is mostly flat and does not have any PHS potential, therefore in an increased flexibility scenario, it would either require high rates of curtailment (which may interfere with current land use patterns) or high interconnections to neighbouring countries. Utilisation factors of technologies also vary across countries, depending on weather conditions. In addition to differences across spatial scales, the temporal scale is also important when considering decarbonisation scenarios: different types of storage services, in fact, are useful for fluctuations occurring at different scales [47]. Current statistics do not allow for this type of analysis. Therefore, it would be advisable for supra-national statistical bodies such as Eurostat to include data across shorter timescales.

The results presented are considered to be conservative, as two elements which have not been included in the model may increase GHG emissions substantially: (i) the change in end-use infrastructure required by an increased electrification of the energy sector (such as the manufacturing of electric cars); and (ii) the turnover of funds. There is uncertainty associated with the possible lifetime of grid-scale batteries [47], however, it is likely that within the 30-year timeframe considered in the study some turnover will be necessary, by either producing new batteries or recycling existing ones.

Accounting for the emission flows associated with funds leads to higher emissions than those envisioned by current scenarios. Thus, results suggest that sustainable production narratives cannot alone lead to a decarbonisation of the energy sector. To be effective, sustainable production efforts must be paired with strong efforts for sustainable consumption [48]. These should not only be spurred by mechanisms such as efficiency and technology but also, and crucially, by radical changes in consumption patterns. This is line with the metabolic view of society [49], which draws a clear connection between production and consumption patterns: changes in the way in which energy carriers are produced inevitably require changes in the way in which they are consumed. This may entail a shift not only in how things are done (structural changes, e.g., technology and efficiency) but also in what is done and why (functional changes, e.g., who is consuming what energy, to do what).

5. Conclusions

Fighting climate change, reducing air pollution and increasing security are three entangled priorities of the EU. Decarbonisation has become a central strategy to deal simultaneously with these disparate targets. However, governing a shift to a decarbonised economy has not been simple. We suggest that this difficulty is partly due to the framing of models used to inform deliberative processes. A focus on the monetary aspects of funds, particularly infrastructure, rather than on the biophysical ones, such as GHG emissions, has minimised discourses linked to the magnitude of the material transformations required to restructure the energy system.

Focusing on the EU power sector in the years 2020–2050, we modelled two decarbonisation pathways in relation to GHG emissions. The scenarios consider operational GHG emissions of electricity generation, as well as those associated with the lifetime of renewable and storage infrastructure. Contrary to the decarbonisation pathways used to inform EU decision-making, the alternative decarbonisation pathways take into account grid flexibility requirements from a biophysical perspective. For the chosen pathways, this entails accounting for the GHG emissions associated either with high rates of curtailment or with storage infrastructure. The results show how emission curves behave differently under different flexibility pathways, and relative peaks of GHG emissions across the years, as well as overall higher cumulative emissions, may emerge depending on the set of assumptions.

Many questions arise from a biophysical problem framing of decarbonisation, for example: What is the best timing to implement technologies? What are the trade-offs among different technological pathways and storage solutions? What trade-offs may emerge between local and global environmental effects? By suggesting that a rapid decarbonisation of the EU power sector by 2050 is "feasible and viable" [14], and therefore glossing over biophysical obstacles to renewable transformations, the scientific tools informing EU decision-making do not open up a space to discuss these crucial issues.

Author Contributions: Conceptualization, M.G., L.J.D.F. and M.R..; Methodology, M.R. and L.J.D.F.; Formal Analysis, L.J.D.F.; Data Curation, L.J.D.F.; Writing-Original Draft Preparation, L.J.D.F. and M.G.; Writing-Review and Editing, L.J.D.F., M.G. and M.R.; Supervision, M.G. and M.R.

funding: The authors acknowledge support by the European Union's Horizon 2020 research and innovation programme under grant agreement no. 689669 (MAGIC). The Institute of Environmental Science and Technology (ICTA) has received financial support from the Spanish Ministry of Economy and Competitiveness through the "María de Maeztu" program for Units of Excellence (MDM-2015-0552). This work reflects the authors' view only; the funding agencies are not responsible for any use that may be made of the information it contains.

Acknowledgments: The authors are very grateful to Ansel Renner for providing support in calculating storage requirements, and to three anonymous reviewers for greatly improving the quality of the paper with their thoughtful feedback.

Conflicts of Interest: The authors declare no conflicts of interest.

References

1. Smil, V. *Energy Transitions: History, Requirements, Prospects*; Praeger: Santa Barbara, CA, USA, 2010; ISBN 9780313381775.
2. Cottrell, F. *Energy and Society: The Relation between Energy, Social Changes, and Economic Development*; McGraw-Hill: New York, NY, USA, 1955.
3. Giampietro, M.; Mayumi, K.; Sorman, A. *The Metabolic Pattern of Societies: Where Economists Fall Short*; Routledge: London, UK, 2011.
4. European Commission. *European Energy Security Strategy*; European Commission: Brussels, Belgium, 2014.
5. Vahtra, P. Energy security in Europe in the aftermath of 2009 Russia-Ukraine gas crisis. In *EU-Russia Gas Connection: Pipes, Politics and Problems*; Pan European Institute: Turku, Finland, 2009; pp. 159–165.

6.   European Commission. *Proposal for a Directive of the European Parliament and of the Council on the Promotion of the Use of Energy from Renewable Sources (Recast)*; European Commission: Brussels, Belgium, 2017; Volume 0382 (COD), pp. 1–116.

7.   Scholz, R.; Beckmann, M.; Pieper, C.; Muster, M.; Weber, R. Considerations on providing the energy needs using exclusively renewable sources: Energiewende in Germany. *Renew. Sustain. Energy Rev.* **2014**, *35*, 109–125. [CrossRef]

8.   Georgescu-Roegen, N. *The Entropy Law and the Economic Process*; Harvard University Press: Boston, MA, USA, 1971.

9.   Giampietro, M.; Mayumi, K.; Ramos-Martin, J. Multi-scale integrated analysis of societal and ecosystem metabolism (MuSIASEM): Theoretical concepts and basic rationale. *Energy* **2009**, *34*, 313–322. [CrossRef]

10.   European Commission. *Energy Roadmap 2050*; European Commission: Brussels, Belgium, 2012.

11.   European Commission. *EU Reference Scenario 2016: Energy, Transport and GHG Emissions Trends to 2050*; European Commission: Brussels, Belgium, 2016; ISBN 978-92-79-52373-1.

12.   Kondziella, H.; Bruckner, T. Flexibility requirements of renewable energy based electricity systems—A review of research results and methodologies. *Renew. Sustain. Energy Rev.* **2016**, *53*, 10–22. [CrossRef]

13.   Eurostat. *Greenhouse Gas Emission Statistics—Emission Inventories*; Eurostat: Luxembourg, 2018.

14.   2050 Low-Carbon Economy | Climate Action. Available online: https://ec.europa.eu/clima/policies/strategies/2050_en (accessed on 26 March 2018).

15.   European Commission. *European Council Conclusions on Jobs, Growth and Competitiveness, as Well as Some of the Other Items (Paris Agreement and Digital Europe)*; European Commission: Brussels, Belgium, 2018.

16.   European Commission. Clean Energy for All Europeans. In *Communication from Commission to European Parliament Council European Economy Society Committee of Committee Regions*; European Commission: Brussels, Belgium, 2016; Volume COM (2016).

17.   Bruckner, T.; Bashmakov, I.A.; Mulugetta, Y.; Chum, H.; De la Vega Navarro, A.; Edmonds, J.; Faaij, A.; Fungtammasan, B.; Garg, A.; Hertwich, E.; et al. In Proceedings of the Energy systems. Climate Change 2014 Mitigation Climate Change Contrib. Work Group III to Fifth Assessment Rep. Intergovernmental Panel Climate Change, Copenhagen, Denmark, 1 November 2014.

18.   European Commission. Modelling Tools for EU Analysis. Available online: https://ec.europa.eu/clima/policies/strategies/analysis/models_en (accessed on 7 February 2018).

19.   Steinke, F.; Wolfrum, P.; Hoffmann, C. Grid vs. storage in a 100% renewable Europe. *Renew. Energy* **2013**, *50*, 826–832. [CrossRef]

20.   Esteban, M.; Zhang, Q.; Utama, A. Estimation of the energy storage requirement of a future 100% renewable energy system in Japan. *Energy Policy* **2012**, *47*, 22–31. [CrossRef]

21.   Denholm, P.; Hand, M. Grid flexibility and storage required to achieve very high penetration of variable renewable electricity. *Energy Policy* **2011**, *39*, 1817–1830. [CrossRef]

22.   Denholm, P.; Margolis, R. *Energy Storage Requirements for Achieving 50% Solar Photovoltaic Energy Penetration in California*; National Renewable Energy Laboratory: Golden, CO, USA, 2016.

23.   Murphy, D.J.; Hall, C.A.S. Energy return on investment, peak oil, and the end of economic growth. *Ann. N. Y. Acad. Sci.* **2011**, *1219*, 52–72. [CrossRef] [PubMed]

24.   Court, V.; Fizaine, F. Long-Term Estimates of the Energy-Return-on-Investment (EROI) of Coal, Oil, and Gas Global Productions. *Ecol. Econ.* **2017**, *138*, 145–159. [CrossRef]

25.   Giampietro, M.; Mayumi, K.; Ramos-Martin, J. Can Biofuels Replace Fossil Energy Fuels? A Multi-Scale Integrated Analysis Based on the Concept of Societal and Ecosystem Metabolism: Part 1. *Int. J. Transdiscip. Res.* **2006**, *1*, 51–87.

26.   Mann, S.; de Wild, M.J. The energy payback time of advanced crystalline silicon PV modules in 2020: A prospective study. *Prog. Photovolt.* **2014**, *22*, 1180–1194. [CrossRef]

27.   Fthenakis, V.; Alsema, E. Photovoltaics energy payback times, greenhouse gas emissions and external costs: 2004–early 2005 status. *Prog. Photovolt. Res. Appl.* **2006**, *14*, 275–280. [CrossRef]

28.   Gibbs, H.K.; Johnston, M.; Foley, J.A.; Holloway, T.; Monfreda, C.; Ramankutty, N.; Zaks, D. Carbon payback times for crop-based biofuel expansion in the tropics: The effects of changing yield and technology. *Environ. Res. Lett.* **2008**, *3*, 034001. [CrossRef]

29.   Mello, F.; Cerri, C.; Davies, C. Payback time for soil carbon and sugar-cane ethanol. *Nat. Clim. Chang.* **2014**, *4*, 605–609. [CrossRef]

30. Barnhart, C.J.; Benson, S.M. On the importance of reducing the energetic and material demands of electrical energy storage. *Energy Environ. Sci.* **2013**, *6*, 1083. [CrossRef]

31. Denholm, P.; Ela, E.; Kirby, B.; Milligan, M. *The Role of Energy Storage with Renewable Electricity Generation*; National Renewable Energy Laboratory: Golden, CO, USA, 2010; pp. 1–53.

32. Nugent, D.; Sovacool, B.K. Assessing the lifecycle greenhouse gas emissions from solar PV and wind energy: A critical meta-survey. *Energy Policy* **2014**, *65*, 229–244. [CrossRef]

33. Cilliers, P. *Complexity and Postmodernism: Understanding Complex Systems*; Taylor & Francis: Abingdon-on-Thames, UK, 2002.

34. European Commission. Energy Modelling. Available online: https://ec.europa.eu/energy/en/data-analysis/energy-modelling (accessed on 22 July 2018).

35. Renner, A.; Giampietro, M. The Regulation of Alternatives in the Electric Grid: Nice Try Guys, But Let's Move On. In *International Conference on Sustainable Energy and Environment Sensing (SEES)*; University of Cambridge: Cambridge, UK, 2018.

36. Kuhn, P. *Iteratives Modell zur Optimierung von Speicherausbau und-Betrieb in Einem Stromsystem mit Zunehmend Fluktuierender Erzeugung*; University of Munchen: Munchen, Germany, 2012.

37. Kougias, I.; Szabó, S. Pumped hydroelectric storage utilization assessment: Forerunner of renewable energy integration or Trojan horse? *Energy* **2017**, *140*, 318–329. [CrossRef]

38. Gimeno-Gutiérrez, M.; Lacal-Arántegui, R. *Assessment of the European Potential for Pumped Hydropower Energy Storage: A GIS-Based Assessment of Pumped Hydropower Storage Potential*; European Commission: Brussels, Belgium, 2013; ISBN 9789279295119.

39. Denholm, P.; Kulcinski, G.L. Life cycle energy requirements and greenhouse gas emissions from large scale energy storage systems. *Energy Convers. Manag.* **2004**, *45*, 2153–2172. [CrossRef]

40. Romare, M.; Dahllöf, L. *The Life Cycle Energy Consumption and Greenhouse Gas Emissions from Lithium-Ion Batteries a Study with Focus on Current Technology and Batteries for Light-Duty Vehicles*; Swedish Environmental Research Institute: Stockholm, Sweden, 2017.

41. Moro, A.; Lonza, L. Electricity carbon intensity in European Member States: Impacts on GHG emissions of electric vehicles. *Transp. Res. Part D Transp. Environ.* **2017**. [CrossRef]

42. Guezuraga, B.; Zauner, R.; Pölz, W. Life cycle assessment of two different 2 MW class wind turbines. *Renew. Energy* **2012**, *37*, 37–44. [CrossRef]

43. Oebels, K.B.; Pacca, S. Life cycle assessment of an onshore wind farm located at the northeastern coast of Brazil. *Renew. Energy* **2013**, *53*, 60–70. [CrossRef]

44. Pehnt, M. Dynamic life cycle assessment (LCA) of renewable energy technologies. *Renew. Energy* **2006**, *31*, 55–71. [CrossRef]

45. Reich, N.H.; Alsema, E.A.; van Sark, W.G.J.; Turkenburg, W.C.; Sinke, W.C. Greenhouse gas emissions associated with photovoltaic electricity from crystalline silicon modules under various energy supply options. *Prog. Photovolt. Res. Appl.* **2011**, *19*, 603–613. [CrossRef]

46. Meyer-Ohlendorf, N.; Voß, P.; Velten, E.; Görlach, B. *EU Greenhouse Gas Emission Budget: Implications for EU Climate Policies*; European Commission: Brussels, Belgium, 2018.

47. Aneke, M.; Wang, M. Energy storage technologies and real life applications—A state of the art review. *Appl. Energy* **2016**, *179*, 350–377. [CrossRef]

48. Jackson, T. Negotiating Sustainable Consumption: A Review of the Consumption Debate and its Policy Implications. *Energy Environ.* **2004**, *15*, 1027–1051. [CrossRef]

49. Sorman, A.H. Metabolism, Societal. In *Degrowth: A Vocabulary for a New Era*; Routledge: London, UK, 2014; Volume 160.

sustainability

MDPI

Article

Latecomers to the Fossil Energy Transition, Frontrunners for Change? The Relevance of the Energy 'Underdogs' for Sustainability Transformations

Anke Schaffartzik [1,2,*] **and Marina Fischer-Kowalski** [1]

[1] Institute of Social Ecology (SEC), University of Natural Resources and Life Sciences (BOKU),
     1070 Vienna, Austria; marina.fischer-kowalski@boku.ac.at
[2] Austria and Institut de Ciència i Tecnologia Ambientals (ICTA), Universitat Autònoma de Barcelona (UAB),
     08193 Bellaterra, Spain
*   Correspondence: anke.schaffartzik@boku.ac.at

Received: 1 June 2018; Accepted: 25 July 2018; Published: 27 July 2018

Abstract: The global energy system subsumes both extreme wealth (and waste) and extreme poverty. A minority of the global population is consuming the majority of the fossil fuel-based energy and causing global warming. While the mature industrialized economies maintain their high levels of energy consumption, the emerging economies are rapidly expanding their fossil energy systems, emulating traditional patterns of industrialization. We take a global, socio-metabolic perspective on the energy transition phases—take-off, maturation, and completion—of 142 countries between 1971 and 2015. Even within our global fossil energy system, the transition to fossil energy is still ongoing; many countries are in the process of replacing renewable energy with fossil energy. However, due to globally limited supplies and sinks, continuing the fossil energy transition is not an indefinite option. Rather than a "Big Push" for renewable energy within pockets of the fossil energy system, a sustainability transformation is required that would change far more than patterns of energy supply and use. Where this far-reaching change requires pushing back against the fossil energy system, the energy underdogs—the latecomers to the fossil energy transition—just might come out on top.

Keywords: energy supply; international inequality; renewable energy; fossil energy system

---

1. The Fossil Energy Transition

" . . . the capital city became the victim of repeated visitations of a thick, yellow, sulphurous vapour that plunged the streets into darkness, choked the lungs, and turned day into night." [1]

" . . . as the sun rose, still the fog didn't disappear, and the visibility was even less then. Everyone around has an uneasiness in their throat due to this kind of smog. Our next step is to keep ourselves inside and step outside only when it is important." [2]

Anthropogenic climate change may not have been on the mind of 19th century Londoners, but the local impacts of fossil fuel combustion certainly were. Today, the deadly smog for which London was renowned hangs over New Delhi (described above) or Beijing [3]. We know that—due to the physical limits to supply—our fossil energy systems have an expiration date [4–6] until which they will have detrimental environmental impacts [7,8]. However, none of this has deterred high and growing reliance on fossil fuels—such as oil, coal, and natural gas—for societies' energy supply [9]. The development of capital-intensive infrastructures and the power-infused institutions of the fossil energy system [10,11] have ushered in "the age of oil" [12] with its "fossil economies" [13].

Under intensified globalization and a rigorous international division of labor, it is no contradiction that this global system subsumes both extreme wealth (and waste) and extreme poverty when it comes to energy. At the turn of the century, 15% of the world population in the Global North used approximately the same amount of energy as the 85% of the population living in the Global South [14]. In 2013, one-tenth of the population caused more than half of the global greenhouse gas emissions [15]. While the mature industrialized economies maintain their high levels of energy consumption, the emerging economies are rapidly expanding their fossil energy systems, emulating traditional patterns of industrialization [16]. Technologies for (renewable) energy are now available that did not exist when the industrialized countries embarked on their energy transitions. But these are not enough of a springboard to leapfrog the colossal fossil energy system [17]. Alternative energy technologies themselves require a boost over the critical barriers posed by the infrastructures and institutions of the fossil energy system [18,19] and the inertia of the fossil energy transition [20]. To enable an alternative energy system, the built infrastructures—predetermining energy demand for decades to come [21]—and the vested, institutionalized interests of powerful political and economic actors [12,13,22] of the fossil energy system would have to be abandoned [10].

Instead, the fossil energy system is solidified by investments and subsidies, and the politics that favor these transactions. Trillions of dollars are globally being earmarked for energy infrastructures in Europe and the United States of America, as well as in countries with much lower energy access [23]. Development banks and private sector companies identify investment opportunities wherever the fossil energy transition has not yet been completed [24,25], and even economies diversifying domestic energy supply favor the fossil energy system in their investment choices. Chinese banks, for example, have surpassed the World Bank in their investments into the infrastructures of coal-fired power plants [26]. High subsidies for fossil energy supply and consumption and the tit-for-tat between mines and power plants maintain a cheap energy source [11,27], despite the associated social and environmental 'costs', and often make it difficult for renewable energy to compete. Despite the unsustainability of the fossil energy system, it is increasingly being bartered politically, in fully industrialized [28] as well as emerging economies [29].

1.1. Renewable Energy in the Pockets of the Fossil Energy System

Compared to the urgency with which a fundamental change to the energy system is now required [7,30,31], the formidable fossil energy system has had a long time to develop. The take-off phase of historical fossil energy transitions alone lasted 58 years on average, and was not systematically shorter for the countries that began their transition later. Only the very early development of fossil infrastructures in the United Kingdom and the Netherlands took longer and provided all other countries with a bit of a piggy-back ride on their innovations [32]. The transition to a fossil energy system is pursued not as a goal in itself, but was and is the by-product of political and economic development enabled by technological innovation and motivated by opportunities to make a profit [33]. In contrast, a transition away from fossil fuels and toward renewable energy would in itself constitute a goal, allowing for big challenges such as climate change and energy security to be met [34,35]. So far, this difference has not materialized as the rapid adoption of renewable energy that might have been hoped for [36]. In the mature industrialized economies, it has taken strong, continuous political and economic support alongside country-specific cultural attitudes and/or resource endowment to allow for renewable energy to develop in pockets of the fossil energy system. By 2015, the German effort to change the tide with an *Energiewende* [37] had amounted to 12% renewable energy in the total primary energy supply (TPES). Higher shares were achieved by countries boasting a unique combination of resource endowment and political will (Sweden: 42%, Iceland: 88%). However, none of these countries have renewable energy systems. What they do have are renewable energy projects within a fossil energy system. The state-owned Swedish power company *Vattenfall* owns and operates almost 100 hydroelectric plants in Sweden, but hydropower only accounts for 30% of the "Waterfall's" electricity generation [38], in which coal and gas play an important role. Iceland has the world's highest electricity generation per capita, which is almost exclusively from geothermal and hydro power plants [39], and mostly used in aluminum smelters [40]. After buildings, the bulk of aluminum is globally engaged in transportation [41], such as in automobiles and airplanes, for example, guzzling fossil fuel.

Countries in which traditional biomass (mainly fuelwood) plays an important role in energy supply have high renewable shares at very low levels of total energy supply per capita; these include Ethiopia (93% renewable in 2015), Tanzania (84%), and Ghana (43%) [40]. The high share of fuelwood limits the possible total energy supply [42] and access to energy is low, especially in sparsely populated rural areas [43–45]. Decentralized electricity generation from renewable sources has been championed as a safe, sustainable, and even cost-effective way to address energy poverty [29,46–48]. However, within the global fossil energy system, renewable energy has had to fall in line with existing power grids and energy use patterns and established institutions and interests [49–52].

1.2. A "Big Push"—But Where?

In 2017, the US–American Energy Information Administration released its International Energy Outlook. One of the major sights on its horizon was how growing Chinese energy consumption would dominate increases in global energy consumption [53]. For many, it was and is a terrifying trifecta: An energy-"hungry" China [54] on the prowl [55], peak oil [5,31], and anthropogenic climate change [8]. The projections according to which population—as an important driver of energy demand—would grow in (energy poor) countries not members of the Organisation for Economic Co-operation and Development [53], conjured a question with unthinkable consequences: billions of people aspiring to US–American levels of energy consumption?

The narrative of the "Big Push"—large-scale, foreign-financed investment to grow countries out of their "poverty trap"—had been making a convenient comeback [56] and was brought into play against energy hunger: Could a "'Big Push' […] to scale up renewable energy in the developing world" prevent countries "get[ing] locked into cheaper, dirtier fossil fuels, [with] no chance of meeting global CO2 reduction targets"? The article from which this question stems [57] is illustrated by an image of a modern-day Sisyphus (cf. Figure 1) in a business suit pushing a boulder up a steep incline. In the world of Greek mythology, that boulder would never reach the top of the hill, but would present our businessman with an afterlife of work and frustration—punishment for having bested the gods. And in the modern-day world? Can a "Big Push" transform our energy system?

Figure 1. "With mighty labour" Sisyphus rolls a millstone up a hill. As soon as he reaches the top, the stone rolls back down, providing him with the opportunity "to keep imployed his afflicted soul" [58].

Energy transitions—from the passive use of solar energy by hunters and gatherers to the active harnessing of that solar energy in agrarian society and the use of fossil fuels in the industrial society—involve fundamental societal transformations of how people live and work, the communities they form, societal values and norms, power relations and hierarchies, and societies' relation to nature [59]. As part of a sustainability transformation, transitions to renewable energy systems will entail equally fundamental societal change, including how much energy we use and for what and how we live and work and organize our societies. Limited to an existence in pockets of the fossil energy system, a "Big Push" for renewable energy might well be a Sisyphusian endeavor.

Push as we may, there is no "quick fix" [60] to the inherent unsustainability of our global resource use patterns. In order to produce knowledge for sustainability transformations, science must address the underlying causes, not only the symptoms, of unsustainability [61]. What we have to offer is a socio-metabolic reading of *currently ongoing energy transitions* with the motivation that better understanding the symptoms of unsustainable development may help in the identification of possibilities for intervention [62]. It seems imperative to have a better idea of what we are up against before we push for change. While it may be clear that the energy system will have to fundamentally change in a sustainability transformation, it is essential to be pushing for change in the right direction. The boulder we're pushing shouldn't roll back to crush those at the bottom of the hill and everyone along the way; renewable energy development shouldn't solidify the fossil energy system.

In that sense, we have our eye not on the transition to renewable energy, but rather on the *transition to fossil energy*. For the period between 1971 and 2015, we examine energy supply patterns for three major country groupings: (1) those countries for which the take-off period of their fossil energy transition falls within this period; (2) those accelerating their transition and maturing their fossil energy systems; and (3) those that have completed this transition. These three groups are in themselves highly heterogeneous, and it is not our aim to provide a definitive analysis of the energy transitions at the national level, much less the subnational, level. The socio-metabolic perspective that we take allows us to show that while we may be eyeing renewable energy, the currently ongoing transition is one to fossil fuels. This seems important in determining where we need to push (back). We focus on the latecomers to the fossil energy transition, referring to them as the 'underdogs' to indicate that in the uphill struggle for a sustainable transformation of not only the energy system, our support lies with the people of these countries. It appears to us that in the deliberation of sustainability transformations, the role of these countries—with their extremely low per capita energy supply—is crucial but often overlooked.

2. Materials and Methods

For our socio-metabolic analysis of energy transitions, we required quantitative data on the amount and composition of primary energy supply per country. We were able to include 142 countries in our sample, achieving good representation of the world population for all of the years between 1971 and 2015 (see Section 2.2). We grouped these countries according to quantitative data on energy supply [40] and on the corresponding phase of their energy transition (see Section 2.1).

2.1. Energy Transition Phases

Following Rotmans et al. [63], we assume that the energy transition, similar to other societal transitions, has four phases of development: (1) predevelopment; (2) take-off; (3) acceleration, and (4) stabilization. The take-off period for the transition to fossil fuels (and later also other modern energy sources, including nuclear) tends to occur at levels of domestic modern energy use between 0.47–7.71 Gigajoules per capita (GJ/cap). This range was identified in the analysis of a large country sample (representing approximately two-thirds of the global population) in a long time series (beginning as early as the 15th and as late as the 18th century) [32]. During the following phase of acceleration of modern energy use and maturation of the energy transition, domestic energy consumption increased up to 50 GJ/cap. In the 20th century, the fossil energy transition in the industrialized economies was largely completed, and modern energy consumption was stabilized. The fossil energy system is global [12,13], but this does not mean that all of countries have concluded their energy transition. In particular, we identified the countries that are latecomers to the transition to fossil fuels, i.e., those for which the take-off period has not yet been concluded by 1970. In this grouping, we included all of the countries with fossil TPES below 8 GJ/cap in 1971. Other countries are still maturing their energy transition, with energy supply above 8 GJ/cap (but below 50 GJ/cap). In this grouping, we included all of the countries in which the fossil TPES grew continuously from above 8 GJ/cap. This acceleration phase applies to many of the successor states of the Soviet Union which had high energy supply from fossil fuels (above 50 GJ/cap) in 1991—indicating a completed energy transition—but then experienced a collapse of their energy systems, and have been accelerating again since and subsequently re-building these energy systems. Countries appearing to be at the precipice between take-off and acceleration with energy supply clearly above 8 GJ/cap but not (yet) continuously growing were classified as maturing energy transition if an energy supply above 8 GJ/cap dominated the time period between 1970 and 2015. Those countries were considered as having completed their fossil energy transition that had fossil TPES above 50 GJ/cap. Table 1 provides an overview of the three country groupings.

Table 1. Between 1970 and 2015, most people lived in countries that either were latecomers to the fossil energy transition or were in the process of maturing that transition, based on their fossil total primary energy supply (TPES). Very high fossil energy consumption following the completion of the energy transition was experienced by only one-fifth of the global population.

Group	Description	N	Population 2015
Late energy transition, *energy underdogs*	Take-off phase of per capita fossil TPES (0.4–8.0 GJ/cap) within 1970–2015 time range	39	3.1 billion people 42% (of world) 44% (of sample)
Maturing energy transition	Transition from above 8.0 to below or equal 50 GJ/cap fossil TPES between 1970–2015	44	2.5 billion people 34% (of world) 35% (of sample)
Completed energy transition	Above 50 GJ/cap fossil TPES during entire 1970–2015 period	59	1.5 billion people 21% (of world) 21% (of sample)

In order to identify the latecomers to the fossil energy transition, it was necessary to define this grouping according to whether the countries were below 8 GJ/cap fossil TPES at *any point* during the period. For the other two country groupings, we included five countries (Algeria, Bosnia and Herzegovina, China, Iraq, and Mongolia) that did not reach 50 GJ/cap until the 2000s in the maturing energy transition and five countries (Cyprus, Greece, Hong Kong, Republic of Korea, and Libya) that reached above 50 GJ/cap during the 1970s in the completed energy transition. With the exception of China, the individual or collective re-assignment of these countries to the respective other possible grouping would not have a significant impact on our results. Which grouping China belongs to significantly affects the per capita results. Since China did not supply more than 50 GJ/cap of TPES from fossil sources until 2005, and 88 GJ/cap in 2015 (compared to 147 GJ/cap in the completed energy transition grouping without China), we considered the maturing period to clearly dominate our period of investigation. This affects the interpretability of our results.

We present and discuss the very heterogeneous energy transition groupings as wholes throughout the article. To make the lack of homogeneity more transparent for our focus on the energy underdogs, we also provide information on ranges of variables within the group. Although the energy underdogs share the trait of still being in the early transition phase to a fossil energy system in the period between 1970 and 2015, their transitions are by no means synchronized.

2.2. Data

Data on national TPES from fossil (coal, oil, natural gas), renewable, and other (mainly nuclear) sources were extracted from the International Energy Agency's World Indicators [40]. These data were available in time series for a sample of 142 countries, accounting for more than 90% of the world population at all points in time between 1970 and 2015 (and until 2050 in the United Nations' low variant population growth projection [64]).

Throughout the article, we refer to the shares of the three country groupings in the total sample as global shares, and ask the reader to bear in mind that—because approximately 10% of the global population is missing from our sample—true global shares would be slightly lower than the sample shares that we discuss (Table 1).

3. Fossil Energy: A Global System that Cannot Be Universal

An energy transition to lower energy use increasingly met from renewable sources must form part of a sustainability transformation. And yet, the fossil energy system is solidified rather than challenged through the combination of sustained high levels of fossil energy supply in the mature industrialized economies, the rapid growth of fossil fuel use in the maturation of the energy transition, and decreasing shares of renewable energy in the transition latecomers.

3.1. Low Energy Supply in Fast-Growing Underdogs

More than 3 billion people—44% of the world's population—live in countries with a late take-off phase of the fossil energy transition and only 10% of global fossil energy supply. Half as many (1.5 billion) live in countries with a complete transition to fossil fuels supplying five times as much primary fossil energy (Figure 2). Per person, fossil TPES in the energy underdogs amounts to one-tenth of that in the countries with a completed energy transition. These international disparities challenge us to identify barriers to more equitable resource distribution: if energy supply in the countries with a completed energy transition could be reduced to half its current level, supply in the energy underdogs could be increased by a factor of 3.5 without increasing global supply, all else remaining equal.

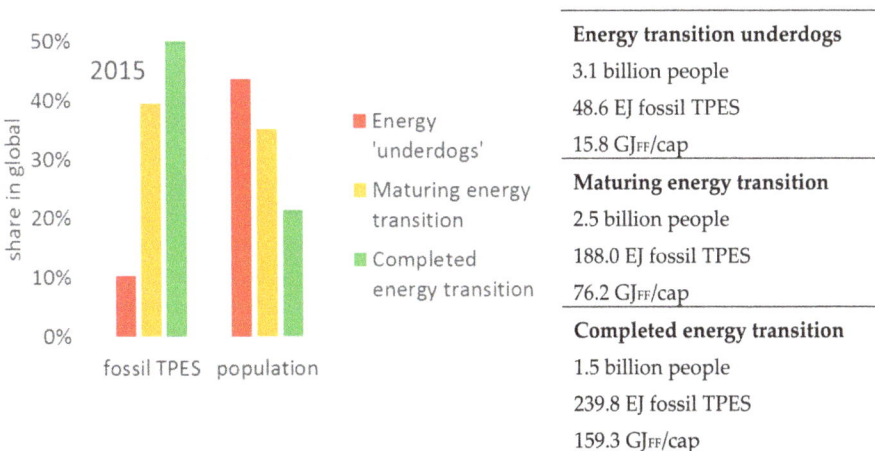

Figure 2. In 2015, the energy underdogs had the lowest share in global total primary energy supply (TPES) from fossil fuels and the highest share in population, while the 21% of the global population that was living in countries that had completed their fossil energy transition accounted for 50% of global fossil TPES. Source of data: International Energy Agency [40].

International inequality in energy supply persists despite gradual reductions since the 1970s of per capita fossil fuel supply in the countries with a completed energy transition and an increasing per capita supply in the underdogs (Figure 3). At only 3.8 GJ/cap in 1971, fossil TPES in the energy underdogs was at a very low level (compared to 14.9 GJ/cap for the maturing and 170.9 GJ/cap for the completed energy transition). At an average of 2.2% per year, population in the energy underdogs grew more strongly than in either of the other two country groupings (1.4% and 1.3% per year). Growth in fossil TPES (averaging 5.5% per year), however, was comparable to that in the countries with a maturing energy transition (5.2%). Only in those countries that had already completed their energy transition did population growth surpass growth in fossil TPES on average, causing a slight decline in the per capita values.

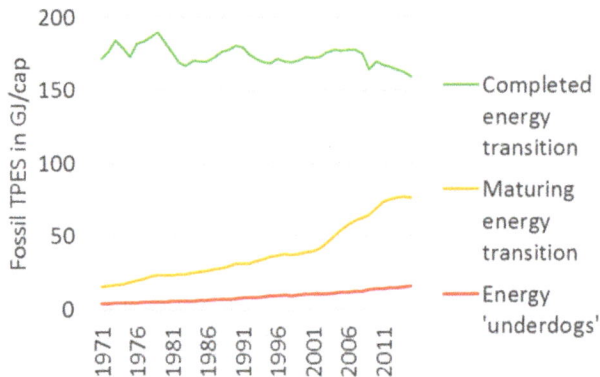

Figure 3. Between 1971 and 2015, fossil total primary energy supply (TPES) in Gigajoules per capita (GJ/cap) stagnated at a very high level in the countries that had completed their energy transition by 1970. The countries in the maturation phase of the energy transition were characterized by high fossil TPES and low population growth, causing per capita values to increase strongly. While fossil TPES growth was even slightly higher in the energy underdogs, their higher population growth and very low initial values did not translate this into the same high per capita gains. Source of data: International Energy Agency [40].

Fossil energy supply beyond 20 GJ/cap is not systematically related to improved access to electricity, but rather to higher levels of consumption [65]. While even well below 20 GJ/cap, countries may provide high levels of access to electricity (in 2015: Tajikistan at 7 GJ/cap, Paraguay at 12 GJ/cap, and Pakistan at 13 GJ/cap, for example), rates of access below 50% are common among the energy underdogs (in Angola at 10 GJ/cap and the Republic of the Congo at 13 GJ/cap, for example). Especially in rural areas and at the fringes of urban areas, unreliable or a lack of access to electricity represents energy poverty with its many implications for the education, health, nutrition, and safety of the population [44,45]. This is not to say that increased energy supply would automatically translate into better energy access and associated improvements for the population. In countries that are integrated into the global economy as suppliers of cheap raw materials and/or labor, the opposite may be true, with gains in energy supply representing increased industrial production for export.

3.2. From Renewable to Fossil Energy and Back? Composition of Energy Supply

Not only the level of fossil energy supply, but also the role it plays in overall energy supply is telling in terms of energy transition phases. Despite the considerable development of renewable energy sources and the increased use of nuclear energy, the energy system in the countries that have completed their transition to the fossil energy system remains dominated by fossil fuels (83% of TPES in 2015; Figure 4). The energy underdogs were characterized by high shares of renewable and low shares of fossil energy in their (comparatively very low) total primary energy supply, especially at the beginning of the period under investigation here. By 2015, the composition and per capita level of energy supply in the underdogs were comparable to the 1971 values for the countries maturing their energy transition.

Can we expect the energy underdogs to do in the next 50 years what the maturing transition countries did in the last half century? Given the biophysical constraints on supply and sinks, this appears increasingly unlikely. As those countries with a maturing energy transition add claims to fossil resources for which demand is already high from the countries with a completed transition, reserves are depleted, and anthropogenic climate change is exacerbated. Between 1971 and 2015, the maturation phase of the energy transition consisted of increasing the energy supply by 64 GJ/cap. The contribution of fossil energy to this growth was almost 15 times as high as the contribution of renewable energy. The completion of the energy transition has—thus far—been characterized by very high levels of energy supply that keep up with low population growth mainly through increased fossil energy use with small contributions from renewable and nuclear energy. Individual countries that strongly decreased the share of fossil energy in their supply were generally able to do so based on a combination of renewable and nuclear energy sources (e.g., France, Switzerland, and Sweden). Only three countries (Iceland, New Zealand, and Norway), representing 0.7% of the population in the grouping with a completed energy transition, currently feature very high levels of renewable energy. Not only is this a small pocket of the world, it is also a pocket of the global fossil energy system. All three countries use hydro and/or geothermal power to generate electricity. Iceland and New Zealand rely on extensive fossil energy systems elsewhere (of which Norway is an example) as sources of their imports of petroleum and natural gas [39]. Neither the economic trajectories nor the resource endowment of these countries can be generalized, not even amongst the high-income industrialized economies. For the majority of the countries in our sample, representing over 90% of the global population in 2015, high shares of renewable energy and high levels of energy supply are incompatible. There is no blueprint for the underdogs to follow.

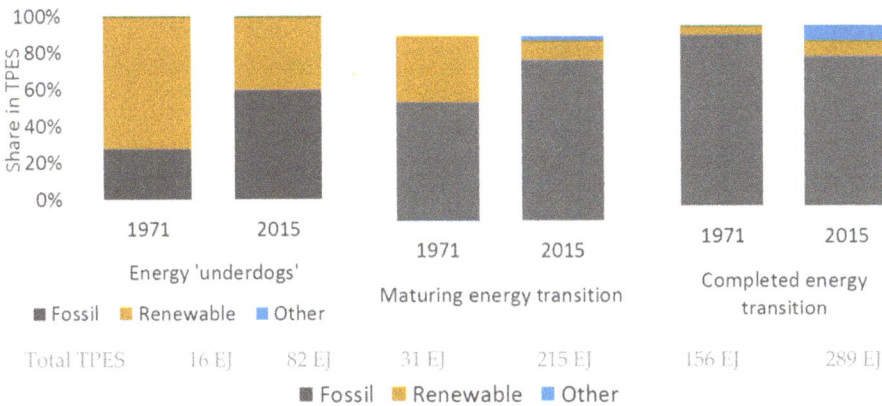

Figure 4. Between 1971 and 2015, the share of renewable sources in the total primary energy supply (TPES) increased only in the countries with a completed energy transition. Here, other energy sources (almost exclusively nuclear energy) have also become relevant. The energy underdogs are characterized by high shares of renewable energy, while the maturing energy transition was marked by renewable energy shares displaced by fossil fuels. In absolute terms, growth in renewable energy supply (in 10^{18} Joules or Exajoules EJ) was most substantial in the energy underdogs, while fossil energy supply increased most strongly during the energy transition maturation phase. Source of data: International Energy Agency [40].

Far be it from us to cite the inherently bad example of the fossil energy transition as pursued by the world's wealthy and wealthier countries as grounds on which the world's poorest countries must not pursue the same path. However, it does appear that the patterns of fossil energy use until today have strained and drained our global environment and its resources to the extent that the option of completing the fossil energy transition will not present itself to all countries [4–6].

3.3. What Would it Take? Thoughts on Completing or Abandoning the Fossil Energy Transition

If the underdogs' fossil energy supply were to continue growing by 3.3% per year as it has done on average since 1971, these countries would embark on the maturation period of their fossil energy transition by 2050, reaching an average of approximately 50 GJ/cap of fossil TPES. Even if the countries with a completed energy transition continue to gradually reduce their fossil TPES and the countries now in the transition maturation follow suit, two things would have happened by 2050:

(1)   The energy underdogs would still be global underdogs, with half of the per capita fossil energy supply of the transition maturation countries, and one-third of the supply of the countries with a completed energy transition.

(2)   Limited reserves and dire environmental consequences of the continued fossil energy transition would—if they had not precluded this development altogether—mean that this transition would occur under conditions of extreme competition in a hazardous, toxic environment.

If the phases of the fossil energy transition were to play out globally, fossil TPES would reach just below 700 EJ/a in 2050 (Figure 5), and would be twice as high as the 350 EJ that have been determined as not altogether eliminating the chances of curbing anthropogenic global warming to two degrees [7]. Our very rough, conservative estimation is based on the United Nations Department of Economic and Social Affairs [64] low variant population forecast until 2050, and would be even higher if we had assumed stronger population growth. What it would take, only in terms of fossil fuel supply, in order for countries to continue along the path of the fossil energy transition, will not realistically be given, or, if so, it will be given under highly adverse conditions.

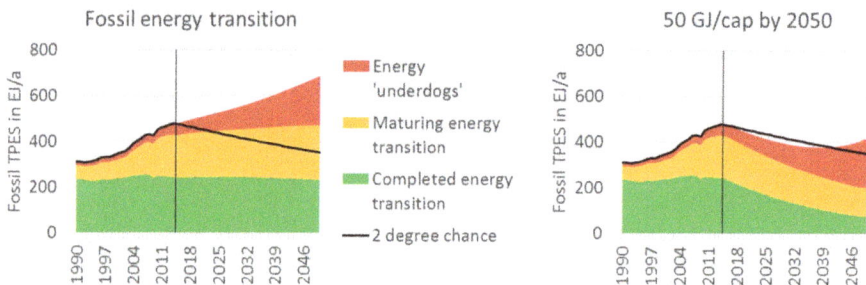

Figure 5. In order for the fossil energy transition to continue (left-hand side), almost 700 Exajoules (EJ) of fossil total primary energy supply (TPES) would be globally required by 2050, which is twice as much as would allow for the possibility of limiting global warming to two degrees [7]. The energy underdogs would barely reach the maturation phase of the transition by 2050. In order to supply an average of 50 Gigajoules (GJ) of fossil energy per person (right-hand side), regardless of the countries' transition phases, just over 400 EJ of fossil TPES would be globally required. All but the energy underdogs would have to drastically reduce their fossil fuel supply. Sources of underlying data: United Nations Department of Economic and Social Affairs [64] population forecast and International Energy Agency [40] World Indicators.

For the energy underdogs to increase their fossil TPES to 50 GJ/cap by 2050 while all other countries reduce their energy supply to this level would take approximately 400 EJ of fossil TPES in

2050 (Figure 5), and generally fall within the overall consumption for a chance at the two-degree target. "50 by 50" is not a target for a more equitable and efficient fossil energy system. It is a generalized outcome that would require the transformation of the global energy system. At 50 GJ/cap, the emerging economies could not continue being the mines, the factories, and the sweatshops of wealthy industrial countries. At 50 GJ/cap, the wealthy industrial countries could not replace the fossil energy reductions with renewable energy. At 50 GJ/cap, the energy underdogs would never develop full-fledged fossil energy systems. If continuing the fossil energy transition is not an option, then alternatives must be sought out and rapidly pursued. The world over, these alternatives require pushing back against the fossil energy system. Maybe this is indeed the chance for the energy underdogs to come out on top, simply because they have less to dismantle and repurpose, less capital tied up in roads and buildings and factories and machines and gadgets that would largely become obsolete at 50 GJ/cap (or less) of fossil energy supply.

4. The Challenge for Change

"50 by 50" (Figure 5) would require transformative change to the global energy system, including the concerted international redistribution and reduction of fossil fuel-based energy. In the current trajectory of the energy transition, we do not find sufficient evidence for the global cooperation, prudence, and willingness to change that would have to precede such transformation.

If the change that might lead us to "50 by 50" is unrealistic, then sustaining the fossil energy transition is just as unrealistic, if not more so. It is already clear that in order to even have a chance of limiting global warming (to two degrees), the combustion of fossil energy carriers will have to be drastically limited, leaving most of the known reserves untouched [7] and accepting the demands of social movements to "leave the coal in the hole, the oil in the soil, and the tar sand in the land" [30,31]. However, the fossil energy transition depends on the unlimited availability of limited energy carriers, the combustion of which threatens the inhabitability of our planet, and the distribution of which is already and will increasingly be controlled violently.

A "Big Push" for renewables [57] that consists in harnessing wind and water to protect fossil capital from shortages in coal and gas or as an investment opportunity for fossil profits may be a more detrimental route up the hill than Sisyphus'. Renewable energy used to maintain the institutions on which the fossil energy system is built further solidifies the fossil energy transition, as exemplified by mega-projects based on large-scale investments and land deals that require access to massive electricity grids with their established issues of access, control, and power [12,49,50,52].

For the energy underdogs to—in the words of our quantitative analysis—succeed in transitioning from traditional to modern renewables at low but sufficient levels of supply and high levels of access would constitute not only transformational but revolutionary change. Abandoning the fossil energy transition is a direct challenge to existing political and economic institutions, both domestically and internationally. Energy supply would focus on households rather than the industry and military. A renewable energy system might not only enable but also necessitate leaving fossil fuels in the ground. The direct [66] and indirect [13,67] provision of energy via trade from the Global South to the Global North and from the *hinterland* to urban areas [68] would not be maintained. The oil supply crisis that almost all of the mature industrialized and emerging economies are facing [4] might be further exacerbated unless these countries, too, transform their energy systems.

It may not feel like we are on the precipice of established power relations toppling in such a transformation. However, why should an energy system failing in a spectacular way to provide "a good life for all within planetary boundaries" [36] even exist? Efforts to systematically reduce and prioritize energy use in order to strengthen decentralized energy systems based on renewable sources to meet people's needs are strategically vital in breaking the momentum of the fossil energy transition [11]. Where established institutions can be challenged to the extent that the fossil energy transition can be abandoned, the global energy underdogs may come out on top. However, the battle to this top—like any—is an uphill one.

Author Contributions: Conceptualization, Methodology, and Analysis, M.F.-K. and A.S..; Writing-Original Draft Preparation, A.S.; Writing-Review & Editing, M.F.-K. and A.S.

funding: This research received no external funding.

Acknowledgments: The BOKU Vienna Open Access Publishing Fund has supported the publication of our work. Anke Schaffartzik acknowledges financial support from the Spanish Ministry of Economy and Competitiveness, through the "María de Maeztu" program for Units of Excellence (MDM-2015-0552).

Conflicts of Interest: The authors declare no conflict of interest.

References

1. Corton, C.L. *London Fog: The Biography*; Harvard University Press: Cambridge, MA, USA, 2015; ISBN 978-0-674-08835-1.
2. "I Feel Helpless": Delhi Residents on the Smog Crisis. Available online: https://www.theguardian.com/world/2017/nov/08/i-feel-helpless-delhi-residents-on-the-smog-crisis (accessed on 24 July 2018).
3. Health Effects Institute. *Health Effects Institute State of Global Air 2018*; Special Report; Health Effects Institute: Boston, MA, USA, 2018.
4. Dittmar, M. A Regional oil extraction and consumption model. Part II: Predicting the declines in regional oil consumption. *Biophys. Econ. Resour. Qual.* **2017**, *2*, 16. [CrossRef]
5. Meng, Q.Y.; Bentley, R.W. Global oil peaking: Responding to the case for 'abundant supplies of oil'. *Energy* **2008**, *33*, 1179–1184. [CrossRef]
6. Murphy, D.J. Fossil fuels: Peak oil is affecting the economy already. *Nature* **2012**, *483*, 541. [CrossRef] [PubMed]
7. McGlade, C.; Ekins, P. The geographical distribution of fossil fuels unused when limiting global warming to 2 °C. *Nature* **2015**, *517*, 187–190. [CrossRef] [PubMed]
8. Stocker, T.F.; Qin, D.; Plattner, G.K.; Tignor, M.M.B.; Allen, S.K.; Boschung, J.; Nauels, A.; Xia, Y.; Bex, V.; Midgley, P.M. *Climate Chang. 2013, The Physical Science Basis. Working Group I Contribution to the Fifth Assessment Report of the Intergovernmental Panel on Climate Change*; Intergovernmental Panel on Climate Change (IPCC); Cambridge University Press: Cambridge, UK; New York City, NY, USA, 2013.
9. Dale, M.; Krumdieck, S.; Bodger, P. Global energy modelling—A biophysical approach (GEMBA) part 1: An overview of biophysical economics. *Ecol. Econ.* **2012**, *73*, 152–157. [CrossRef]
10. Day, J.W.; D'Elia, C.F.; Wiegman, A.R.H.; Rutherford, J.S.; Hall, C.A.S.; Lane, R.R.; Dismukes, D.E. The energy pillars of society: Perverse interactions of human resource use, the economy, and environmental degradation. *Biophys. Econ. Resour. Qual.* **2018**, *3*, 2. [CrossRef]
11. Schmidt, T.S.; Matsuo, T.; Michaelowa, A. Renewable energy policy as an enabler of fossil fuel subsidy reform? Applying a socio-technical perspective to the cases of South Africa and Tunisia. *Glob. Environ. Chang.* **2017**, *45*, 99–110. [CrossRef]
12. Mitchell, T. *Carbon Democracy: Political Power in the Age of Oil*; Verso Books: London, UK; New York City, NY, USA, 2011; ISBN 1-84467-745-1.
13. Malm, A. *Fossil Capital: The Rise of Steam Power and the Roots of Global Warming*; Verso Books: London, UK; New York City, NY, USA, 2016; ISBN 1-78478-130-4.
14. Haberl, H.; Fischer-Kowalski, M.; Krausmann, F.; Martinez-Alier, J.; Winiwarter, V. A socio-metabolic transition towards sustainability? Challenges for another great transformation. *Sustain. Dev.* **2011**, *19*, 1–14. [CrossRef]
15. Chancel, L.; Piketty, T. *Carbon and Inequality: From Kyoto to Paris Trends in the Global Inequality of Carbon Emissions (1998–2013) & Prospects for an Equitable Adaptation Fund*; Paris School of Economics: Paris, France, 2015.
16. Asif, M.; Muneer, T. Energy supply, its demand and security issues for developed and emerging economies. *Renew. Sustain. Energy Rev.* **2007**, *11*, 1388–1413. [CrossRef]
17. Van Benthem, A. *Has Energy Leapfrogging Occurred on a Large Scale?* Social Science Research Network: Rochester, NY, USA, 2010.
18. Unruh, G.C. Understanding carbon lock-in. *Energy Policy* **2000**, *28*, 817–830. [CrossRef]
19. Vergragt, P.J.; Markusson, N.; Karlsson, H. Carbon capture and storage, bio-energy with carbon capture and storage, and the escape from the fossil-fuel lock-in. *Glob. Environ. Chang.* **2011**, *21*, 282–292. [CrossRef]

20. Unruh, G.C.; Carrillo-Hermosilla, J. Globalizing carbon lock-in. *Energy Policy* **2006**, *34*, 1185–1197. [CrossRef]
21. Krausmann, F.; Wiedenhofer, D.; Lauk, C.; Haas, W.; Tanikawa, H.; Fishman, T.; Miatto, A.; Schandl, H.; Haberl, H. Global socioeconomic material stocks rise 23-fold over the 20th century and require half of annual resource use. *Proc. Natl. Acad. Sci. USA* **2017**, *114*, 1880–1885. [CrossRef] [PubMed]
22. Mori, A. Socio-technical and political economy perspectives in the Chinese energy transition. *Energy Res. Soc. Sci.* **2018**, *35*, 28–36. [CrossRef]
23. Bridge, G.; Özkaynak, B.; Turhan, E. Energy infrastructure and the fate of the nation: Introduction to special issue. *Energy Res. Soc. Sci.* **2018**, *41*, 1–11. [CrossRef]
24. Naqvi, A. Energy Infrastructure: Seizing the Opportunity in Growth Markets | McKinsey & Company. Available online: https://www.mckinsey.com/industries/electric-power-and-natural-gas/our-insights/energy-infrastructure-seizing-the-opportunity-in-growth-markets (accessed on 23 February 2018).
25. PwC. *Power in Indonesia: Investment and Taxation Guide 2017*; Pricewaterhouse Coopers: London, UK, 2017.
26. Gallagher, K.P. China's global energy finance: Poised to lead. *Energy Res. Soc. Sci.* **2018**, *35*, 15–16. [CrossRef]
27. Hvelplund, F.; Lund, H. Rebuilding without restructuring the energy system in east Germany. *Energy Policy* **1998**, *26*, 535–546. [CrossRef]
28. Trump, D.J. President Donald J. Trump's State of the Union Address. Available online: https://www.whitehouse.gov/briefings-statements/president-donald-j-trumps-state-union-address/ (accessed on 11 May 2018).
29. Sareen, S. Energy distribution trajectories in two Western Indian states: Comparative politics and sectoral dynamics. *Energy Res. Soc. Sci.* **2018**, *35*, 17–27. [CrossRef]
30. Bond, P. Social movements and corporate social responsibility in South Africa. *Dev. Chang.* **2008**, *39*, 1037–1052. [CrossRef]
31. Bridge, G. Geographies of peak oil: The other carbon problem. *Geoforum* **2010**, *41*, 523–530. [CrossRef]
32. Fischer-Kowalski, M.; Rovenskaya, E.; Krausmann, F.; Pallua, I.; McNeill, J.R. Energy transitions and social revolutions. *Technol. Forecast. Soc. Chang.* **2018**. under review.
33. Sovacool, B.K. How long will it take? Conceptualizing the temporal dynamics of energy transitions. *Energy Res. Soc. Sci.* **2016**, *13*, 202–215. [CrossRef]
34. Kern, F.; Rogge, K.S. The pace of governed energy transitions: Agency, international dynamics and the global Paris agreement accelerating decarbonisation processes? *Energy Res. Soc. Sci.* **2016**, *22*, 13–17. [CrossRef]
35. Sovacool, B.K.; Geels, F.W. Further reflections on the temporality of energy transitions: A response to critics. *Energy Res. Soc. Sci.* **2016**, *22*, 232–237. [CrossRef]
36. O'Neill, D.W.; Fanning, A.L.; Lamb, W.F.; Steinberger, J.K. A good life for all within planetary boundaries. *Nat. Sustain.* **2018**, *1*, 88–95. [CrossRef]
37. Beveridge, R.; Kern, K. The energiewende in Germany: Background, developments and future challenges. *Renew. Energy Law Policy Rev. RELP* **2013**, *4*, 3.
38. Vattenfall Hydro Power Operations. Available online: http://corporate.vattenfall.com/about-energy/renewable-energy-sources/hydro-power/hydro-power-at-vattenfall/ (accessed on 11 July 2018).
39. IEA Energy Atlas. Available online: http://energyatlas.iea.org/#!/tellmap/-1118783123/1 (accessed on 11 July 2018).
40. IEA World Indicators. Available online: http://dx.doi.org/10.1787/data-00514-en (accessed on 22 March 2018).
41. Liu, G.; Müller, D.B. Centennial evolution of aluminum in-use stocks on our aluminized planet. *Environ. Sci. Technol.* **2013**, *47*, 4882–4888. [CrossRef] [PubMed]
42. Sieferle, R.P. *The Subterranean Forest: Energy Systems and the Industrial Revolution*; The White Horse Press: Cambridge, MA, USA, 2001.
43. Davidson, O.; Mwakasonda, S.A. Electricity access for the poor: a study of South Africa and Zimbabwe. *Energy Sustain. Dev.* **2004**, *8*, 26–40. [CrossRef]
44. Doll, C.N.H.; Pachauri, S. Estimating rural populations without access to electricity in developing countries through night-time light satellite imagery. *Energy Policy* **2010**, *38*, 5661–5670. [CrossRef]
45. Tully, S. The human right to access electricity. *Electr. J.* **2006**, *19*, 30–39. [CrossRef]
46. Alstone, P.; Gershenson, D.; Kammen, D.M. Decentralized energy systems for clean electricity access. *Nat. Clim. Chang.* **2015**, *5*, 305–314. [CrossRef]

47. Chaurey, A.; Ranganathan, M.; Mohanty, P. Electricity access for geographically disadvantaged rural communities—Technology and policy insights. *Energy Policy* **2004**, *32*, 1693–1705. [CrossRef]

48. Nouni, M.R.; Mullick, S.C.; Kandpal, T.C. Providing electricity access to remote areas in India: An approach towards identifying potential areas for decentralized electricity supply. *Renew. Sustain. Energy Rev.* **2008**, *12*, 1187–1220. [CrossRef]

49. Del Bene, D.; Scheidel, A.; Temper, L. More dams, more violence? A global analysis on resistances and repression around conflictive dams through co-produced knowledge. *Sustain. Sci.* **2018**, *13*, 617–633. [CrossRef]

50. Howe, C.; Boyer, D. Aeolian extractivism and community wind in Southern Mexico. *Public Cult.* **2016**, *28*, 215–235. [CrossRef]

51. Scheidel, A.; Sorman, A.H. Energy transitions and the global land rush: Ultimate drivers and persistent consequences. *Glob. Environ. Chang.* **2012**, *22*, 588–595. [CrossRef]

52. Sovacool, B.K.; Bulan, L.C. They'll be dammed: the sustainability implications of the Sarawak Corridor of Renewable Energy (SCORE) in Malaysia. *Sustain. Sci.* **2013**, *8*, 121–133. [CrossRef]

53. EIA. *International Energy Outlook*; U.S. Energy Information Administration: Washington, DC, USA, 2017.

54. Kynge, J. *China Shakes the World: The Rise of a Hungry Nation*; Hachette UK: London, UK, 2010; ISBN 978-0-297-85693-1.

55. Zweig, D.; Jianhai, B. China's global hunt for energy. *Foreign Aff.* **2005**, *84*, 25–38. [CrossRef]

56. Easterly, W. Reliving the 1950s: the big push, poverty traps, and takeoffs in economic development. *J. Econ. Growth* **2006**, *11*, 289–318. [CrossRef]

57. AtKisson, A. The "Big Push" Transforming the World's Energy Systems. Available online: https://www.greenbiz.com/article/big-push-transforming-worlds-energy-systems (accessed on 15 March 2018).

58. Burton, R. *Choice Emblems, Divine and Moral, Antient and Modern, or, Delights for the Ingenious, in above Fifty Select Emblems, Curiously Ingraven upon Copper-Plates: With Fifty Pleasant Poems and Lots, by Way of Lottery, for Illustrating Each Emblem to Promote Instruction and Good Counsel by Diverting Recreation*, 6th ed.; Edmund Parker at Bible and Crown: London, UK, 1732.

59. Fischer-Kowalski, M.; Schaffartzik, A. Energy Availability and Energy Sources as Determinants of Societal Development in a Long-term Perspective. Available online: https://www.cambridge.org/core/journals/mrs-energy-and-sustainability/article/energy-availability-and-energy-sources-as-determinants-of-societal-development-in-a-longterm-perspective/095970C15255B4F19F034894B6107EDA (accessed on 26 July 2018).

60. Ehrenfeld, J.R. Searching for sustainability: No quick fix. *Reflections* **2004**, *5*, 1–13.

61. Abson, D.J.; Fischer, J.; Leventon, J.; Newig, J.; Schomerus, T.; Vilsmaier, U.; von Wehrden, H.; Abernethy, P.; Ives, C.D.; Jager, N.W.; Lang, D.J. Leverage points for sustainability transformation. *Ambio* **2017**, *46*, 30–39. [CrossRef] [PubMed]

62. Meadows, D. Leverage Points: Places to Intervene in a System. Available online: http://donellameadows.org/archives/leverage-points-places-to-intervene-in-a-system/ (accessed on 27 July 2018).

63. Rotmans, J.; Kemp, R.; van Asselt, M. More evolution than revolution: transition management in public policy. *Foresight* **2001**, *3*, 15–31. [CrossRef]

64. United Nations, Department of Economic and Social Affairs, Population Division. World Population Prospects: The 2017 Revision. Available online: https://www.un.org/development/desa/publications/world-population-prospects-the-2017-revision.html (accessed on 25 July 2018).

65. World Bank World DataBank. World Development Indicators. Available online: https://data.worldbank.org/products/wdi (accessed on 25 July 2018).

66. Schaffartzik, A.; Pichler, M. Extractive economies in material and political terms: Broadening the analytical scope. *Sustainability* **2017**, *9*, 1047. [CrossRef]

67. Peters, G.P.; Minx, J.C.; Weber, C.L.; Edenhofer, O. Growth in emission transfers via international trade from 1990 to 2008. *Proc. Natl. Acad. Sci. USA* **2011**, *108*, 8903–8908. [CrossRef] [PubMed]

68. Decker, E.H.; Elliott, S.; Smith, F.A.; Blake, D.R.; Rowland, F.S. Energy and material flow through the urban ecosystem. *Annu. Rev. Energy Environ.* **2000**, *25*, 685–740. [CrossRef]

sustainability

MDPI

Article

Sustainability Indicators Past and Present: What Next?

Simon Bell [1] and Stephen Morse [2,*]

[1]   Bayswater Institute and the Science, Technology, Engineering and Mathematics Faculty, Open University, Milton Keynes MK7 6AA, UK; S.G.Bell@open.ac.uk
[2]   Centre for Environment and Sustainability, University of Surrey, Guildford GU2 7XH, UK
*   Correspondence: s.morse@surrey.ac.uk; Tel.: +44-(0)1483-686079; Fax: +44-(0)1483-686671

Received: 27 March 2018; Accepted: 16 April 2018; Published: 20 April 2018

Abstract: This paper discusses the current state of thought amongst the Sustainability Indicator (SI) community, what has been achieved and where we are succeeding and failing. Recent years have witnessed the rise of "alternative facts" and "fake news" and this paper discusses how SIs fit into this maelstrom, especially as they are themselves designed to encapsulate complexity into condensed signals and it has long been known that SIs can be selectively used to support polarized sides of a debate. This paper draws from chapters in a new edited volume, the "Routledge Handbook of Sustainability Indicators and Indices", edited by the authors. The book has 34 chapters written by a total of 59 SI experts from a wide range of backgrounds, and attempts to provide a picture of the past and present, strengths and weaknesses of SI development today. This paper is an "analysis of those analyses"—a mindful reflection on reflection, and an assessment of the malign and benign forces at work in 2018 within the SI arena. Finally, we seek to identify where SIs may be going over the coming, unpredictable years.

Keywords: sustainability indicators; gross domestic product; GDP; fake news; tweets

1. Introduction

"The moment we begin to fear the opinions of others and hesitate to tell the truth that is in us, and from motives of policy are silent when we should speak, the divine floods of light and life no longer flow into our souls".

Elizabeth Cady Stanton

We argue in this paper, without trying to be alarmist, that a truly existential issue faces all of us in the sustainable development community and, in this crisis of truth, Sustainability Indicators (SIs) are at the epicentre, especially as given the breadth of concerns within sustainable development the variety of what can be an SI is understandably immense. Here, we use the term "Sustainability Indicator" to encompass indices (amalgams of indicators). We have also taken a liberal view of what could be considered to be an "SI" given that sustainability spans the three pillars of social, economic and environmental dimensions. Similarly, there is "no one SI to rule them all" (although some agencies have arguably exhibited a Mordor-esqe attitude to SIs on occasion) but a wide diversity of approaches and indicators, each emerging in their own time and space and designed to meet a defined set of objectives. Thus, we have seen indices such as the Human Development Index (HDI), Ecological Footprint (EF) and Environmental Performance Index (EPI) becoming popular and, at the time of writing, we have the emergence of the targets and indicators linked to the Planetary Boundaries concept [1] as well as the Sustainable Development Goals (SDGs). Indices (aggregations of indicators) such as the HDI and EPI have evolved over time in response to feedback from researchers and practitioners, and the ever-increasing availability of data (albeit of varying qualities and arguably still not enough) also acts as a spur to change. However, at their heart, we all know that indicators and indices are simplifying tools designed to capture complexity and help convey information to specialists and non-specialists alike. This is, of course, well known and there are many published examples spanning decades as to how this process of simplification results in trade-offs; decisions to exclude and include; and to manipulate data (for an early review, please see [2]). These are human decisions and, while they are rationalized by their "owners", they are nonetheless inherently subjective. It is acknowledged that not all will agree with those decisions and the reader need look no further than the numerous debates that have resonated over the years regarding the HDI let alone the EPI and its precursor called the Environmental Sustainability Index (ESI). Morse [2] provided a summary of the debates surrounding indices such as the HDI and EPI/ESI. We must accept that SIs are not "laws of nature" but human constructs that reflect the biases, failings, intentions and worldview of their creators. In that sense, because of the inherent subjectivity all indicators and indices can be labelled as "fake" by at least someone and they can provide "evidence" (based on different biases, intentions, assumptions and worldviews) to back it up. Needless to say, this "home truth" may be uncomfortable reading for those of us in the indicator business.

The SI landscape is certainly a constantly shifting one, and, while much of what we have said in the previous paragraph is well known, there are still many questions that need answers. Amongst them are:

- What is the current state of thought amongst the SI community?
- What has been achieved and where were we succeeding and failing?
- What challenges and threats face the informing agency at the heart of the SI process?
- Most seriously and existentially for the indicator oeuvre, is there evidence of a fight on-going for what we might call "the soul of facts"?

These were questions we had been asking ourselves, especially with the recent rise of "alternative facts" and "fake news" [3], which take highly selective stances on what are "facts" and the Twitter phenomenon where complexity is condensed into tweets of just a few hundred characters. "Fake news" can be believed as "truth" by many people; it can indeed become "realer than real" [4]. At one level, the rise of the fake news phenomenon in the 2000s is but a recent manifestation of the hoaxes portrayed by writers such as Edgar Allan Poe in the 19th century. For example, Poe published a short story (called the "Balloon Hoax") in the form of a newspaper article that purported to describe the first crossing of the Atlantic by a manned balloon. The story was very detailed and had a ring of plausibility about it, hence it was believed by many who first read it in the Sun newspaper published in New York. It was only later revealed to be a hoax. While Poe certainly did not invent hoaxes, he was one of the first writers of science fiction and clearly had a fertile mind, even if some have since suggested that the balloon hoax was derived from other written and contemporary sources [5]. What is different about the fake news of today compared to the 19th century is its rapid spread and indeed democratization via social media such as Facebook and Twitter [6]. Anyone with a Twitter account can now make up their own news and the system facilitates its rapid spread via "re-tweeting". Re-tweeting has a cascade, even domino effect which means that a news item can literally be spread to millions of Twitter users in seconds. How do SIs fit into all of this, especially as they are themselves designed to encapsulate complexity into condensed signals and it has long been known that SIs can be selectively used to support polarized sides of a debate? Indeed, are SIs the sustainability equivalent of "tweets", fulfilling an innate human thirst for rapid information that simplifies complexity? In addition, do SIs under certain circumstances play into a desire amongst some for "alternative facts" which can be in some way customized, even weaponized, to create "formations of terror" in receiving communities [7]? Are we in a fight about the nature of facts without even knowing it? This post-truth debate has been going on for a while now. In 2006, Steven Poole [8] and Anthony O'Hear [9] anticipated the rise of trivialization and the demise of "truth" in public discourse in their respective books. The debates contained in these books could now be said to have matured. An apparent "easy" answer to these questions rests with motivation. Those of us in the "indicator business" think of ourselves as having a good motive; we want to help bring about a positive change. Hence, the indicators we develop and encourage others to use are there with the very best of intentions. Poe knew he was writing a hoax and while the offices of the Sun were besieged with people looking to get the "news" about the balloon crossing, Poe would no doubt argue that he did not set out to hurt anyone. However, are the modern purveyors of fake news purposely setting out to cause damage? Some may well, but it might surprise us how genuine the motives are of those who create and spread such news. It should be noted here that this apparent similarity between SIs and Twitter/Facebook domain of "quick" and "fake" news is not a similarity the authors see as a fact, but that it is a fact that (biased) consumers in their echo chambers, and thus significant parts of the public, may be unable to recognize the difference.

In 2014, a major publisher—Routledge—approached us and asked if we would be interested in editing a book on SIs. With a combined experience of over 35 thirty years of effort and learning from responses to our previous books and papers, we felt that this may well be an ideal opportunity to reflect the history and theory of sustainability measurement, approaches and methods used, agencies involved and critiques of where we are today and their intended use for "measuring the immeasurable", especially the awkward question as to whether SIs play into a desire for "alternative facts". We begin this paper with our analysis of the book and in particular the major points which emerged regarding the future of SIs, and what the authors felt was needed going forward from here. Following that, we discuss some of the thoughts regarding the point we make above about the future of SIs in this new era of "fake news" and "tweets". These thoughts were informed by various points made throughout the book as well as numerous email communications we have had with contributors since 2014, especially by some authors who were clearly frustrated with what they regarded as the current state-of-play regarding "non-use" or arguably "misuse" of SIs. As we have noted above, this raises some uncomfortable (perhaps) issues for those of us in the SI community. Without wishing to be overly-provocative, are we also playing the same game as those who readily use the term "fake news" at every opportunity that suits them and use "tweets" to get their messages out? Are we not in a glass box and perhaps should we stop throwing stones?

2. The Book: An Analysis

2.1. A Brief Tour

In the book, 59 distinguished authors, many of them with decades of experience working on the "coal face" of SI development, have contributed to map out their past experiences of SIs and reflect on the future. To provide a summary of the topics covered in the book is never really an adequate exposition of the richness of the original, and here we can only really set out some brief outlines of the material and messages. We divided the book into four sections and 34 chapters, as shown in Figure 1. The topics spanned the theory and history of SIs through to methods, agency experiences and critical reflections. As editors we sought to avoid a book which simply acted as a shop window for many "favourite" SIs, but wished to include a more nuanced perspective regarding the many years of experience the indicator community has amassed with their use. Hence, there are two sections in the book on experience and reflection.

We should emphasize here that our intention in this paper is not to offer a kind of book editorial or summary, but instead we have utilized the material in the book as a source of information to address the questions we set out regarding the future of SIs. In effect, this paper is an "analysis of analyses", and, given the material in the book is contemporary and reflective, it does provide a unique resource on SIs.

Authors in the collection made various and wide-ranging suggestions regarding future work on SIs, and we have focused on those points that stood out from the various conclusions reached by the contributors. The points span the following:

1. More case studies on the development/use of SIs

2.   Alternatives to Gross Domestic Product (GDP)
3.   The growing confusion around data provision
4.   The essential need for a more systemic perspective
5.   Top-down versus bottom-up
6.   Issues around the aggregation of indicators

All of these cover long-established debates in the SI arena, of course, even if some have arguably received more attention than others. Indeed, it should perhaps not be surprising that they emerged again as strong points of discussion within the book. However, it was also clear from the chapters that the debates had moved on and it is useful to set out some of the conclusions that were reached and what we as editors can conclude from those conclusions.

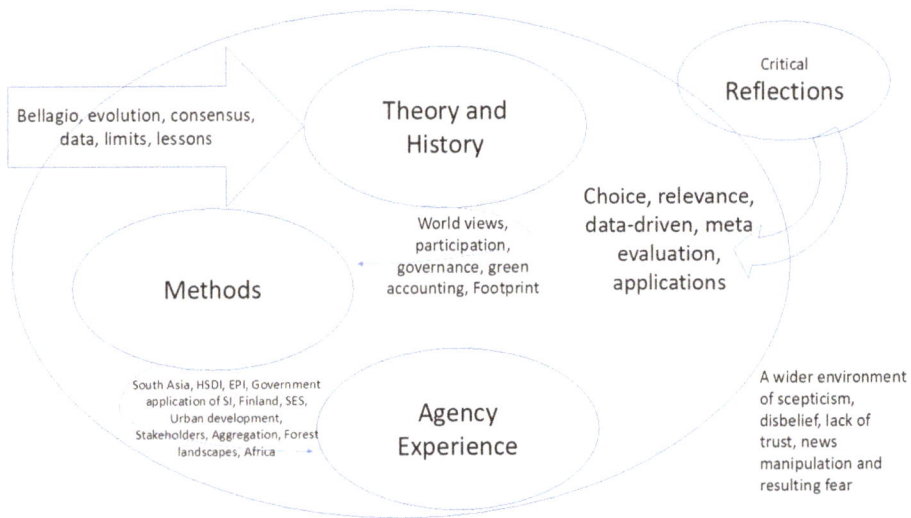

Figure 1. The structure of our book set in its environment.

2.2. More Case Studies on the Development/Use of Sustainability Indicators

Pintér et al. called for a *"richer selection of case studies"* to help create *"practical and more useful guidance"* regarding Sustainability Assessment and Measurement Principles (STAMP) [10] and the book had several "case study" chapters which discussed the development and application of SIs; examples are chapters on experiences with the EPI in Malta [11] and SIs in Finland [12]. There is certainly a need for more research of this type to allow for the identification of potential generic patterns as to what works best, or not. However, case study-based research certainly has its critics and challenges, as those of us who have tried to publish case study-based research findings have repeatedly found. The dilemma, and one that is so often espoused by paper reviewers and journal editors, is that case study findings are often not readily generalizable. Hence, they can be dismissed as being "context specific", and linked to a specific place and time. How can we derive more universal "truths" from such work, especially in a world of publication metrics where impact factor (at the level of the journal) and H-Index (at the level of the individual researcher) increasingly seem to dominate? Competition for space in the best journals is increasingly intense and journal editors are looking for those papers that will amplify the journal itself (often by promoting those who are already successful and therefore less risky) and boost ratings? Given this competition for space, it is easy to appreciate how negative comments from some reviewers can readily be seized upon and used to reject case study-based work.

This is not the case for all case-study based papers, of course, and some reviewers and editors are more amenable and supportive than are others, but we do nonetheless wonder how much is missed.

However, case studies have a place, and in the case of Sis, they allow us to understand much more about that critical interface with SI users albeit, we accept, in what can be quite context-specific spaces. Case studies can provide early examples of experiences which may become general trends, weird results which provoke curiosity, even contradictions to the established opus of "truth". Hence, we agree with Pintér et al that a case-study based body of knowledge regarding SIs can allow for new patterns to emerge (and old ones to be questioned) and that is why we were keen to include case study experiences in the book [10]. What we perhaps need is a meta-analysis of SI use experiences, but, to do this, we need the case studies to be peer reviewed and placed in the public domain. This is very challenging work, as we note later in this paper, but also very valuable. The dilemma, of course, is how to get such case study-based material on SIs reviewed and published. Maybe there is a need for a new journal devoted to case studies in sustainability.

2.3. Alternatives to Gross Domestic Product

Dahl, in his chapter on the Contributions to the "Evolving Theory and Practice of Indicators of Sustainability" [13], reiterated the need for alternative indicators to GDP and suggests material flow analysis as an integrating approach in sustainability assessment. There are echoes here with an intriguing call for a *"New Bretton Woods"* to help achieve a broad consensus regarding alternative indicators to allow us to move beyond GDP and achieve *"measures of what we really want and to achieve these goals"* [14]. However, while the *"New Bretton Woods"* idea is tantalizing, these calls to explore alternatives to GDP have been with us for some years with little obvious success to date. Indeed, one of the rationales for the HDI was as a counter-weight to the economic-based indicators that were perceived by the United Nations Development Programme (UNDP) to be so dominant in assessing development. Nonetheless, economic-based indicators still dominate in a world desperate to see the return of economic growth and prosperity. We flag this issue to contribute to the amassing weight of evidence that GDP does not provide the necessary or sufficient resilience for twenty first century needs. However, the question is arguably not whether other indicators are needed but what they should be and how to get them accepted in the light of experience to date.

2.4. Confusions in Data Provision

Some contributors to the book note the potential of indicators to help support environmental decision-making but point to continuing problems of data limitation, even if there has been much improvement and data are no longer as scarce as they once were [15–17]. We very much agree, as without an adequate availability of good quality indicators there is a likelihood that indicators may be deeply flawed and hence readily dismissed. Ulla Rosenström made the interesting observation about how digitization has done little to improve the timeliness of data provision or it "created new opportunities to measure sustainable development. Too much of the data is still presented on an annual basis when more real-time databases could be created" [12].

The question, of course, is what it would take to achieve this. Collecting necessary data of the required quality is likely to be resource-demanding and/or imagination challenging. At one level, we have a profusion of data being collected of a good quality on a daily basis on mobile phones. However, how do we lever this for SI purposes? It may be that what we have witnessed so far with digitization is but a reflection of the limited capability of machines on the one hand and the creative imaginations of researchers on the other, and as machines become more sophisticated, machine learning begins to expand and researchers become more aware of the wealth of data incidentally collected second by second by millions of people, then we may pass into a new age of automation, with machine and human, digital and analogue combining to revolutionize the concept of the data needed for SIs. Jean et al. provided an example of using machine learning to help predict poverty, using another tool (satellite imagery) which may well grow in importance for populating SIs especially in places where resources to collect good quality data in the field may be lacking [18].

2.5. A systems Perspective

Walter Vermeulen suggested that "we need to build indicators and index systems based on a clear guiding vision and key elements" [19] and, in a related vein, Rotz and Fraser called for a greater acknowledgement that "conceptual and instrumental challenges" of sustainability and resilience are deeply linked and that "indicators need to be nested in a broader analysis that helps to make sense of context specific dynamics" [20]. Gilberto Gallopin also called for a more integrated approach that considers linkages, synergies and antagonisms between goals and targets (and their associated SIs of course) rather than simple listings under themes as we see with the Sustainable Development Goals (SDGs) [21]. It is hard to disagree with that or indeed his sombre conclusion that "given that linear thinking is still dominant in most institutions (including governments), the outlook is rather pessimistic, at least in the short and medium term". Herein rests a significant challenge that has been with us for some time. It has been relatively easy for us to "talk the talk" of such systems approaches to SIs, and we have also added out voices to this over the years, but linear thinking and desires to strict accountability over relatively short time periods can work against "walking the talk". Clearly, the issues involved here are proving to be far more intractable than we would have thought over 20 years ago when we first began working on SIs. Breaking out of the "linear thinking" cultural mindset arguably dominant since the advent of the first industrial revolution and prevalent as a knee-jerk against risky ideas in most institutions clearly requires much more analysis as to why such thinking has become so dominant in the first place. Some of it is no doubt driven by a legacy of innate distrust of the individual in the world of work to "deliver" and a commensurate push for an apparent accountability that makes sure "delivery" can be assessed. In this sense, SIs could be seen to be part of a more general drive to crudely equate measurement with outcomes relating to inputs (no matter how spurious the measurement method applied); as if any single input were ever responsible for one single output. This delusion propagated by the management classes to spuriously link outcomes to expenditure has been exemplified in the past by planning frameworks such as the "logical framework" approach [22–26]. The "square peg" mindset of the "log frame" as developed in the 1980s and 1990s might be said to have found a refined form in the SIs of recent times.

2.6. Top-Down vs. Bottom-Up

A further point linked to the systems perspective is the role of SIs in helping to facilitate the development of an appreciation of what sustainability and resilience are in any particular context. Hence, it is not solely a case of SIs being created as an operational output after an understanding of sustainability and resilience has been arrived at, but SIs as a catalytic precursor to help facilitate such an understanding. SIs can help ground such discussions and provide tangible representations of what is seen as relevant and important. We have often advocated such a dialectic and others in the book have also made the point. For example, Dwi Amalia Sari and colleagues in their chapter on SIs in complex, multi-functional forest landscapes suggested that "the role of criteria and indicator processes in these complex and contested situations is perhaps more to allow a structuring of the debate than to provide a set of boxes to be ticked" [27].

However, one of the dilemma's here is what to do with the SIs that emerge out of such a dialectic. Once the SIs have allowed an "arrival" at an understanding and have no doubt passed through a process of discussion, sieving and modification, then it is possible that they may not necessarily match the SIs that have been set in a more "top-down and one-way" process by government or other experts. This is certainly not to say that "top-down and one-way" SIs are bad or irrelevant; they may well have a strong antecedence of their own and offer advantages such as cross-country and timeline comparison. Simon Joss and Yvonne Rydin addressed this "bottom-up and dialectic"–"top-down and one-way" space in the context of urban sustainability and come to understandable conclusion that: "What constitutes an appropriate balance between the standard aspects of urban sustainability frameworks and the local variation of particular applications remains an open discussion in need of ongoing conceptual and practical exploration" [28].

We very much agree with this sentiment and would postulate that, while much progress has been made with participatory methodologies and their acceptance within interventions, there does indeed still seem to be something of an unexplored boundary between SIs developed via such approaches and those derived "top down" by experts. The dualism implicit in this may be false and, in the "space" between experts and "people", emerge many of the intriguing problems which provide the wider environment for the SI discourse and project. This is surely a space in deep need of mindful exploration. Either by intent or accident, experts can be perceived (perhaps even presented) as callous and unworldly, indicators as symptoms of authority and even demagoguery, and the entire SI project as an example of an educated and liberal elites conspiracy to enforce an agenda at variance with common sense and social/economic needs. This remains a contaminating issue for the field but maybe one which could be most richly mined in future research. Where there is contention, there should research cluster.

2.7. Aggregation of Indicators

One of the fascinating aspects that emerges from the book chapters is the varied views on aggregation of indicators into indices. Many of the chapters include examples where this has been done, for example with the EPI [15] and a derivative of the HDI called the Human Sustainable Development Index (HSDI) [29], but there are some stark warnings as well. As Jesinghaus passionately put it, "Aggregation is evil when it gives mediatic power to numbers that do not deserve it" [30]. However, and perhaps surprising to us, we do not detect a clear consensus amongst the authors that more integration is required, and Dahl when summarizing the outcomes of a UN Commission on Sustainable Development (CSD) led process to identify SIs reflects this by noting that "despite repeated requests from governments, reviews of progress, and the best efforts of the scientific community, no consensus emerged on highly aggregated indices" [31]. This raises an interesting dilemma. On the one hand, one of the "givens" often assumed in the indicator world is that aggregated indices are useful tools as they help present complexity in simple ways. On the other hand, we all seem to know the risks involved as aggregation can "hide" key decisions over what to aggregate and how that can, in turn, significantly influence the result and any conclusions that emerge from it. Indeed, the creators of the HDI say that they have resisted major changes to the index for that very reason and go to great lengths to present "standardized" (in methodological terms) versions of the HDI to allow for time-series comparisons [2]. However, it seems that the experts have yet to arrive at a clear consensus, although this is not for the want of trying. We would argue that the work of Dahl regarding what "consumers" of SIs want needs to be more fully developed: is there demand for aggregated indices and are there patterns which exist in this demand between types of SI consumer?

However, the issue of aggregation takes us to the equally contentious issue of what is a fact? How is an "aggregation of facts" contrived to be meaningful and how does meaning result in an action/response which is in some way commensurate to the "fact" outlined in the aggregation? What is real and what is fake in the SI world? This is a question that drives at the very heart of our interests in SIs, and we provide some thoughts in the next section.

3. Fake Indicators?

Given that SIs occupy that nexus between developers and users, it seems almost inevitable that there could be an element of selection-bias by the latter [32]. No matter the motives of the SI developers, some people may indeed want to make selective use of them to convey a message. However, this is a complex landscape. For example, in one of the first published studies of the use of SIs by government, Herzi suggested that there are five categories of use [33]:

- Instrumental: Indicators inform decisions that have impacts

- Conceptual: Catalyse learning and understanding
- Tactical: Substitute for action and deflect criticism
- Symbolic: Ritualistic assurance
- Political: Support a pre-determined position

The first two in the list are arguably the most "positive" uses in the sense that the SIs seemed to be linked to a desire for genuine improvement, while the other three are arguably more "negative" in the sense that they seem to be about deflection, false assurance and support of entrenched positions that may not necessarily be to the benefit of society as a whole. However, while the categories may seem to be neat, the boundaries between them are blurred, and what one user may genuinely regard as "instrumental" use of an SI another may vigorously regard as "political". Thus, in any one context, and with a suite of SIs available, it is not hard to imagine that different users would select different SIs to address any of these uses. For the researcher, this may be something of an intriguing and bewildering minefield, and an attempt to categorize the use of an SI cherished by one group as "political", while others may see it as "instrumental" or "conceptual", can leave him/her open to the claim of spreading "fake news". Even if the process of categorization was opened-up to a kind of democratic decision-making where the majority view rules, it is not guaranteed that those in the minority would accept it and it is highly likely that at least some of them would not. Even so, we may argue that it is the majority view which counts and a minority, even if vociferous, is still a minority. After all, science may not be based on fiat but, in the world of SIs, fiat is arguably the only game in town. However, here is another symptom of the complexity masked by indicators. Indicator intention and application relates to psychological choices and these are deep waters worthy and in need of exploration. For a topical example, the reader need look no further that the June 2016 "Brexit" referendum and heated debate in the UK associated with it that continues to the time of writing. One of the most oft-quoted phrases by those on the "leave" campaign (those in favour of Brexit) was that the UK was the "5th largest economy" in the world and thus, by extrapolation, well-able to flourish outside of the EU. The phrase was often repeated and is still a key element of the Brexiteers (those who support Brexit) lexicon. The phrase is claimed to be based on a metric and statistics but is it true?

Well, of course, much depends on the measures one uses to represent the size of the "economy". Economies can be measured in various ways and the World Bank has been collating such information for many years with data readily available at https://data.worldbank.org/. Several indicators could be employed but here we have focused on just four. In each case, the indicator is founded upon the Gross Domestic Product (GDP) where, using the World Banks definition:

> GDP is the sum of gross value added by all resident producers in the economy plus any product taxes and minus any subsidies not included in the value of the products. It is calculated without making deductions for depreciation of fabricated assets or for depletion and degradation of natural resources. [34]

In effect, GDP calculated on the basis of expenditure is given by:

$$GDP \text{ (expenditure)} = C + G + I + (EX - IM) \tag{1}$$

where C is the consumers' expenditure on goods and services; G is the government expenditure on goods and services; I is investment; EX is exports; and IM is imports.

The balance of these components will vary across economies [2]. In essence, the assumption here is that the higher the level of GDP then the greater the "size" of the economy, with an additional implied assumption that, the bigger the GDP, the better. Jesinghaus certainly made a good case for treating GDP with care when it comes to sustainable development and care does need to be taken in assuming that GDP growth is always a good thing, at least for most of a population, as much depends on distribution [30]. As Peter Bartelmus has noted, the GDP has often been "accused of being a misleading measure of well-being" [35]. Clearly, it is not such a measure and was never intended to be; unfortunately, it has become the key barometer of national economic performance and, in the minds of many, this is very much associated with well-being. However, is GDP an SI? It does, of course, sit within the economic domain often included in sustainable development. However, it needs to be noted here that, while GDP may not be unanimously regarded as an SI, it has certainly found its way into indices often considered to be part of the SI stable, such as the HDI (where GDP/capita is regarded as a measure of "income") and even within components of the Environmental Sustainability Index (ESI), the precursor of the EPI. In addition, GDP is often used as an independent variable for exploring environmental performance, as with the Environmental Kuznet Curve models [2]. It needs to be stressed that GDP is not itself a "bad" indicator, and, as Bartelmus noted, we do need to be careful not to discard the GDP: "There is indeed no other place where standardized measures of economic activities can be found and presented to policy makers in a meaningful "nutshell". Individuals, corporations, and trade unions can compare information on their economic situation and prospects with those of their own country and other nations" [35].

One can indeed use the GDP for international comparisons by converting local currencies to the U.S.$ using exchange rates (GDP current U.S.$). However, a complication, of course, is that the size of a country's GDP expressed as U.S.$ could fluctuate over time as the exchange rate fluctuates. To allow for fluctuations in relative currency value over time, caused by inflation for example, GDP could be based on a single reference point and the World Bank provide an estimate of GDP using exchange rates for 2010. A further refinement is to adjust the GDP to allow for changes in the "purchasing power" of currencies, which is referred to as Purchasing Power Parity (PPP). Purchasing Power Parity is much more than a simple adjustment for exchange rate and is based on the knowledge that one US$ will buy different quantities of goods and services across the globe. As the World Bank define it: "Purchasing Power Parity GDP is gross domestic product converted to international dollars using purchasing power parity rates. An international dollar has the same purchasing power over GDP as the U.S. dollar has in the United States."

Purchasing Power Parity adjusted GDP could also be based on current exchange rates and an exchange rate fixed to one particular year (as above). Table 1 provides a summary of the four indicators. Using these four indicators of economy "size", the ranking of the UK amongst the countries of the globe is shown in Figure 2. The numbers of newspaper articles published each year that mention the phrases "5th largest economy" and "fifth largest economy" in relation to the UK are also shown. These data have come from the Nexis database of global media publications (https://www.lexisnexis.com/en-us/products/nexis.page) but specifically searching newspapers where these phrases appears in English referring to the UK. The Nexis database has been applied in several published studies designed to explore reporting of indicators in the media [36–39]. Unsurprisingly, the number of "mentions" of the phrase surged in 2016, and is also higher than the 2010–2014 norm in 2015 when speculation over the referendum was rife and in 2017 as the UK started negotiating the terms of its exit from the EU. Prior to the 2015–2017 period, the terms appeared in the press, but the incidence was less than 100 articles per annum. Immediately after the referendum result in 2016, the value of the Pound Sterling fell by 10% against the U.S.$; indeed, it hit a 31 year low, and this would have affected the value of the GDP calculation expressed in US$ and the country's ranking in the "size of the economy" league tables.

However, does the use of the "5th largest economy" term match the reality? Well, with GDP (expressed as current U.S.$) and GDP (expressed as constant 2010 US$), the answer seems to be "no" The UK tends to fluctuate between 6th and 7th between 2010 and 2016, although it did hit a peak of 5th in 2015 for the GDP (current U.S.$) indicator. Nonetheless the "5th largest economy" claim that was so loudly proclaimed in 2016 is hardly convincing. However, let us provide some benefit of the doubt here, as such calculations are complex and say that the GDP (current U.S.$) and GDP (constant 2010 U.S.$) are at least in the right ballpark and the ranking based on GDP (current U.S.$) is close to being true. Nonetheless, "fifth" does obviously sound better than claims of "sixth" or "seventh".

Table 1. Summary of four indicators of economic "size". Purchasing Power Parity (PPP) [40] .

Indicator Name	Notes (as Provided by the World Bank for Each Indicator)
GDP (constant 2010 U.S.$)	Data are in constant 2010 U.S. dollars. Dollar figures for GDP are converted from domestic currencies using 2010 official exchange rates. For a few countries where the official exchange rate does not reflect the rate effectively applied to actual foreign exchange transactions, an alternative conversion factor is used.
GDP (current U.S.$)	Data are in current U.S. dollars. Dollar figures for GDP are converted from domestic currencies using single year official exchange rates. For a few countries where the official exchange rate does not reflect the rate effectively applied to actual foreign exchange transactions, an alternative conversion factor is used.
GDP, PPP (constant 2011 international $)	Data are in constant 2011 international dollars.
GDP, PPP (current international $)	Data are in current international dollars. For most economies PPP figures are extrapolated from the 2011 International Comparison Program (ICP) benchmark estimates or imputed using a statistical model based on the 2011 ICP. For 47 high- and upper middle-income economies, conversion factors are provided by Eurostat and the Organisation for Economic Co-operation and Development (OECD).

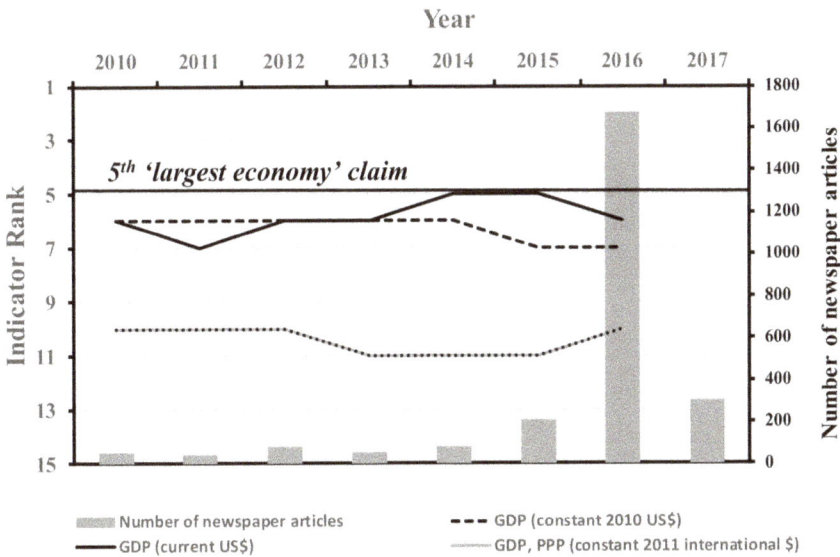

Figure 2. Four indicators of measuring the size of the UK economy and the rank of the UK in the global "league table" using those measures [40].

However, the same cannot be said of the two GDP indicators adjusted for purchasing power, a commonly applied technique for adjusting GDP over many years [41]. With these PPP-adjusted measures, the UK typically ranks between 9th and 10th—some considerable distance away from the "5th largest economy" claim. However, in fairness, it should be noted that PPP has attracted criticism from some economists [42], although there is logic in the notion that PPP adjustments allow for differing purchasing power across economies, and hence reduce any distortions that might arise. However, there is little, if any, evidence to suggest that the PPP adjustment GDPs were employed by those advocating for Brexit. Similarly, while Figure 2 does not include the figures if the GDP and GDP PPP are calculated on a per capita basis, the UK ranks even lower in those "league table". Per capita adjustments allow for the fact that the value of the GDP may be linked to population size: the more people there are then the greater the flow of money in the system. This is not always the case, of course, and can distort the rankings as countries with small populations and low corporate tax regimes can rank very high purely because companies introduce processes to ensure that a lot of their taxable income flows through them, but it is a widely used adjustment of GDP nonetheless. The HDI, for example, uses the GDP PPP adjusted on a per capita basis and has long argued in favour of that as an indicator of income even if the HDI engineers have sought to cap high values of GDP PPP/capita in various ways to prevent a distorting effect on the index [37]. However, all of these adjustments were ignored by the Brexit supporters and instead the focus was on the most "favourable" measure for their case—the GDP based on current US$. They would regard this as an "instrumental" use of the indicator as it was being used by them to help inform an important decision. Others, based upon the evidence presented above, may see it as more of a symbolic or ritual use.

We as SI developers and practitioners should not be surprised by any of this, and indeed it does have to be stressed that, while we have used the Brexit "hot house" period of intense debate to illustrate the selective used of indicators, this is by no means an issue solely linked to that time and place. It goes with the "indicator territory" and we must accept, whether we like it or not, that the indicators we develop or promote may be "used" in ways that we did not intend or that users may be highly selective in their choices [32]. Indicators do not have any special privileges in the complex, "messy" real world of decision making where those who take the decisions are being influenced by implicit and explicit concerns and pressures, and it would naïve to think that an SI, no matter how well-crafted or presented, would be a sole, pure source of influence. Even efforts to develop neat looking typologies of SI use have to contend with a multitude of interactions and forces as well as multiple perspectives on what our apparently "well defined" categories mean. In a sense, we are part of that mess and are playing the same game as everyone else; maybe we just do not reflect on it as much as we should. As Rotz and Fraser noted: "we must remain focused on understanding the conditions within which sustainability and resilience get manipulated in the interests of political-economic and social empowerment and capital accumulation. How are these concepts deployed by different groups, and for what possible ends?" [20].

If we wish to produce an SI that will somehow be above all of this, then maybe we would be chasing the end of a rainbow—we would be seeking to "know" in a manner which is culturally and ethically "neutral". As social and psychological actors in the world with innumerable stakes in outcomes of diverse kinds this can never be possible. In the same vein, if we are in the business of producing indicators to help make a difference by influencing those with power then we must expect that power to also have an impact on the uses it puts to those indicators. We cannot have it both ways. Decision-making is a complex process and decision-makers will be subject to many influences and motives. However, does this mean that we have to stop trying and accept that we will always be producing and promoting "fake" indicators, at least in the eyes of some? Well no—not at all. We live in a world where many (rapidly becoming "most") people get their news from social media outlets such as WhatsApp, LinkedIn, Twitter and Facebook. This context demands that complex events be reduced to "Tweets" of just a few hundred characters. Such simplifications are pernicious and viral. They can influence the thinking of many people. At the time of writing, Twitter has over 300 million "active" users across most countries of the globe, and the President of the USA (perhaps the most influential global citizen) is using it to get highly subjective points over directly to the public—presenting as truth—and it seems will readily re-tweet "news" without necessarily checking its veracity.

There is an appetite for communication tools that seek to present complexity in ways that busy people can interact with but with simplification come consequences. To some extent SIs are trying to do the same thing and there is also an appetite for them, but as with Twitter there are profound dangers to the consumers of such simplification. This brings us neatly into what we think the messages in the book tell us about the future of SIs.

4. Discussion and Tentative Conclusions

What conclusions can we come to regarding the future of SIs based upon material provided by contributors to the new book on SIs? Do we see any resonance between SIs and the world of "fake news" and "tweets"? Do SIs play into a desire amongst some for "alternative facts"? Are we in the SI community living in a glass box and should we stop throwing stones? Indeed, what is the future of SIs? Well, it would appear we are in something of a fight on a number of fronts, spanning familiar battlefields such as aggregation, stakeholder participation and the need for good quality data to less-well trodden territory such as the need for more published case studies on the use of SIs so insights can be drawn. There is no other way of putting it. However, perhaps the front that is of greatest concern to us is a fight of an existential nature in terms of *reasonably* objective and verifiable facts as counters to the "fake news" agenda. We recognize the reality that interest groups will always make selective and distorted use of indicators. That is the price we pay for being human beings involved in the objective/ subjective indicator business. Thus, we would like to see a greater emphasis in research on the space between production and use. Specifically, the uses to which SIs are put and how that information can feed back into the development and presentation of SIs. As Giangiacomo Bravo succinctly put it: "Any index inevitably is the product of a number of more or less arbitrary choices (not only scientific ones, since politics often plays a major role)" [29].

From what we have seen before, clearly, there is no magic bullet or one-size-fits-all here; no SI can ever be made immune to all manner of intended and accidental distortion and we need to be aware of our own biases. This is a point echoed by Joachim H. Spangenberg:

> Indicator users should be aware of the limitations each indicator, index or indicator system has, partly from the method of calculation, but also from the often-hidden assumptions inherent to the world views from which they have been derived. Practitioners should choose and combine the indicators they use carefully, being fully aware of these biases and their impacts on both the measurement and the messages derived from it, implicitly or explicitly [43].

SIs are, after all, human constructs and their development and use can be subject to the same biases that drive the "echo chambers" we see in Twitter and Facebook. However, that human fallibility must not dissuade us for further development of SIs and seeking new ways for presenting them to a defined group (or groups) of consumer(s). We just need to be more reflective in our assumptions, smarter in our use and have a better sense who our consumers are, what they are looking for and how we can best help. To date, SI development has been almost entirely "creator-led" with little, if any, input from consumers of those SIs—those we intend to use them. That balance needs to shift so that we as creators move towards a model of co-creation with the voices of SI consumers being part of the process. This is not a new call, of course, and we amongst many others have been saying it for years, including Almassy and Pinter [44], but we still feel that much more progress is required and for us this is a key element in the future of SIs. As Ulla Rosenström has noted: "good indicators are of little influence and importance if they are not used in any way. Although use does not guarantee the desired influence, aiming at use is well argued for. Hence efforts to create opportunities for use and disseminating information remain crucial" [12].

The "Indicator Policy Fact Sheets" proposed by Janoušková et.al are one tangible suggestion to "help SI users (most often decision- and policy-makers) choose and use the most appropriate indicators for assessing particular sustainability issues" [45]. However, maybe there is a deeper issue at the heart of this issue. Maybe the indicator community (along with many other areas of rationalism) were labouring under a misapprehension that we are, as Steven Pinker suggested in his opus—"The Better Angels of our Natures" [46]—living in a more rational world. A world where instinctive and knee jerk reactions are beginning to fade out in the on-rush of rational and objective decision making. Of course, this has been a dream for time out of mind. Since Plato's "Philosopher Kings" through to Saint Simon and Auguste Comte's concepts of a new social doctrine based on science and today's algorithmic governance by global data corps such as Facebook, humankind has sought what we may consider to be an illusion of a rational world. A world governed by clear data, un-contestable facts and wise administration. To some extent the whole SI debate might be seen as a sub-set of this project—a rationalizing project to save human beings from their instinctive and irrational selves.

Sadly, this does not seem to be working terribly well. Plato's Republic remains a paper dream only, Saint Simon and Comte's technocracy could not dispel the terror of the French Revolution and the power of global algorithms raise as much "1984" and "Brave New World" angst as they do hopes for a better world. Indeed, the total transparency which Facebook might be argued and provoking, mimicked and played to horrific levels in David Egers book "The Circle" appears only as a nightmare of algorithm-led social engineering. Knee-jerk reactions, the denial of "evidence-based facts" with disdain, the assumption of subjective "truth" and the trust in instinct seems to be prevalent and has been argued to lead to more terror and even an amplification of terror based on compounding cycles of unreasonable social fear [7].

The experiences of the authors of this book with the complexity of the indicator/indices fields, the short comings of any statistical means to address complex truths, the uneven and evolving nature of the field and the issues of objectivity and subjectivity remain as on-going strategic and tactical issues, logistic complexities set against a much more troubling background—the human proclivity to the irrational and the dupes of the sellers of snake oil. While the challenges arising from the (necessary and intentional) simplification, and the questions of manipulation and instrumentalisation associated with SIs are not new, they have arguably gained new urgency far beyond the statistical and policy advisory professions in the context of the age of "fake news".

The arguments we set out in this paper bear witness to the long, hard and arduous task of understanding—understanding how human beings interact with social, technical and environmental issues, and how the psychology of the human attempts to measure the immeasurable and make sense of the world so that in the future there will be a world to make sense of. It is a testimony to the noble attempt at the measurement of the immeasurable. They are a step towards sustainability, resilience and what we have called elsewhere *"the saving of the human project"* [47]. On the road so far, great progress has been made. Hosts of indicators and indices have been constructed to try and influence people with power (including the public) to do wiser things. There remains important second order work to engage with. This can be framed in terms of continuing reflection on the formulation of indicators by experts and communities, the strategic, tactical and operational value and targeting of indicators and the development of forms of assessment. All of these have been mulled over but the mulling is in its infancy and has not as yet taken into account the fearsome push-back of those hostile to the sense of the SI project. We must not forget, we are in an existential fight.

We are not at the end of the SI process, but we may be at the end of the beginning. Battle lines are still being drawn up.

Acknowledgments: The authors would like to thank the anonymous reviewers for their suggestions regarding the improvement of this paper. They would also like to thank the editor of the Special Edition—Joachim Spangenberg—for his kind invitation to write this paper and for the advice he provided to us.

Author Contributions: S.B. and S.M. made equal contributions to the development and writing of this paper.

Conflicts of Interest: The authors declare no conflict of interest.

References

1. Steffen, W.; Richardson, K.; Rockström, J.; Cornell, S.E.; Fetzer, I.; Bennett, E.M.; Biggs, R.; Carpenter, S.R.; de Vries, W.; de Wit, C.A.; et al. Planetary boundaries: Guiding human development on a changing planet. *Science* **2015**, *347*, 1259855. [CrossRef] [PubMed]

2. Morse, S. *Indices and Indicators in Development: An Unhealthy Obsession with Numbers*; Earthscan: London, UK, 2004.

3. Mitchell Waldrop, M. News Feature: The genuine problem of fake news. *Proc. Natl. Acad. Sci. USA* **2017**, *114*, 12631–12634. [CrossRef] [PubMed]

4. Berkowitz, D.; Asa Schwartz, D. Miley, CNN and the Onion. *J. Pract.* **2016**, *10*, 1–17.

5. Wilkinson, R.S. Poe's "Balloon-Hoax" Once More. *Am. Lit.* **1960**, *32*, 313–317.

6. Carruthers, K.; Ballsun-Stanton, B. #c3t An Agreeable Swarm: Twitter, the Democratization of Media & Non-localized Proximity. In Proceedings of the 5th International Conference on Computer Sciences and Convergence Information Technology, Seoul, Korea, 30 November–2 December 2010; pp. 166–169.

7. Bell, S. *Formations of Terror*; Cambridge Scholars Publishing: London, UK, 2017.

8. Poole, S. *Unspeak*; Little, Brown: London, UK, 2006.

9. O'Hear, A. *Plato's Children: The State We Are in*; Gibson Square: London, UK, 2006.

10. Pinter, L.; Hardi, P.; Martinuzzi, A.; Hall, J. Bellagio STAMP: Principles for Sustainability Assessment and Measurement. In *Routledge Handbook of Sustainability Indicators*; Bell, S., Morse, S., Eds.; Routledge: London, UK, 2018; pp. 21–41.

11. Conrad, E.; Cassar, L.F. The Environmental Performance Index: Does this reflect reality. In *Routledge Handbook of Sustainability Indicators*; Bell, S., Morse, S., Eds.; Routledge: London, UK, 2018; pp. 294–307.

12. Rosenstrom, U. Sustainable development indicators. In *Routledge Handbook of Sustainability Indicators*; Bell, S., Morse, S., Eds.; Routledge: London, UK, 2018; pp. 321–328.

13. Dahl, A.L. Contributions to the Evolving Theory and Practice of Indicators of Sustainability. In *Routledge Handbook of Sustainability Indicators*; Bell, S., Morse, S., Eds.; Routledge: London, UK, 2018; pp. 42–58.

14. Costanza, R.; Hart, M.; Kubiszewski, I.; Posner, S.; Talberth, J. Lessons from the History of GDP in the Effort to Create Better Indicators of Prosperity, Well-being, and Happiness. In *Routledge Handbook of Sustainability Indicators*; Bell, S., Morse, S., Eds.; Routledge: London, UK, 2018; pp. 117–123.

15. Esty, D.C.; Emerson, J.W. From Crises and Gurus to Science and Metrics: Yales Environmental Performance Index and the Rise of Data-Driven Policymaking. In *Routledge Handbook of Sustainability Indicators*; Bell, S., Morse, S., Eds.; Routledge: London, UK, 2018; pp. 93–102.

16. Esty, D.C. Toward Data-Driven Environmental Policy-making. In *Routledge Handbook of Sustainability Indicators*; Bell, S., Morse, S., Eds.; Routledge: London, UK, 2018; pp. 494–506.

17. Hsu, A. Governing by Numbers: China, Viet Nam, and Malaysia's Adaptation of the Environmental Performance Index. In *Routledge Handbook of Sustainability Indicators*; Bell, S., Morse, S., Eds.; Routledge: London, UK, 2018; pp. 167–283.

18. Jean, N.; Burke, M.; Xie, M.; Davis, W.M.; Lobell, D.B.; Ermon, S. Combining satellite imagery and machine learning to predict poverty. *Science* **2016**, *353*, 790–794. [CrossRef] [PubMed]

19. Vermeulen, W.J.V. Substantiating the rough consensus on concept of sustainable development. In *Routledge Handbook of Sustainability Indicators*; Bell, S., Morse, S., Eds.; Routledge: London, UK, 2018; pp. 59–92.

20. Rotz, S.; Fraser, E. The Limits of Sustainability and Resilience Frameworks: Lessons from agri-food systems research. In *Routledge Handbook of Sustainability Indicators*; Bell, S., Morse, S., Eds.; Routledge: London, UK, 2018; pp. 103–116.

21. Gallopin, G.C. The socio-ecological system (SES) approach to sustainable development Indicators. In *Routledge Handbook of Sustainability Indicators*; Bell, S., Morse, S., Eds.; Routledge: London, UK, 2018; pp. 329–346.

22. Coleman, G. Logical Framework Approach to the Monitoring and Evaluation of Agricultural and Rural Development projects. *Proj. Apprais.* **1987**, *2*, 251–259. [CrossRef]

23. Cordingley, D. Integrating the Logical Framework into the Management of Technical Co-operation Projects. *Proj. Apprais.* **1995**, *10*, 103–112. [CrossRef]

24. Girma, M.; Sartorius, R.; Silansky, C.; Thompson, R.M. *The Project Cycle Management Resource Guide: A Logical Framework Approach*; Team Technologies Inc.: Chantilly, France, 1996.

25. Baccarini, D. The Logical Framework Method for Defining Project Success. *Proj. Manag. J.* **1999**, *30*, 25–32.

26. Bell, S. Logical frameworks, Aristotle and soft systems: A note on the origins, values and uses of logical frameworks, in reply to Gasper. *Public Adm. Dev.* **2000**, *20*, 29–31. [CrossRef]

27. Sari, D.A.; Margules, C.; Boedhiharton, A.K.; Sayer, J. Criteria and indicators to audit the performance of complex, multi-functional forest landscapes. In *Routledge Handbook of Sustainability Indicators*; Bell, S., Morse, S., Eds.; Routledge: London, UK, 2018; pp. 407–426.

28. Joss, S.; Rydin, Y. Prospects for Standardising Sustainable Urban Development. In *Routledge Handbook of Sustainability Indicators*; Bell, S., Morse, S., Eds.; Routledge: London, UK, 2018; pp. 364–378.

29. Bravo, G. The Human Sustainable Development Index. In *Routledge Handbook of Sustainability Indicators*; Bell, S., Morse, S., Eds.; Routledge: London, UK, 2018; pp. 284–293.

30. Jesinghaus, J. How Evil is Aggregation? Lessons from the Dashboard of Sustainability. In *Routledge Handbook of Sustainability Indicators*; Bell, S., Morse, S., Eds.; Routledge: London, UK, 2018; pp. 392–406.

31. Dahl, A.L. UNEP and the CSD Process for Sustainable Development Indicators. In *Routledge Handbook of Sustainability Indicators*; Bell, S., Morse, S., Eds.; Routledge: London, UK, 2018; pp. 347–363.

32. Frederiksen, F.; Gudmundsson, H. Policy use and influence of indicators. *Ecol. Indic.* **2013**, *35*, 1–2. [CrossRef]

33. Herzi, A.A. Sustainability indicators system and policy process in Malaysia: A framework for utilisation and learning. *J. Environ. Manag.* **2004**, *73*, 357–371.

34. Coyle, D. *GDP: A Brief but Affectionate History*; Princeton University Press: Princeton, NJ, USA; Oxford, UK, 2014.

35. Bartelmus, P. Green accounting: Balancing environment and economy. In *Routledge Handbook of Sustainability Indicators*; Bell, S., Morse, S., Eds.; Routledge: London, UK, 2018; pp. 236–244.

36. Morse, S. Out of sight, out of mind. Reporting of three indices in the UK national press between 1990 and 2009. *Sustain. Dev.* **2013**, *21*, 242–259. [CrossRef]

37. Morse, S. Stirring the pot. Influence of changes in methodology of the Human Development Index on reporting by the press. *Ecol. Indic.* **2014**, *45*, 245–254. [CrossRef]

38. Morse, S. Measuring the success of sustainable development indices in terms of reporting by the global press. *Soc. Indic. Res.* **2016**, *125*, 359–375. [CrossRef]

39. Morse, S. Focusing on the extremes of good and bad: Media reporting of countries ranked via index-based league tables. *Soc. Indic. Res.* **2017**. [CrossRef]

40. Bell, S.; Morse, S. What next? In *Routledge Handbook of Sustainability Indicators*; Bell, S., Morse, S., Eds.; Routledge: London, UK, 2018; pp. 543-555

41. Officer, L. The purchasing power parity theory of exchange rates: A review article. *Int. Monet. Fund Staff Pap.* **1976**, *23*, 1–60. [CrossRef]

42. Hyrina, Y.; Serletis, A. Purchasing power parity over a century. *J. Econ. Stud.* **2010**, *37*, 117–144. [CrossRef]

43. Spangenberg, J.H. World views, interests and indicator choices. In *Routledge Handbook of Sustainability Indicators*; Bell, S., Morse, S., Eds.; Routledge: London, UK, 2018; pp. 143–155.

44. Almassy, D.; Pinter, L. Environmental governance indicators and indices in support of policy-making. In *Routledge Handbook of Sustainability Indicators*; Bell, S., Morse, S., Eds.; Routledge: London, UK, 2018; pp. 204–223.

45. Janoušková, S.; Hák, T.; Moldan, B. Relevance—A neglected feature of sustainability indicators. In *Routledge Handbook of Sustainability Indicators*; Bell, S., Morse, S., Eds.; Routledge: London, UK, 2018; pp. 477–493.

46. Pinker, S. *The Better Angels of Our Nature: A History of Violence and Humanity*; Penguin: London, UK, 2011.

47. Bell, S.; Morse, S. *Resilient Participation: Saving the Human Project?* Earthscan: London, UK, 2012.

sustainability

MDPI

Article

Sustainability Assessment: Exploring the Frontiers and Paradigms of Indicator Approaches

Tomás B. Ramos

CENSE, Center for Environmental and Sustainability Research, Department of Environmental Sciences and Engineering School of Sciences and Technology, School of Science and Engineering, NOVA University Lisbon, Campus da Caparica, 2829-519 Caparica, Portugal; tabr@fct.unl.pt

Received: 27 October 2018; Accepted: 28 January 2019; Published: 5 February 2019

Abstract: Sustainability assessment approaches could support all levels of decision-making and policy processes (including strategies, policies, plans, programs, projects, and activities/operations), thus improving the management of natural and human systems. Sustainability Indicators (SIs) have been extensively used to assess and communicate the progress toward sustainable development. However, despite all the SI initiatives and the well-known advantages and popularity, several risks have been pointed out, so there is a need to rethink the current state of SIs and build visions that could reshape the indicator reality. The main goal of this research is to develop a constructive debate around the possible futures and paths of SIs', by conducting a critical analysis of a set of challenges and opportunities identified by the literature. This was explored through a critical perspective and viewpoint article that discusses what could be some of the new frontiers and paradigms in SIs. Exploratory research supported by a combination of methods was conducted, consisting of a search of the literature and qualitative document analysis, followed by an assessment procedure based upon an evaluation ranking scale. The classification scale integrated three main criteria of valuation: Relevancy, feasibility, and societal impacts. The findings showed that most of the challenges and opportunities analyzed are old and mainly technically oriented, with a low potential impact on society, including end-users and practitioners. The majority of the challenges have low-to-medium feasibility, showing that there would be difficulty in implementing them, and so they should be improved or redesigned. A set of key questions on SIs' futures is proposed, aiming to represent a critical view of the relevant challenges and opportunities analyzed, but underpinned and observed from a crosscutting angle, represented by the societal role. The SI research community should be ready to adapt ways of thinking and doing, responding to new global and local paradigms and using transdisciplinary collaborative scientific development and innovation as the foundations for the change process, wherein communities and the individual have central roles to play.

Keywords: sustainable development; indicators; stakeholders; goals; challenges; opportunities; societal impact

---

1. Introduction

In the monitoring, assessment, and reporting of sustainability, one of the main ends is to support decision-making and policy processes, thus improving the management of socio-ecological systems and achieving more sustainable outcomes with fewer negative effects, as discussed by several authors [1–3]. In addition, to support policy development and management strategies, sustainability evaluation, reporting, and governance initiatives should integrate and reflect the uncertainty and complexities of human and natural system interactions, and face global challenges toward sustainable development [4]. Despite the existence of several non-consensual definitions, interpretations, and methods [5], the term "sustainability assessment" is often used to refer to ex post and forward-looking ex ante approaches [6], aiming to characterize the sustainability state (covering the environmental, social, economic, and institutional/governance dimensions) of a current implemented situation or to predict the potential effects of an activity prior to its implementation, respectively. Sustainability assessments can support decision-making processes, playing a role in the strategic and operational levels of planning and project processes, including policies, plans, programs, projects, and activities or operations that address sustainable development goals and targets, independently of their specific context and mission.

There is a significant diversity of methods and tools to assess and report sustainable development (SD). However, indicators are one of the approaches most used, playing a central role in the sustainability assessment of every decision-making process, as noted by Sala [7] and Pope [5], in particular to communicate sustainability performance to stakeholders [8]. Nevertheless, at the same time, sustainability assessment theoretical approaches and practice are currently in a relative initial phase of development [9], where early practice is being adapted to fit new situations and new contexts. Practice has not yet reached a situation where particular methods or approaches are proven to work well.

Despite the current importance and popularity of indicators at an international level [10,11], their development and use is not very recent, since some of the first important references date from the 1970s, for instance, [12–14] mainly focusing on the environmental aspects. In the last decades, there has been a proliferation of sustainability indicator initiatives worldwide (e.g., [15–17]), often labelled and criticized as an "indicator factory" that produces countless initiatives, which mainly serve the individuals or organisations closely involved in designing, producing, and disseminating indicators, as discussed by Rinne et al. [18]. They range from global to local and citizen levels, including transnational, national (countries), regional (e.g., states, regions, provinces), local (e.g., municipalities, cities, localities), organizational (e.g., companies, public agencies, universities, non-governmental organizations), economic sectors (e.g., energy, transports, agriculture), households, communities/families, and individuals, as well as ecosystems.

The massive literature and the uncoordinated and independent practice on sustainability indicators (SIs) have brought no consensus around methodologies—not even agreements on conceptual frameworks, or clarifications of the different terms. As noted by Bell and Morse [19], numerous books, articles and reports have been written, attesting to the popularity and relevance of the field, and yet very few resources exist that tell the full story of the SI phenomenon. Several authors insist that the way forward for SIs should be stronger harmonization at different territorial/organization levels and functions (e.g., [20,21]). Others argue that sustainability indicators must incorporate sufficient flexibility, yet still be culturally and universally appropriate, emphasizing the need to develop tailor-made approaches [22]. There is a will to channel diversity and at the same time standardize some concepts and methods. SIs have also been criticized for trying to assess sustainability complexities through quantitative and restricted indicator approaches, but mostly for being ineffective in changing decision-making processes and outcomes [23].

Related to the specific challenges, threats, and opportunities of the past, current and future roles for SIs are the use of different definitions of the terms sustainable development (SD), sustainability, and indicators, which have been explored over the past decades. As discussed by Bolis et al. [24], the conceptual complexity is significant when dealing with sustainability, since this concept means many things to different people, and this diversity of meaning tends to increase over time. The concept of SD is charged with uncertainties and complexities, as it involves and balances several different dimensions. As stressed by Hussey et al. [25] and Lozano [26], SD-related terms have been considered subjective, complex, controversial, and open-ended, and the indicator terminology is still rather confusing and not well established [27]. Since the indicator movement and boom that started in the early 1990s [24], the term "indicator" has been used rather loosely to include almost any sort of quantitative information or statistic [28].

SIs reflect the issues and paradigms that have been most studied in practice. However, as highlighted by Ramos [17] and Viegas et al. [29], sustainability frontiers should also be built upon non-traditional aspects of sustainability, including immaterial values of sustainability, such as ethics, culture, esthetics, justice, compassion, mutual help, moderation, and solidarity. Sustainability indicator research and practical approaches have to be transdisciplinary and flexible in order to include emerging issues and deal with aspects that have been overlooked in previous research. As explored by Lang et al. [30], to deal with real-world problems, as well as with the goals of sustainability science as a transformational scientific field, approaches like transdisciplinary, community-based, interactive, or participatory research are often suggested as appropriate means.

Conventional SIs and related tools have long been used to assess sustainability, and much progress has been achieved. However, it has become necessary to start rethinking their roles and applicability. The approval of the 2030 Agenda for Sustainable Development at the United Nations (UN) with 17 Sustainable Development Goals (SDGs), 169 targets, and 232 indicators [31] represents a paramount opportunity for transitions to new paradigms and ways of thinking in assessing sustainability. Despite their weaknesses and limitations (see, e.g., Spangenberg [32]), SGDs create visibility for SIs, where indicator-based assessments are presented as key evidence-based approaches to support SDG implementation and benchmarking [33], giving room for research, innovation, and change.

As noted by Bell and Morse [19] (pp. 1), "we have never been so much in need of indicators to assess, in an impartial and confirmable manner, the outlines of our changing, developing, resilient, and threatened world," in a growing "post-truth reality." There is a decline in official data and information credibility, where objective facts are less influential in shaping public views. Therefore, desires and opinions appeal to emotion and personal beliefs, calling for a sustainability assessment change of paradigm. The official truth provided by raw data, statistics, and indicators should be able to integrate and weight non-official inputs, such as societal values, aspirations, desires, perceptions, opinions, and ultimately data collected by stakeholders, as explored by Coutinho et al. [34] and Domingues et al. [35], in a balanced and trustworthy approach. Social or multi-stakeholder collaborative networks, as presented in Kelly and Moles [36], could play an important role is these processes.

In the last 40 years, various studies have identified and discussed the strengths and weaknesses of SIs, addressing the most relevant challenges. Some of those major challenges are related to the use of indicators [3,37], with the need to define clear, simple, and robust frameworks for presenting the indicators, and supported by the engagement of those who are involved in the indicator process, including the potential users. Recent works repeated these attempts and systematized a vast array of challenges and opportunities for SIs, e.g., [38]. However, when analyzing those lists, and despite the value of several of the identified items noted by the international literature analyzed in the work of Verma and Raghubanshi [38], several of them are too general, outdated, redundant, and somewhat blurred. This is also true for the discussion around the specific challenge of SI selection criteria, where most related indicator studies keep using and recommending a substantial number of criteria. As demonstrated by several authors, e.g., [39–42], the vast number of SI selection criteria causes significant complexity and ineffectiveness, and is often associated with subjectivity, redundancy, and alienation from the reality of indicator practice. Therefore, it has been increasingly assumed that indicator development and selection criteria should be tested and evaluated, through assessment by the end-users and other stakeholders [41,43], for example to ascertain their importance to select SIs, confronting their theoretical grounds and the potential relevance versus their practical effectiveness and usefulness.

The main goal of this research was to develop a constructive debate around the possible futures and paths of SIs', conducting a critical analysis of a set of challenges and opportunities identified by the literature. This was explored through a critical perspective and viewpoint article that discusses what could be some of the new frontiers and paradigms in SIs.

This paper is organized as follows: After the introduction, which presents an overview of and international context for the research, the research gap is presented, including the fundamentals to discuss indicator challenges and opportunities. Then the main research goal is detailed. In Section 2, the methods used to develop the research are outlined, followed by Section 3, with the main findings and discussion of new SIs frontiers and paradigms. In Section 4, final remarks are presented, and the contribution to knowledge and the paper's implications are highlighted.

2. Methodological Approach

Inductive-exploratory research was conducted through a combination of methods, consisting of a search of the literature and qualitative document analysis, followed by an assessment procedure supported by an evaluation ranking scale, as discussed by Saunders et al. [44].

The document analysis focused mainly on the scientific literature on approaches, concepts, methods, and frameworks, or case study applications that deal with assessing and reporting sustainability through indicator initiatives. This analysis was essentially comparative of the main SI challenges and opportunities identified. It was explored whether and how they overcome the major drawbacks and limitations of SIs, looking at differences, highlights, and novelties between documents. Although the search procedure mainly followed a subjective approach, rather than systematic, it took into consideration a minimum level of regularity in the analyzed literature that covered SIs' challenges and opportunities. Issues that are seldom pointed out, not clearly presented, or not well grounded were not included in the analysis. To identify and review the selected documents, the keywords *challenges, limitations, drawbacks, opportunities, strengths, weaknesses, threats, sustainability indicators,* and *sustainable development indicators* were particularly considered to support this exploratory analysis.

A critical evaluation of a set of challenges and opportunities was then conducted. The criteria used to support the analysis were Relevancy, covering technical and scientific importance, Feasibility, covering the possibility of implementation and operability, as explored by Ramos et al. [27], and Societal Impacts, related to the usefulness to society in terms of SD desires, aspirations, values, and needs. Therefore, elements such as potential community added value, contribution to public policies, and initiatives and contribution to community sustainable development objectives, as identified in Bornmann (2012) [45], were included in the analysis of this third criterion. A ranking scale of Poor, Moderate, and High, varying from low to high values of Relevancy, Feasibility, and Societal Impacts, was used to evaluate each challenge and opportunity. The evaluation process was mainly supported by the insights collected in the document analysis and weighted through qualitative expert knowledge.

There are limitations associated with exploratory qualitative research design and the inherent flexibility and adaptability. Validity, reliability, and generalizability [44,46] are limitations of this type of approach, and were weighed up in the qualitative assessment and discussion of the results, and when drawing the conclusions.

3. Findings and Discussion of New Frontiers and Paradigms

3.1. Evaluation of the Indicator Challenges and Opportunities

Findings make clear that the analyzed set of SI challenges and opportunities have high relevancy (Table 1), and are considered a significant priority for action in the literature, e.g., [38] and [47], as demonstrated by the rationale that supported this evaluation (see the Appendix A for more details).

In all, few of the identified challenges and related opportunities simultaneously received a classification of high relevancy, feasibility, and societal impact. Most of the current challenges and opportunities are old and repeated by the literature (see, for example, the limitations and questions raised in the 1970s by the work of Ott [14]).

Table 1. Evaluation of the selected sustainability indicator (SI) challenges and opportunities, according to the three main criteria (Relevancy, Feasibility, and Societal Impacts), ranked in the following categories.

Selected Challenges and Opportunities	Relevancy	Feasibility	Societal Impacts
#1. Richer selection of case studies	M	H	H
#2. Specific cultural context	H	M	H
#3. Adequate level of standardization	H	M	H
#4. Meta-evaluation	H	L	L
#5. Alternatives to move beyond GDP	H	L	H
#6. Data limitations and provision problems	H	L	L
#7. Integrated and systemic and holistic perspective	H	M	L
#8. *Optimum* level of indicator aggregation	M	L	H
#9. Better mechanisms for indicator use in practice	H	L	H
#10. Integration or non-traditional aspects of sustainability	H	L	H
#11. Use of information tools and systems	H	L	H
#12. Find the best selection criteria	H	M	H
#13. Institutionalisation process and governance models	H	M	L
#14. Satellite remote sensing and other observing technologies	H	M	L
#15. Intergenerational equity information transfer	H	L	L
#16. The lack of an endogenous indicator's theory	H	L	L

High (H) ; Moderate (M) ; Low (L) .

Overall, they are technically oriented, and are meaningless or too complex for end-users' understanding, even for practitioners who are non-indicator experts, following the same pattern identified for SIs themselves and the surrounding discourse, which is often developed by scientists and expressed in abstruse language [43,48], and mainly useful for the people who designed them. Almost half of the analyzed challenges have a potential low impact on society, since their opacity or technicality move them away from users' perceptions and interests. Therefore, a central topic to deal with low social understanding and usefulness could be the promotion of societal collaborative networks, involving decision makers, researchers, practitioners, communities, and individuals, as also explored by Domingues et al. [35] and Kelly and Moles [36]. These networks could provide mutual support and learning, and mitigate the low social impact.

Overall, despite the high relevancy, they have low-to-medium feasibility, showing that there will be great difficulty in implementing them, often due to their inherent complexity and operability, or the resources needed. The current state shows that it has become necessary to rethink SI priorities to overcome old and new barriers, and to make future steps toward the Sustainable Development Goals, as established by the United Nations [31]. Several of the analyzed challenges and opportunities remain unanswered or are still in the early stages of development, and are not yet covered by sufficient theoretical and empirical knowledge and evidence.

Two of the challenges ("#1. A richer selection of case studies" and "#8. Optimum level of indicator aggregation") were classified with medium relevancy mainly because, despite their relative importance, they represent aspects that are already well covered by the existing literature and practice, or their importance is not confirmed (see Table A1 in the Appendix A).

3.2. Exploring New Frontiers and Paradigms

Despite important progress and the existing vast amount of literature, SIs are still an underexplored field of study. The analyzed set of indicator challenges and opportunities call for a critical analysis of some specific challenges. Exploring new frontiers and paradigms of SIs leads to unanswered epistemological questions, such as "How was the original development of SIs conceived?" and "Why do serious-minded communities of decision makers and theorists still believe sustainability can be measured in an objective sense?" [49] (pp. 205).

A crosscutting challenge for SIs is that the lack of an endogenous indicator's theory hinders the development of the indicator's research into an autonomous scientific field and limits indicators to the ecological, social, or economic fields [50], meaning that researchers can only conduct the study of indicators within their subjects of expertise. Therefore, SI evolution is often stuck in sectoral frontiers (ecological, sociocultural, economic, institutional) and facing different barriers, depending on the angle from which they are viewed. They are often not grounded in effective integrated and interdisciplinary sustainability studies, which are not just a sum of different parts, and usually do not include the time dimension and intergenerational equity evaluation, which is a fundamental SD pillar [51,52].

Another central issue to consider in this discussion is related to indicator data, where SIs have a key part to play in the crisis of truth: "We are in a fight, and we recognize the reality that interests will always make selective and distorted use of indicators. That is the price we pay for being in the indicator business" [47] (pp. 553). SIs need to deal with reality, where the value of official data is in question. Furthermore, some other related drawbacks from the existing indicator approaches are that oftentimes, and in spite of the investment put into the compilation of SIs and respective data, stakeholders feel that either the information is not easily accessible or usable, or it is incomplete or sometimes obsolete by the time it reaches the user [53], and therefore not useful.

SIs should be ready to rethink the "old" and "new" world challenges, and deal with the complexity, scale, and unpredictability of many of the current SD questions: A multifaceted mix of post-truth reality, scientific developments, global changes, globalization, social crises (e.g., environment, poverty, and war refugees), economic growth pressures versus de-growth thinking, and new technological opportunities and risks. SIs should also be able to respond to non-traditional aspects of sustainability [17,29], also referred to as a less tangible "fourth pillar" or "missing dimension" of sustainability [29,54], particularly those involving sustainability ethics, culture, esthetics, justice, compassion, mutual help, moderation, solidarity, and general non-material values, as well as goal and target uncertainty, new and old limits of natural-human systems, or the blurred distinction between peacetime and wartime, collaborative learning, voluntary monitoring, and crowd sourcing.

Besides a community perspective, where each community has to develop its individual set of indicators [55] and be an actor in a multi-stakeholder collaborative network [36], each individual should play a central role in sustainability assessment [56], being more ambitious than "simply" measuring and reporting. Each one should be a pivotal asset, using and assessing their own selection of Sis and applying them at any desired and feasible scale, from households to ecosystems, following a stakeholder-driven approach for sustainability assessment [34,35] as previously stressed. This diversity of concepts, approaches, methods, and frameworks for SIs is usually presented as the root of the increased difficulty in providing reliable and robust comparisons among different situations. This should be used as an opportunity to face SD complexities and singularities, improving and developing the use of tailor-made approaches conducted by citizen volunteers.

In this context, academia has a paramount role to play [17], including as an example for the rest of society through its scientific knowledge, independence, transparency, and proactive and facilitating behavior. Higher education institutions could help stakeholders deal with the new opportunities and risks of sustainability [57], including teaching and educating for observing, listening, understanding, and following up the progress toward SD.

The evolutionary stages of adherence between future indicator paths and reality will guide initiatives in several major areas, as identified in the previous section (see also Table A1 and the Appendix A). Regardless of the importance of all those topics identified and evaluated, it is proposed here that indicator progress should particularly address the angles that will impact society, as already emphasized by other works, e.g., [48,56], and assuming the individual as a central dimension for future developments in SIs (e.g., using a technological device to collect, upload, and report SIs, tagging and interacting in real-time word situations, such as noise level, water quality data, urban degradation, or street poverty and crime). This will be underpinned by an unpredictable changing world of new technologies and platforms of gathering, sharing, and spreading data and information [53,58,59].

In the context of the current critical perspective and viewpoint paper, and supported by the evaluation conducted previously, a set of key questions on SIs' futures are proposed (Figure 1). These questions aim to represent an integrated view of the relevant challenges and opportunities analyzed, but are underpinned and observed from a crosscutting angle, represented by the societal role.

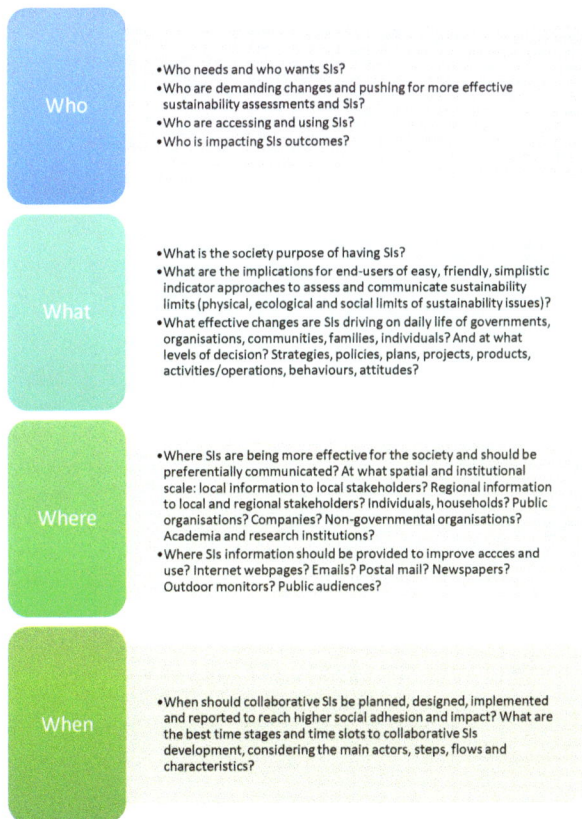

Who
- Who needs and who wants SIs?
- Who are demanding changes and pushing for more effective sustainability assessments and SIs?
- Who are accessing and using SIs?
- Who is impacting SIs outcomes?

What
- What is the society purpose of having SIs?
- What are the implications for end-users of easy, friendly, simplistic indicator approaches to assess and communicate sustainability limits (physical, ecological and social limits of sustainability issues)?
- What effective changes are SIs driving on daily life of governments, organisations, communities, families, individuals? And at what levels of decision? Strategies, policies, plans, projects, products, activities/operations, behaviours, attitudes?

Where
- Where SIs are being more effective for the society and should be preferentially communicated? At what spatial and institutional scale: local information to local stakeholders? Regional information to local and regional stakeholders? Individuals, households? Public organisations? Companies? Non-governmental organisations? Academia and research institutions?
- Where SIs information should be provided to improve access and use? Internet webpages? Emails? Postal mail? Newspapers? Outdoor monitors? Public audiences?

When
- When should collaborative SIs be planned, designed, implemented and reported to reach higher social adhesion and impact? What are the best time stages and time slots to collaborative SIs development, considering the main actors, steps, flows and characteristics?

Figure 1. *Cont.*

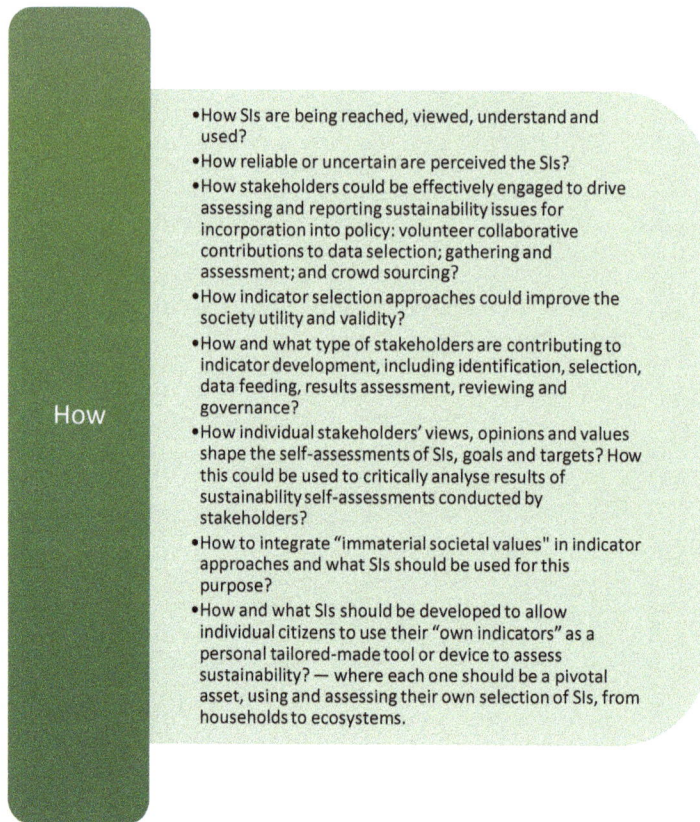

Figure 1. Key questions to be addressed by SIs in a societal-oriented approach.

To respond to these questions, significant further work should be conducted based upon theoretical and empirical research approaches. The SIs community should work on the qualitative values and societal dimensions of sustainability, trying to minimize the time delay to start dealing with these challenges and contribute to the truth value of the SIs in place. Transdisciplinary, community-based, interactive, or participatory research approaches [30] should be major options to conduct the necessary review of the current sustainability monitoring, assessing, and reporting systems, and reach the next level of SIs. Also, major indicator guidelines, such as the Bellagio Principles, now reviewed and renamed the Bellagio STAMP (Sustainability Assessment and Measurement Principles) [60], in particular, should be considered.

Empowerment approaches in sustainability assessment should be further studied, including the type of stakeholders to integrate in different SI initiatives [35], which indicators are more suitable, and what practices could guide the use of SIs. This step can result in a new level of effectiveness and active engagement, and increase the inclusiveness, transparency, and accountability of SIs.

4. Final Remarks

In the near future, SI researchers and practitioners should be ready to adapt their ways of thinking and doing. Sustainability assessments must respond to new global and local paradigms, and use collaborative scientific development and innovation as the foundations for change. Indicators should evaluate what really matters to track progress toward a sustainable society, and be able to deal with new information traps, post-truth reality, and volatile contradictory societal values. The term "sustainability" and its related topics are wrapped up in a blurred web of contrary meanings, despite several important events and initiatives, including the 2030 Agenda for Sustainable Development of the United Nations as a major SD roadmap at the global level.

The critical review and qualitative evaluation conducted in this research allowed us to trace the pragmatic profile of the analysed SIs' challenges and benefits, where the majority of them are still not implemented or answered, and a significant amount will probably have a low impact on society if operationalized. Therefore, the need for new developments on SIs to effectively assess and report SD in a robust and, at the same time, collaborative and open way, has never been so great.

There are limitations associated with this kind of critical review and qualitative evaluation, and those limitations should be weighed up in the use of the obtained findings, and when drawing conclusions. However, since a critical perspective and viewpoint paper is clearly assumed as a particular view on a specific topic of research, where views differ, this should not be considered a major constraint. The objective was to promote constructive debate around SIs' possible futures and paths.

As proposed in this research, the individual should have a central role to play in all the SIs' challenges, in particular the ones related with societal impact dimension. Individual citizens should be leading actors, collecting, analyzing, evaluating, and communicating sustainability data and related SI information, from households and daily activities to "upper scales," including rural and urban ecosystems. A crowdsourcing mindset for SIs will be a central piece in this process, associated with tailor-made approaches conducted by volunteer individuals.

Funding: CENSE is financed by Fundação para a Ciência e Tecnologia, I.P., Portugal (UID/AMB/04085/2019). The funding sources played no part in the design, analysis, interpretation, or writing-up of the paper or in the decision to publish.

Acknowledgments: A special thanks to all the friends, colleagues, and co-workers who participated actively with their work, thoughts, insights, and questions, in the Topic Group and Annual Conference Track—*Assessing Sustainability (indicators and reporting)*—of the International Sustainable Development Research Society (ISDRS), which I have been pleased to co-lead with Professor Anne Wallis, from Deakin University, Australia, for the last eight years.

Conflicts of Interest: The author declare no conflict of interest.

Appendix A

Table A1. Identification of the set of challenges and opportunities and remarks that supported the value given to each criterion: Relevancy, Feasibility, and Societal Impacts.

Selected Challenges and Opportunities	Summary of Rationale		
	Relevancy	Feasibility	Societal Impacts
#1. Richer selection of case studies: Call for a richer selection of case studies to help create practical and more useful guidance regarding sustainability assessment [60]. Allow the identification of patterns of what works best and the understanding and designing of context-specific approaches.	A significant amount of the existing SI work is related to case study-based approaches.	Despite their being resource-intensive, there are several SI systems being implemented, at national, regional, local and organisational levels, that can be used as case studies.	Proximity and visibility to stakeholders.
#2. Specific cultural context: Indicators should be placed in a specific cultural context with a clear understanding of previous interventions; if indicators are used without understanding the processes and people they are relevant to, they may be easily misused (even if an indicator is good itself) [61]. SIs should not be "context-free."	The need to understand the context that will tailor the SIs (e.g., the type of decision-making assessed, the institutional system, the context of professional practice and capacity, the territorial context and their specific natural and human-cultural aspects).	Requires additional resources to adopt this approach. Local context data, including cultural/social, should be collected and integrated.	Increased sense of ownership and commitment from everyone involved.
#3. Adequate level of standardization: Identify the adequate level of standardization for indicator sets versus context-specific sets [21]. Related to this aspect is the need to consider the vertical integration between SIs at different spatial scales (national, regional, local/organizational), and to examine the common sets of indicators between scales [62,63].	Facilitate comparability and benchmarking between different cases and scales, and optimize the resources to conduct a sustainability assessment.	The operational process is not consensual, and the approaches are still under discussion. Further methodological development and practical evaluations are required.	Improve the communication with stakeholders, and the governance of different SIs.

Table A1. *Cont.*

Selected Challenges and Opportunities	Summary of Rationale		
	Relevancy	Feasibility	Societal Impacts
#4. Meta-evaluation: The evaluation of an evaluation and analysis of SI experiences [64,65]. Allows us to do a critical assessment of the strengths and weaknesses of the SIs, and draw conclusions about the overall utility, accuracy, validity, feasibility and propriety.	Several research initiatives that show how to accomplish this task and demonstrate the need and benefits of adopting meta-evaluation and reviewing approaches, with practical and theoretical implications.	The implementation of a formal meta-evaluation process could be technically complex, where the approaches are still not well established. Practical difficulties can arise in their implementation due to the complexity of prioritizing the implementation of the "key good-practice factors" and developing "meta-evaluation indicators" can also be a hard task [65].	Too technical to be understood by most of the stakeholders, in particular the general public.
#5. Alternatives to move beyond GDP: Development of alternative indicators, to move beyond GDP [66,67], to obtain clear and robust sustainability measures and "achieve measures of what we really want" [67].	To provide a global SD shared vision, using new ways of measuring progress towards new goals.	Despite several attempts to propose GDP substitutes with the same popularity and impact, this is still ongoing work, and there is no consensus among the existing proposals.	Global communication implications and significant visibility to citizens.
#6. Data limitations and provision problems: Overcome the data limitations and provision problems to better support decision-making processes, as well as reporting and communication initiatives, e.g., [68,69].	Access to reliable data or justifiable proxies for the relevant themes is a paramount step, as well as providing open access to data.	In some cases, this could be difficult to overcome in a short term, in particular in territories/institutions that are less developed. It is a resource-intensive and complex task, with moving targets.	In an era of "post-truth" where the value of data and information is very volatile, data accuracy and reliability could be not perceived or valued by stakeholders.
#7. Integrated and systemic and holistic perspective: Develop a more integrated and systemic/holistic perspective for SI, considering linkages, synergies, and antagonisms between SI, goals and targets [70]. SI integrated sets should include integrated or interlinkage indicators that cover different sustainability dimensions, i.e., one single indicator includes several dimensions, in particular environmental, economic, social, cultural and institutional/governance [51,65,71].	Analyse, understand and report the integrated/systemic sustainability views and perspectives, and avoid a fragmented assessment, in particular for indicators that cover more than one thematic area and dimension (environmental, economic, social).	The implementation process is technically complex, where the approaches are still not well established. According to some authors (e.g., [50]), the interdisciplinary hypostasis of sustainability that traverses environmental, economic and societal issues may be an operational drawback instead of an advantage. This holistic approach, which encompasses more aspects than necessary, orients the use of indicators to vast collections of statistics that rarely influence policy-making.	Despite it being too technical to be perceived by stakeholders, the indirect effects of using integrated sustainability measures could be significant for communication and awareness purposes.
#8. Optimum level of indicator aggregation: Raise the optimum level of indicator aggregation, as discussed in Singh [8]. Help present complex information in a synthetic way and at the same time avoid manipulation and "fake news," with distorted indicators.	Several authors, e.g. [50], stress that instead of focusing on the construction of composite indicators that cover different areas of knowledge, we should try to summarise a complex situation in a single number (difficult to be attained in the absence of an appropriate indicator theoretical framework); "research should be focused on the identification of key indicators that can be linked together through verbal, statistical, or mathematical relationships and equations, contributing to a better understanding of the linkages among the different areas of knowledge that compose the aforementioned fields … " [50] (pp. 426).	Despite several attempts to propose the adequate level of indicator aggregation, this is still an ongoing work, and there is a lack of consensus among the existing approaches.	Improve communication standards, with significant visibility to stakeholders. Support the main indicator goals of synthesizing complex phenomena and transmit them in an easy and understandable way to stakeholders, and support decision-making processes.
#9. Better mechanisms for indicator use in practice: Explore the mechanisms for indicator use in practice, e.g., [48,56,72], and understanding by different actors, creating opportunities for use and reporting indicator information. Approaches and methods need further development to understand the most effective ways to influence processes at different levels, including policy making and organisational strategies and operations, likewise citizens' behaviours and attitudes towards sustainable goals.	As emphasized by Ronseström [73], good indicators are of little influence and importance if they are not used in any way. Information can feed back into the development and presentation of SIs.	Despite the existence of several works that explore technical issues of indicators and how they could support decision-making processes, few of them address the how, if, when, and who questions about indicators. The work of Morse [48] shows the emergence of this topic.	The most significant impact for stakeholders is when they use the tool that was developed for them.
#10. Integration or non-traditional aspects of sustainability: SIs should cover general non-material values or non-traditional aspects of sustainability, such as ethics, culture and arts, aesthetics, effectiveness of governance, legislation and norms, spirituality, solidarity, compassion, mutual help [17,29,54,71], which represent less tangible dimensions of human society.	Until we have appropriate indicators to assess these intangible but fundamental aspects of SD, they will be invisible for assessment purposes [71].	It may be very difficult to use direct indicators to evaluate these non-tangible aspects. Qualitative survey approaches are most likely to support these indicators, and therefore difficult to operate in a continuous way.	Increased sense of ownership, commitment and communication from everyone involved.

Table A1. *Cont.*

Selected Challenges and Opportunities	Summary of Rationale		
	Relevancy	Feasibility	Societal Impacts
#11. Use of Information tools and systems: Use of information tools and systems that condense the huge flows of information to report SIs, e.g., [74]. SI systems should respond to the growing access to information provided by modern information technologies and ensure rapid assessment.	New technologies, including geographic information systems and the Internet, are enabling web-based platforms for information sharing and gathering [57,58,59], enabling the desired stakeholders' input.	The implementation process could be technically complex, and the approaches are still not well established. These more demanding information and communication technologies still face pending challenges that need further research. Examples of such limitations comprise data quality, use and sharing policies and expertise.	Increased sense of ownership, commitment and improved communication with stakeholders and access/use to data and indicators. Information systems designed to use/report sustainability data and indicators provide tools that could have significant positive impacts at individual/ community levels.
#12. Find the best selection criteria: What indicator selection criteria should be used without compromising credibly and accuracy and at the same time avoiding redundancy and complexity. Indicator selection is usually made by experts and/or through participatory approaches, in combination with literature reviews of existing indicator sets, and often little is known about the robustness of the selection stage [43].	It is fundamental to evaluate the indicator selection process, regarding their utility, accuracy, validity and feasibility, e.g., [41,75]. The selection stage will impact the ability of the indicator system to be institutionalised and therefore used and maintained [76].	Despite various works discussing these aspects, the implementation process is technically complex, and the approaches are still not well established.	When stakeholders are effectively involved, it could increase the sense of ownership, commitment and improve the evaluation and communication stages.
#13. Institutionalisation process and governance models: SI governance models should be improved and clarified. Also, SIs need to become institutionalised in certain governmental processes to provide stability and credibility [17].	The management model and institutional cooperation is a fundamental component of SIs; identifying the institution(s) and their roles and the leadership structures is essential to an understanding of the feasibility and societal influence of the indicator system [66].	Despite no significant additional resources being required to implement this component, an institutional/political commitment of the involved decision-makers is a fundamental step, and in many cases is difficult to achieve.	Low visibility and usually not being perceived as a very important aspect by the general public and practitioners – "somebody is certainly in charge" but few people really care who is and what they do.
#14. Satellite remote sensing and other observing technologies: New approaches to indicators using satellite remote sensing and other observing technologies to evaluate sustainability goals, as explored by [77].	SIs supported by satellite data could be an important solution to mitigate data limitations and provision, in particular for certain scales of analysis.	Despite various related works that explore this field, the use of remote sensing data for SIs is still relatively underexplored, e.g., [77].	The value of data and information is very volatile, and data availability, accuracy and reliability could be not perceived or valued by stakeholders, probably even more so in the case of remote sensing data.
#15. Intergenerational equity information transfer: Indicators that capture the effectiveness with which intergenerational equity information transfer is taking place and how are pushing social and cultural evolution. However, several questions arise: How do we know what future generations will value? In that respect, how can one define what is a "fair," ethical and "sustainable" thing to do? [61])	One of the SD dimensions should be "time" [52], when assessing progress towards sustainability goals, so consider time preservation or intergenerational equity. As noted by ([31]), the time dimension should be taken into account where long-term changes towards sustainability are evaluated, like global warming, ecological disruption and social equity issues	Despite the existence of several attempts to explore this topic, it is still an open and complex question, needing further theoretical and practical scientific work.	Low visibility and too technical to be perceived by stakeholders.
#16. The lack of an endogenous indicator's theory The inexistence of an endogenous indicator's theory is an important barrier to the enhancement of indicator research into an autonomous scientific field and relegates indicators to the ecological, social or economic field [50]	An integrated SI theory could be a fundamental step to respond to several of the most important needs and related challenges, weakness and limitations, and reach the next stage of indicator evolution.	Despite some works that explore this topic, there is a significant lack of progress and consensus on how to approach this complexity.	Low visibility and too technical to be perceived by stakeholders.

References

1. Bond, A.; Morrison-Saunders, A.; Howitt, R. *Sustainability Assessment: Pluralism, Practice and Progress*; Routledge: New York, NY, USA, 2013; ISBN 9780203112625.
2. Gibson, R.B.; Hassan, S.; Holtz, S.; Tansey, J.; Whitelaw, G. *Sustainability Assessment: Criteria and Processes*; Routledge: New York, NY, USA, 2013; ISBN 9781849772716.
3. Gibson, R.B. Why Sustainability Assessment? In *Sustainability Assessment: Pluralism, Practice and Progress*; Routledge: New York, NY, USA, 2013; pp. 3–17.
4. Ramos, T.B.; Wallis, A.; Track, B. Sustainability Assessment and Indicators. In Proceedings of the 25st Annual International Sustainable Development Research Society Conference, Nanjing, China, 26–28 June 2019.

5. Pope, J.; Bond, A.; Hugé, J.; Morrison-Saunders, A. Reconceptualising sustainability assessment. *Environ. Impact Assess. Rev.* **2017**, *62*, 205–215. [CrossRef]
6. Pope, J.; Annandale, D.; Morrison-Saunders, A. Conceptualising sustainability assessment. *Environ. Impact Assess. Rev.* **2004**, *24*, 595–616. [CrossRef]
7. Sala, S.; Ciuffo, B.; Nijkamp, P. A systemic framework for sustainability assessment. *Ecol. Econ.* **2015**, *119*, 314–325. [CrossRef]
8. Singh, R.K.; Murty, H.R.; Gupta, S.K.; Dikshit, A.K. An overview of sustainability assessment methodologies. *Ecol. Indic.* **2012**, *15*, 281–299. [CrossRef]
9. Bond, A.; Morrison-Saunders, A.; Pope, J. Sustainability assessment: The state of the art. *Impact Assess. Proj. Apprais.* **2012**, *30*, 53–62. [CrossRef]
10. Agol, D.; Latawiec, A.E.; Strassburg, B.B.N. Evaluating impacts of development and conservation projects using sustainability indicators: Opportunities and challenges. *Environ. Impact Assess. Rev.* **2014**, *48*, 1–9. [CrossRef]
11. Holman, N. Incorporating local sustainability indicators into structures of local governance: A review of the literature. *Local Environ.* **2009**, *14*, 365–375. [CrossRef]
12. Thomas, W.A. (Ed.) *Indicators of Environmental Quality*; Plenum Press: New York, NY, USA, 1972.
13. Inhaber, H. *Environmental Indices*; John Wiley and Sons: New York, NY, USA, 1976.
14. Ott, W.R. *Environmental Indices—Theory and Practice*; Ann Harbor Science: Ann Arbor, MI, USA, 1978.
15. Hezri, A.A.; Hasan, M.N. Management framework for sustainable development indicators in the State of Selangor, Malaysia. *Ecol. Indic.* **2004**, *4*, 287–304. [CrossRef]
16. Wilson, J.; Tyedmers, P.; Pelot, R. Contrasting and comparing sustainable development indicator metrics. *Ecol. Indic.* **2007**, *7*, 299–314. [CrossRef]
17. Ramos, T.B. Development of regional sustainability indicators and the role of academia in this process: The Portuguese practice. *J. Clean. Prod.* **2009**, *17*, 1101–1115. [CrossRef]
18. Rinne, J.; Lyytimäki, J.; Kautto, P. Beyond the "indicator industry": Use and potential influences of sustainable development indicators in Finland and the EU. *Prog. Ind. Ecol. Int. J.* **2012**, *7*, 271. [CrossRef]
19. Bell, S.; Morse, S. Introduction: Indicators and Post Truth. In *Routledge Handbook of Sustainability Indicators*; Bell, S., Morse, S., Eds.; Routledge: New York, NY, USA, 2018; pp. 1–17.
20. Tasaki, T.; Kameyama, Y. Sustainability Indicators: Are We Measuring What We Ought to Measure? *Glob. Environ. Res.* **2015**, *19*, 147–154.
21. Moreno Pires, S.; Fidélis, T.; Ramos, T.B. Measuring and comparing local sustainable development through common indicators: Constraints and achievements in practice. *Cities* **2014**, *39*, 1–9. [CrossRef]
22. Mickwitz, P.; Melanen, M.; Rosenstro, U.; Seppa, J. Regional eco-efficiency indicators e a participatory approach. *J. Clean. Prod.* **2006**, *14*, 1603–1611. [CrossRef]
23. Holden, M. Sustainability indicator systems within urban governance: Usability analysis of sustainability indicator systems as boundary objects. *Ecol. Indic.* **2013**, *32*, 89–96. [CrossRef]
24. Bolis, I.; Morioka, S.N.; Sznelwar, L.I. When sustainable development risks losing its meaning. Delimiting the concept with a comprehensive literature review and a conceptual model. *J. Clean. Prod.* **2014**, *83*, 7–20. [CrossRef]
25. Hussey, D.M.; Kirsop, P.L.; Meissen, R.E. Global Reporting Initiative Guidelines: An Evaluation of Sustainable Development Metrics for Industry. *Environ. Qual. Manag.* **2001**, *11*, 1–20. [CrossRef]
26. Lozano, R. Envisioning sustainability three-dimensionally. *J. Clean. Prod.* **2008**, *16*, 1838–1846. [CrossRef]
27. Ramos, T.B.; Caeiro, S.; de Melo, J.J. Environmental indicator frameworks to design and assess environmental monitoring programs. *Impact Assess. Proj. Apprais.* **2004**, *22*, 47–62. [CrossRef]
28. RIVM (National Institute of Public Health and the Environment). *A General Strategy for Integrated Environmental Assessment at the European Environment Agency*; RIVM: Bilthoven, The Netherlands, 1995.
29. Viegas, O.; Caeiro, S.; Ramos, T.B. Conceptual Model for the integration of Non-Material components in Sustainability Assessment. *Rev. Ambient. Soc.* **2018**, *21*.
30. Lang, D.J.; Wiek, A.; Bergmann, M.; Stauffacher, M.; Martens, P.; Moll, P.; Swilling, M.; Thomas, C.J. Transdisciplinary research in sustainability science: Practice, principles, and challenges. *Sustain. Sci.* **2012**, *7*, 25–43. [CrossRef]
31. United Nations. Sustainable Development Goals—Knowledge Platform. Available online: https://sustainabledevelopment.un.org/sdgs (accessed on 13 January 2019).

32. Spangenberg, J.H. Hot Air or Comprehensive Progress? A Critical Assessment of the SDGs. *Sustain. Dev.* **2017**, *25*, 311–321. [CrossRef]

33. Allen, C.; Metternicht, G.; Wiedmann, T. Initial progress in implementing the Sustainable Development Goals (SDGs): A review of evidence from countries. *Sustain. Sci.* **2018**, *13*, 1453–1467. [CrossRef]

34. Coutinho, V.; Domingues, A.R.; Caeiro, S.; Painho, M.; Antunes, P.; Santos, R.; Videira, N.; Walker, R.M.; Huisingh, D.; Ramos, T.B. Employee-Driven Sustainability Performance Assessment in Public Organisations. *Corp. Soc. Responsib. Environ. Manag.* **2017**, *25*, 29–46. [CrossRef]

35. Domingues, A.R.; Lozano, R.; Ramos, T.B. Stakeholder-driven initiatives using sustainability indicators. In *Routledge Handbook of Sustainability Indicators*; Bell, S., Morse, S., Eds.; Routledge: London, UK, 2018; pp. 379–391.

36. Kelly, R.; Moles, R. The Development of local Agenda 21 in the mid-west region of Ireland: a case study in interactive research and indicator development. *J. Environ. Plan. Manage.* **2002**, *45*, 889–912. [CrossRef]

37. Bell, S.; Morse, S. *Measuring Sustainability: Learning by Doing*; Routledge: London, UK, 2013; ISBN 9781849771962.

38. Verma, P.; Raghubanshi, A.S. Urban sustainability indicators: Challenges and opportunities. *Ecol. Indic.* **2018**, *93*, 282–291. [CrossRef]

39. Hardi, P.; Zdan, T. *Assessing Sustainable Development: Principles in Practice*; International Institute for Sustainable Development: Winnipeg, MB, Canada, 1997; ISBN 1895536073.

40. Kurtz, J.C.; Jackson, L.E.; Fisher, W.S. Strategies for evaluating indicators based on guidelines from the Environmental Protection Agency's Office of Research and Development. *Ecol. Indic.* **2001**, *1*, 49–60. [CrossRef]

41. Cloquell-Ballester, V.-A.; Cloquell-Ballester, V.-A.; Monterde-Díaz, R.; Santamarina-Siurana, M.-C. Indicators validation for the improvement of environmental and social impact quantitative assessment. *Environ. Impact Assess. Rev.* **2006**, *26*, 79–105. [CrossRef]

42. Donnelly, A.; Jones, M.; O'Mahony, T.; Byrne, G. Selecting environmental indicator for use in strategic environmental assessment. *Environ. Impact Assess. Rev.* **2007**, *27*, 161–175. [CrossRef]

43. Mascarenhas, A.; Nunes, L.M.; Ramos, T.B. Selection of sustainability indicators for planning: Combining stakeholders' participation and data reduction techniques. *J. Clean. Prod.* **2015**, *92*, 295–307. [CrossRef]

44. Saunders, M.N.K.; Thornhill, A.; Lewis, P. *Research Methods for Business Students.*, 6th ed.; Pearson Education Limited: Harlow, Essex, England, 2012; ISBN 9780273750758.

45. Bornmann, L. What Is Societal Impact of Research and How Can It Be Assessed? A Literature Survey. *J. Am. Soc. Inf. Sci. Technol.* **2013**, *64*, 217–233. [CrossRef]

46. Bryman, A. *Social Research Methods Bryman*; Oxford University Press: Oxford, UK, 2012; ISBN 9788578110796.

47. Bell, S.; Morse, S. Whats Next? In *Routledge Handbook of Sustainability Indicatorsu*; Bell, S., Morse, S., Eds.; Routledge: New York, NY, USA, 2018; pp. 453–555.

48. Morse, S. Measuring the Success of Sustainable Development Indices in Terms of Reporting by the Global Press. *Soc. Indic. Res.* **2016**, *125*, 359–375. [CrossRef]

49. Bell, S.; Morse, S. *Sustainability Indicators: Measuring the Immeasurable?* 2nd ed.; Routledge: New York, NY, USA, 2008; ISBN 9781849772723.

50. Pissourios, I.A. An interdisciplinary study on indicators: A comparative review of quality-of-life, macroeconomic, environmental, welfare and sustainability indicators. *Ecol. Indic.* **2013**, *34*, 420–427. [CrossRef]

51. Lozano, R.; Huisingh, D. Inter-linking issues and dimensions in sustainability reporting. *J. Clean. Prod.* **2011**, *19*, 99–107. [CrossRef]

52. Seghezzo, L. The five dimensions of sustainability. *Environ. Polit.* **2009**, *18*, 539–556. [CrossRef]

53. Ramos, T.B.; Martins, I.P.; Martinho, A.P.; Douglas, C.H.; Painho, M.; Caeiro, S. An open participatory conceptual framework to support State of the Environment and Sustainability Reports. *J. Clean. Prod.* **2014**, *64*, 158–172. [CrossRef]

54. Burford, G.; Hoover, E.; Velasco, I.; Janoušková, S.; Jimenez, A.; Piggot, G.; Podger, D.; Harder, M.K. Bringing the "Missing Pillar" into sustainable development goals: Towards intersubjective values-based indicators. *Sustainable* **2013**, *5*, 3035–3059. [CrossRef]

55. Valentin, A.; Spangenberg, J.H. A guide to community sustainability indicators. *Environ. Impact Assess. Rev.* **2000**, *20*, 381–392. [CrossRef]

56. Dahl, A.L. Achievements and gaps in indicators for sustainability. *Ecol. Indic.* **2012**, *17*, 14–19. [CrossRef]
57. Disterheft, A.; Caeiro, S.S.; Leal, W.; Azeiteiro, U.M. The INDICARE-model–measuring and caring about participation in higher education's sustainability assessment. *Ecol. Indic.* **2016**, *63*, 172–186. [CrossRef]
58. Jankowski, P. Towards participatory geographic information systems for community-based environmental decision making. *J. Environ. Manag.* **2009**, *90*, 1966–1971. [CrossRef]
59. Green, D.R. The role of Public Participatory Geographical Information Systems (PPGIS) in coastal decision-making processes: An example from Scotland, UK. *Ocean Coast. Manag.* **2010**, *53*, 816–821. [CrossRef]
60. Pintér, L.; Hardi, P.; Martinuzzi, A.; Hall, J. Bellagio Stamp. In *Routledge Handbook of Sustainability Indicators*; Bell, S., Morse, S., Eds.; Routledge: London, UK, 2018; pp. 21–41.
61. Latawiec, A.E.; Agol, D. 13 Conclusions-Sustainability Indicators In Practice: Lessons Learned From The Past, Directions For The Future. *Sustain. Indic. Pract.* **2016**, 16–18. [CrossRef]
62. Mascarenhas, A.; Coelho, P.; Subtil, E.; Ramos, T.B. The role of common local indicators in regional sustainability assessment. *Ecol. Indic.* **2010**, *10*, 646–656. [CrossRef]
63. Coelho, P.; Mascarenhas, A.; Vaz, P.; Dores, A.; Ramos, T.B. A framework for regional sustainability assessment: Developing indicators for a Portuguese region. *Sustain. Dev.* **2010**, *18*, 211–219. [CrossRef]
64. Ramos, T.B.; Alves, I.; Subtil, R.; Joanaz de Melo, J. Environmental performance policy indicators for the public sector: The case of the defence sector. *J. Environ. Manag.* **2007**, *82*, 410–432. [CrossRef]
65. Ramos, T.B.; Caeiro, S. Meta-performance evaluation of sustainability indicators. *Ecol. Indic.* **2010**, *10*, 157–166. [CrossRef]
66. Dahl, A. Contributions to the Evolving Theory and Practice of Indicators of Sustainability. In *Routledge Handbook of Sustainability Indicators*; Bell, S., Morse, S., Eds.; Routledge: London, UK, 2018; pp. 42–58.
67. Costanza, R.; Hart, M.; Kubiszewski, I.; Posner, S.; Talberth, J. Lessons from the History of GDP in the Effort to Create Better Indicators of Prosperity, Well-being, and Happiness. In *Routledge Handbook of Sustainability Indicators*; Bell, S., Morse, S., Eds.; Routledge: London, UK, 2018; pp. 117–123.
68. Hildén, M.; Rosenström, U. The use of indicators for sustainable development. *Sustain. Dev.* **2008**, *16*, 237–240. [CrossRef]
69. Mascarenhas, A.; Nunes, L.M.; Ramos, T.B. Exploring the self-assessment of sustainability indicators by different stakeholders. *Ecol. Indic.* **2014**, *39*, 75–83. [CrossRef]
70. Gallopin, G. The socio-ecological system (SES) approach to sustainable development Indicators. In *Routledge Handbook of Sustainability Indicators*; Bell, S., Morse, S., Eds.; Routledge: London, UK, 2018; pp. 329–346.
71. Dahl, A.L. Integrated Assessment and Indicators. In *Sustainability Indicators*; Tomás, H., Moldan, B., Dahl, A.L., Eds.; Island Press: Washington, DC, USA, 2007; pp. 163–176.
72. Gudmundsson, H. The Policy Use of Environmental Indicators-Learning from Evaluation Research. *Environ. Stud.* **2003**, *2*, 1–12.
73. Ronseström, U. Sustainable Development Indicators, Finland: Going from Large Descriptive Sets to Target-Oriented Actively Used Indicators. In *Routledge Handbook of Sustainability Indicators*; Bell, S., Morse, S., Eds.; Routledge: London, UK, 2018; pp. 321–328.
74. Myhre, O.; Fjellheim, K.; Ringnes, H.; Reistad, T.; Longva, K.S.; Ramos, T.B. Development of environmental performance indicators supported by an environmental information system: Application to the Norwegian defence sector. *Ecol. Indic.* **2013**, *29*, 293–306. [CrossRef]
75. Van Zeijl-rozema, A.; Ferraguto, L.; Caratti, P. Comparing region-specific sustainability assessments through indicator systems: Feasible or not? *Ecol. Econ.* **2010**, *70*, 475–486. [CrossRef]
76. Moreno Pires, S.; Fidélis, T. Local sustainability indicators in Portugal: Assessing implementation and use in governance contexts. *J. Clean. Prod.* **2015**, *86*, 289–300. [CrossRef]
77. Andries, A.; Morse, S.; Murphy, R.; Lynch, J.; Woolliams, E.; Fonweban, J. Translation of Earth observation data into sustainable development indicators: An analytical framework. *Sustain. Dev.* **2018**, 1–11. [CrossRef]

sustainability

MDPI

Article

Indicators on the Impacts of Climate Change on Biodiversity in Germany—Data Driven or Meeting Political Needs?

Rainer Schliep [1,*], Ulrich Walz [2], Ulrich Sukopp [3] and Stefan Heiland [1]

1   Technische Universität Berlin, Institut für Landschaftsarchitektur und Umweltplanung, Fachgebiet Landschaftsplanung und Landschaftsentwicklung, Sekr. EB5, Straße des 17. Juni 145, 10623 Berlin, Germany; stefan.heiland@tu-berlin.de
2   Hochschule für Technik und Wirtschaft Dresden, Fakultät Landbau/Umwelt/Chemie, Professur Landschaftsökologie, Pillnitzer Platz 2, 01326 Dresden, Germany; ulrich.walz@htw-dresden.de
3   Bundesamt für Naturschutz, Fachgebiet II 1.3 „Monitoring", Konstantinstraße 110, 53179 Bonn, Germany; ulrich.sukopp@bfn.de
*   Correspondence: rainer.schliep@tu-berlin.de; Tel.: +49-(0)30-314-29196; Fax: +49-(0)30-314-23507

Received: 21 September 2018; Accepted: 25 October 2018; Published: 31 October 2018

Abstract: When developing new indicators for policy advice, two different approaches exist and may be combined with each other. First, a data-driven, bottom-up approach determines indicators primarily by the availability of suitable data. Second, indicators can be developed by a top-down approach, on the basis of political fields of action and related normative goals. While the bottom-up approach might not meet the needs of an up-to-date policy advice, the top-down approach might lack the necessary data. To discuss these problems and possible solutions, we refer to the ongoing development of an indicator system on impacts of climate change on biodiversity in Germany, where a combination of both approaches has been successfully applied. We describe suitable indicators of this system and discuss the reasons for the remaining gaps. Both approaches, mentioned above, have advantages, constraints, and shortcomings. The scientific accuracy of the indicators, the availability of data and the purpose of policy advice have to be well-balanced while developing such indicator systems.

Keywords: indicators; climate change; biodiversity; data needs; monitoring; policy advice; Germany

1. Introduction

The task of the ongoing project, presented in this article, is to design and implement an indicator system that describes the direct and indirect impacts of climate change, on the state and development of biodiversity in Germany, in a summarized and easily-understandable way, so that conclusions for the shaping of nature conservation policy and related policy areas can be drawn. The article focuses on the crucial role of data availability and quality, for the development of such indicators.

The term "indicator" is ambiguous and linked to a number of different meanings, in many different contexts [1,2]. As a prerequisite for the conceptual design of indicator systems, an understanding of what is meant by the term is, therefore, necessary. We have based our work on the following definition:

Indicators in the context of nature conservation summarize empirical data from monitoring programs, in order to depict relevant pressures, states, impacts, or measures related to biodiversity, in an easily-understandable manner. They show successes and failures in achieving previously defined nature conservation objectives, provide policy advice, and inform the public [3]. This definition clearly differs from an older scientific concept of indicators, which is purely descriptive [2]. Our indicators are designed for policy advice and refer to normative standards that require political legitimacy, in advance. Their statements are based on a comparison of target and actual values. The necessary data and information for setting a target as the assessment standard must indeed be based on scientific knowledge. However, the decision on the actual target value or direction of development is beyond the scope of descriptive natural science and is part of a social or political process [2,3].

Data on state and changes of biodiversity provide fundamental information for planning and decision-making, in modern conservation policy [4]. In recent years, much effort has been spent to improve the communication of monitoring results, particularly towards politicians and the public. For this purpose, many different biodiversity indicators and indicator systems have been developed. The main objective of monitoring programs is to produce precise and reliable information on the state and trends of different biodiversity components. Reports based on comprehensive indicator systems are then used to make monitoring results known not only to experts but also to decision-makers and the public, cf. [3,5]. Such indicators need to reduce complex biological information to simple and easily-understandable messages of political concern.

Environmentally relevant phenomena can be classified in line with the Driving Forces-Pressures-States-Impacts-Responses (DPSIR) model (see Section 3) to systematically structure indicator systems representing an environmental issue, within its social and political context. The single indicators should measure distinct parts of the issue and represent phenomena of interest on various temporal and spatial scales. The realization of such an indicator system, however, is often confronted with, first, the need to select thematically and politically appropriate indicators and, second, an incomplete database that does not meet the needs of purposeful indicator systems [6]. Regarding biodiversity issues this is illustrated by current efforts to define the so-called "Essential Biodiversity Variables (EBVs)" as a set of key variables for detecting major dimensions of biodiversity change, bridging the gap between biodiversity data and policy reporting needs [7–9]. Schmeller and colleagues [10] (p. 2970) point out that the "development of indicators and the understanding of the causes of the documented change do not fall within the EBV framework, but are a logical next step in using the EBV data".

When developing new indicators for policy advice, two different approaches exist and must be combined with each other [3]. First, there is a data-driven bottom-up approach, primarily determining indicators by the availability of suitable data. By contrast, indicators can be developed by a top-down approach, on the basis of political fields of action and related normative goals, e.g., nature conservation or biodiversity goals, for which meaningful indicators and suitable data, for their calculation, are sought. Ideally, if a top-down approach is successfully applied, policy advice can use tailor-made indicators [2,3]. Each of the two approaches, taken individually, is insufficient. While the bottom-up-approach might not meet the needs of an up-to-date policy advice, the top-down approach might lack the necessary data.

In the following sections, we outline the requirements for biodiversity monitoring programs and data (Section 2), as well as for indicators and indicator systems (Section 3). Based on these findings, we introduce an indicator system on direct and indirect impacts of climate change, on biodiversity in Germany, as a practical example for the feasibility and constraints of developing an indicator system. Successfully developed indicators, based on the requirements outlined before, will be presented as well (Section 4). Finally, we discuss the data-related factors which hampered the development of the indicator system (Section 5) and summarize the experiences gained (Section 6).

2. Monitoring Data as a Basis for Developing Indicators

In the context of nature conservation, monitoring comprises empirical records (observations, counts, and measurements) of selected elements of species, communities, habitats, and landscapes in regular long-term spatiotemporal sequences gained by standardized scientific methods. These records are designed to achieve reliable data on the state and changes of these elements and are directed to nature conservation objectives [3,11–13]. In order to enable a regular reporting system, consistent, trustworthy, and accessible data are a prerequisite [14]. More precisely, the requirements for monitoring programs, as a sound database for indicators are [15]:

- permanent surveys in order to enable continuous availability of data from monitoring programs;
- ensured financing of the monitoring programs;
- functional organization of the monitoring (consolidation and analysis of data and transfer of results);
- sufficient update interval, depending on the variable;
- data series over long periods of time;
- full area coverage or representative sample;
- sufficient resolution which allows for spatially different findings (administrative units like counties, federal states, etc.);
- differentiation between different sub-issues, e.g., different habitat types, species, etc.;
- standardized reliable survey methods; and
- accurate data.

Regarding the impacts of climate change on biodiversity, there are hardly any specific monitoring activities. Consequently, a corresponding indicator system has to be based predominantly on data that were originally collected for other purposes–in our case for biodiversity and climate change issues separately. Several examples for ongoing monitoring activities or the development of such monitoring programs concerning different components of biodiversity do already exist, e.g., for bees, locusts, butterflies, dragonflies, birds, fish, and plankton at the species level, as well as high nature value farmland and inland and coastal waters at the habitat level. Monitoring of the natural environment in Germany is carried out by governmental agencies, administrations, or non-governmental organizations (often in combination with citizen science). These efforts, however, cover, only selected groups of species and habitats, so far, and the resulting data sets are often incomplete and heterogeneous, e.g., in data quality and sampling intensity. Climate data and phenological phases (annually recurring growth and development phenomena) of plants are gathered within the monitoring programs of the German Weather Service (Deutscher Wetterdienst—DWD) and provided, e.g., through its Climate Data Center (CDC) and the German Climate Service (Deutscher Klimadienst—DKD).

3. Indicators and Indicator Systems for Biodiversity—Balancing Information and Communication Needs

An indicator system for assessing the state of biodiversity and the trends in the development of its components, caused, inter alia, by climate change, should reflect the impacts of all relevant drivers on the biological diversity and the associated cause-effect chains, as well as the success of nature conservation strategies and measures for adaptation to climate change. It is also intended to provide political advice [2]. To this end, the single indicators as well as the entire indicator system must meet certain requirements [1,2,14–21], like that of relevance, data sufficiency, and suitability for policy advice.

1. **Relevance:** The indicator system must address a representative sample of relevant key topics in the context of biodiversity changes caused by climate change, which includes direct and indirect impacts of climate change on biodiversity. The relation between climate and biodiversity change, as described by every single indicator, has to be evident or of high probability. Consequently, it is not sufficient to merely represent changes in either biodiversity or climatic parameters, but the connection between both should also be illustrated. Species and habitats with distinct sensitivity for climatic changes, such as alpine, marine, and coastal species and habitats, are particularly suitable for indication, in order to fulfill this requirement. Selecting species and habitats predominantly sensitive to climate change is crucial for the conception of purposeful indicators. In our project, scientific literature surveys have validated such choices.

2. **Data sufficiency:** This includes different basic requirements of the data used for forming the single indicators: Availability, stability, and regular collection, based upon scientifically reliable and standardized methods. To allow for area-covering findings of single indicators and the indicator system, data should cover Germany's entire terrestrial and marine territory.

3. **Suitability for policy advice:** This comprises the following criteria.

- Relation to politically defined targets: The indicators should relate to targets politically agreed upon, e.g., as laid out in strategies and legal norms, in order to inform about the degree of target achievement.
- Relation to politically controllable issues: In general, the indicator subject should be influenceable by policy measures. However, there are indicator subjects which can only be influenced on a global scale or very indirectly, over long periods of time, such as phenological changes.
- Comprehensibility and clarity: As soon as an indicator system is designed for policy advice, the single indicators, as well as the entire indicator system have to be as understandable, transparent and simple as possible, without simplifying facts in a way that may lead to misinterpretation or scientific incorrectness.
- The indicators should have a high spatial resolution to allow for the implementation of specific and appropriate measures in different parts of Germany, at least, at the federal states level.

4. Developing an Indicator System for the Impacts of Climate Change on Biodiversity in Germany

Man-made climate change is leading to significant changes in global biodiversity altering the biosphere in marine, limnic, and terrestrial environments, on large and small scales. Species ranges are shifting in response to climate change, and species interactions are changing due to climate driven shifts, in abundance or distribution of species, for example. Consequently, entire ecosystems are rearranged. Trends that are expected to intensify in the coming decades, for Germany, include poleward and upslope range shifts, formation of novel ecosystems, decline and extinction of species and habitats, and expansion of new species [22]. Major losses are expected with respect to freshwater and marine habitats [23–26]. Climate change is considered to be a critical threat to many components of biodiversity and is generally expected to have an increased impact on biodiversity, in the future. Numerous examples from scientific studies have shown complex relationships between climate change and biodiversity. Campbell and colleagues, as well as Bellard and colleagues, provided a comprehensive overview on this matter [24,27].

However, there is still a vast need for research in order to obtain a more detailed picture of the changes and to develop a full understanding of the underlying processes. Since climate change occurs over relatively long time-scales of several decades and resulting changes in biodiversity also show time lags, long-term, systematic observation programs of the environment are of outstanding importance. This has been demonstrated by McMahon and colleagues, for the global scope, and by Dröschmeister and Sukopp, for Germany [4,28]. For Germany, however, monitoring programs with a long-term perspective, which aim to provide data on the impacts of climate change on biodiversity, are largely lacking or cover only selected aspects of biodiversity, at federal or federal state level. Heiland and colleagues point out this problem and emphasize the necessity of long-term surveys [29].

Among other policy measures, the German government is taking into account the ongoing biodiversity loss and climate change by the ambitious goals of the National Strategy on Biological Diversity ("Nationale Strategie zur biologischen Vielfalt"—NBS) [30] and the German Strategy for Adaptation to Climate Change ("Deutsche Anpassungsstrategie an den Klimawandel"—DAS) [31]. To achieve the goals of these strategies, monitoring programs and indicator systems are required which are suitable for comprehensively assessing the broad spectrum of climate-change-related impacts on biodiversity, as well as the effectiveness of adaptation measures. Indicator systems delivering a broad picture of climate-change impacts on biodiversity, however, are, so far, largely missing at national levels, which is also true for Germany.

In 2011, the German Agency for Nature Conservation (BfN) initiated the development of a comprehensive indicator system on the impacts of climate change, on biological diversity. Hereby, the BfN aimed at gaining new knowledge on the relation between climate change and biodiversity, but mainly at an improved editing of already existing knowledge on the issue for policy advice and decision making. Two consecutive research and development projects have been funded to this end. The first project ("Indicator system for depicting direct and indirect impacts of climate change on biodiversity", FKZ 3511 82 0400, 2011–2015) aimed at developing an expert information system for the federal level, but also included the calculation and implementation of five indicators for policy advice (see below). An extensive report explains the reasons why and how indicators could be implemented or not [21,32]. In the second project ("Further development of indicators on the impact of climate change on biodiversity", FKZ 3517 81 1000, 2017–2019), seven indicators from the first project, which could not be realized then, are currently being further developed, calculated, and implemented, if possible.

During the first project, a systematic structure of the indicator system was developed. It is based on the DPSIR model (see Section 1) [33] and comprises three indicator domains (Figure 1) with nine indicator fields (Table 1). The DPSIR model is useful for describing the origins and consequences of environmental problems and allows for exploring the links between the different elements of the model. According to the model [33], (p. 6), "social and economic developments exert Pressure on the environment and, as a consequence, the State of the environment changes, such as the provision of adequate conditions for health, resources availability and biodiversity. Finally, this leads to Impacts on human health, ecosystems and materials that may elicit a societal Response that feeds back on the Driving forces, or on the state or impacts directly, through adaptation or curative action."

The indicator system to be developed should focus on mapping direct and indirect impacts of climate change on species and habitats, but also include some pressure, state, and response indicators. Accordingly, Column 1 in Figure 1 (direct impacts) comprises impact indicators only, Column 2 comprises predominantly pressure indicators, while Column 3 (adaptation of nature conservation strategies and measures) represents response indicators only. Depending on the context, some of the proposed indicators may also be interpreted as state indicators.

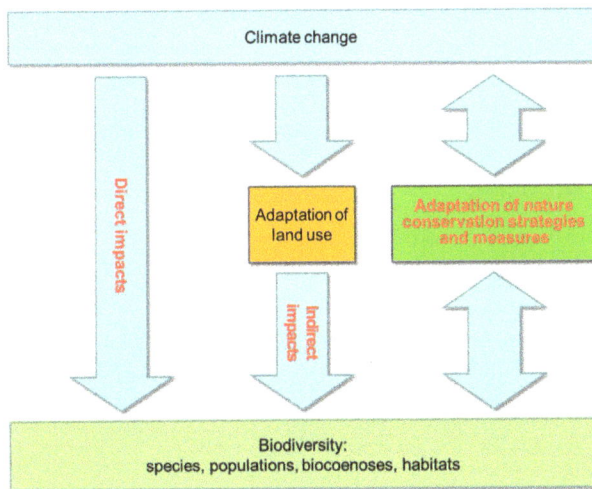

Figure 1. Structure of the indicator system with three indication domains (**red color**).

The first indication domain deals with changes of biodiversity, directly resulting from climate change, and addresses three thematically distinct indication fields: (i) Phenological changes of plant and animal species, (ii) changes in species distribution areas, populations and biocoenoses, and (iii) changes of habitats. It is intended to reflect as many changes in biodiversity caused by climate change as possible and to cover terrestrial, limnic, and marine ecosystems, as well as different groups of species (plants, birds, mammals, amphibians, reptiles, insects, and possibly microorganisms).

The second indication domain discusses indirect changes in biodiversity due to climate change and includes indicators addressing pressures on biodiversity caused by sectoral adaptation measures of different land uses, such as forestry, agriculture, and water management. Indirect climate-change impacts, including changes in land use, have a major effect on biological diversity. An exact quantification of these indirect impacts on species and habitats is, however, hardly possible at present, as the interaction of the various influencing factors is too complex and consequently does not allow for a clear analytical isolation of each factor.

The third indication domain contains indicators which relate to the adaptation of nature conservation strategies, measures to climate change, its direct and indirect impacts on biodiversity, and reflect the success of such adaptations. This indication domain also addresses three thematically distinct indication fields: (i) The adaptation of nature conservation policies and landscape planning to climate change, (ii) the implementation of adaptation measures, and (iii) the physical effectiveness of such measures.

Potentially suitable indicators were either selected from existing indicator systems (e.g., the SEBI—Streamlining European Biodiversity Indicators initiative and the Climate Change Indicators of the European Environment Agency), or were newly developed [21], resulting in a set of forty-four indicators which have been examined, in depth, for their feasibility at the German national level. Out of these, five indicators could be fully calculated ("realized" in Table 1) and nine indicators could be developed as "prototypes"; meaning that they could be fully developed on a conceptual level, but the necessary data for their calculation have not been available due to different reasons. Six out of these nine indicator prototypes are currently to be calculated and realized ("prototype in development" in Table 1). Thirty indicators, due to different reasons (see Section 4.2 and 5 and Reference [21]), could not be feasibly developed further. Indicator factsheets for all realized indicators and indicator prototypes describe the indicator and include all relevant information, such as suitability of the indicator, legal references and existing political targets, calculation algorithms, data sources, spatial and temporal resolution, as well as graphical and textual representations of the determined indicator values. All newly developed indicators have been included in the indicator set of the DAS [34] and one of them (phenological changes in wild plant species) has been added to the indicator set of the NBS [35].

Table 1. Indicators and indicator prototypes for an indicator system on climate-change impacts on biodiversity in Germany (status: May 2018).

Indicator Name	Status
Indication domain I: Direct climate-change-induced changes in biological diversity	
Indication field I.1 Phenological changes in species and communities	
Phenological changes in wild plant species	Realized
Phenological changes in animal species	Prototype in development
Indication field I.2 Changes in populations, areas and biocenoses	
Temperature index of the bird species community	Realized
Changes in the species inventory of high nature value farmland	Prototype
Distribution of marine fish species	Prototype
Climate-change-induced shifts in plant distribution	Prototype in development
Temperature index of the butterfly species community	Prototype in development
Changes in the flora on Alpine summits	Prototype in development
Climate-change-induced changes in dragonflies	Prototype
Indication field I.3 Changes in habitats	
No realizable indicators	

Table 1. *Cont.*

Indicator Name	Status
Indication domain II: Indirect climate-change-induced changes in biological diversity	
Indication field II.1 Changes in biodiversity due to climate-change adaptations in the agricultural sector	
No realizable indicators	
Indication field II.2 Changes in biodiversity due to climate-change adaptations in the forestry sector	
No realizable indicators	
Indication field II.3 Changes in biodiversity due to climate-change adaptations in water management	
Restoration of natural flood plains	Realized
Indication domain III: Adaptation of nature conservation strategies and measures to climate change	
Indication field III.1 Adaptation of nature conservation strategies to climate change	
Consideration of climate change in landscape planning (state / district level)	Realized
Indication field III.2 Adaptation of nature conservation measures to climate change	
Nationwide biotope network	Prototype in development
Habitat diversity and landscape quality	Prototype in development
Protected areas	Realized
Indication field III.3 Successes of climate-change-induced adaptations of nature conservation strategies and measures	
No realizable indicators	

The assignment of the proposed indicators to the indication domains and fields (see Table 1), the indicator data sheets with all the necessary information for a transparent documentation of calculation, the employed data, and the spatial and temporal resolution make it easy to understand the structure of the system. The graphical and textual representations of the computed indicator values included in the indicator factsheets are easy to understand and the indicators mainly comply with all requirements presented in Section 3.

4.1. Successfully Developed Indicators

The five realized indicators listed in the table above have been briefly explained below (see [21,29,34] for additional information).

4.1.1. Phenological Changes in Wild Plant Species

The newly developed indicator shows climate-change-related changes in the annual entry date of the phenological seasons, since 1951. The beginning of these seasons is marked by the occurrence of certain phases in the development of selected native wild plant species. For example, the beginning of the early spring as a phenological season, is indicated by the beginning of the flowering of the coltsfoot (*Tussilago farfara*). The shifts of entry of all ten recognized phenological seasons can be graphically illustrated by a phenological clock. The nationwide mean values of the entry data and the resulting duration of each of the ten phenological seasons from a thirty-year reference period (1951–1980) have been compared with the corresponding current values, which are available for the last thirty years. In 2017, the comparison shows an earlier entry of the phenological seasons of spring (early spring, first spring, full spring), summer (early summer, midsummer, late summer) and early autumn [36].

4.1.2. Temperature Index of the Bird Species Community

This index is based on the Community Temperature Index developed by Devictor and colleagues [37] and has been modified for the purposes mentioned above. The index adds up temperature indices of eighty-eight common breeding bird species, occurring in Germany, based on the average temperature in the European breeding range of these species, from March to August. The index shows the changes in the relative abundances of these species in relation to a reference year, linking it to the adaptation of the species to a colder or warmer climate. In the years 1990 to 2016, the relative frequencies of bird species have shifted in a statistically significant way in favor of species adapted to warmer conditions, consequently, to the disadvantage of species adapted to colder conditions [38].

4.1.3. Restoration of Natural Flood Plains

This newly developed indicator shows the annual cumulative increase in natural flood plains due to dike relocations in the main catchment areas of the Meuse, Rhine, Ems, Weser, Elbe, Oder, Danube, and their direct tributaries, to the North and the Baltic Seas. Land use changes that can be linked to climate change, include adaptation measures in water management. In addition to technically-oriented measures, the permanent restoration of natural flood plains is regarded as an effective flood protection strategy. The re-connection to the water bodies and the restoration of the natural flood dynamics have created new habitats of high conservation value for a large number of rare and endangered animal and plant species. Through different restoration measures on seventy-nine rivers, from 1983 to 2018, 4951 hectares of former floodplain area have been reconnected to the natural flooding dynamics of watercourses, and these areas are now flooded in an uncontrolled way during flood events. However, these measures were generally not planned, primarily, to adapt to climate change [39].

4.1.4. Consideration of Climate Change in Landscape Planning

This newly developed indicator describes if, how, and to what extent, the impacts of climate change on biodiversity are taken into account in landscape programs and landscape framework plans, which landscape plans are at the federal state or at the regional level. The indicator presents the percentage share of plans addressing climate change in the total number of evaluated plans. The evaluation of a hundred and seventy-nine plans that were in force, in 2018, showed that that the impacts of climate change and the resulting planning requirements have not yet been widely taken into account, as the mainstreaming of climate change issues, in landscape planning, takes its time, due to the fact that landscape plans are usually updated only every 15–20 years. However, climate-change-related statements have increased significantly, between 2000 and 2018 [40].

4.1.5. Protected Areas

This indicator assesses the total size of strictly protected areas in Germany. The area of land designated as nature conservation areas (NCAs) and national parks (NLPs) is expressed as a percentage of the German land surface. Natura 2000 sites and core areas and buffer zones of biosphere reserves are included, if designated as NCAs or NLPs.

The area of these strictly protected areas has increased significantly from 1.1 million hectares, in 2000, to 1.6 million hectares in 2016, which is an increase from 3.2% to 4.4% of Germany's land area. Even though the designation of new strictly protected areas was not mainly driven by it, it also has to be assessed positively in terms of adaptation of species to climate change. However, the formal designation of a protected area is only a first, albeit important, step towards adapting the system of protected areas to the requirements associated with climate change. In addition to the protection of suitable areas on a sufficiently large scale, effective management of these areas is an additional important requirement [41].

4.2. Gaps in the Indicator System

Despite these successes, certain indication fields could not be supported by indicator proposals. This concerns all indication domains and in particular indication fields, such as "changes in habitats" and "successes of climate-change-related adaptations to nature conservation strategies and measures", which were classified as central to the structure of the indicator system, within the framework of the projects, and are, therefore, listed as indication fields to be further developed in the future. Tracing impacts of climate change via indirect pathways in Indication Domain II, turned out to be particularly difficult and yielded only one appropriate indicator (Restoration of natural flood plains). Against the background of the ongoing expansion of wind power, changes in biological diversity, as a result of energy generation from wind power, and the associated, nationwide-expected considerable impacts on species groups, such as birds and bats, as well as on marine ecosystems, would have been of particular interest to the indicator system. However, the lack of data recorded in sufficient update intervals and gained on a uniform methodological basis, over long periods of time, does not allow for developing an appropriate indicator on this important issue.

In summary, the gaps in the indication fields are mainly caused by three factors:

- **Knowledge deficits on the direct impacts of climate change on biological diversity, at the habitat level:** In this area, scientific knowledge and data from monitoring programs are still unsatisfactory in many cases [4]. The links between climate change, on the one hand, and climate-change-induced changes in habitats, on the other, have not yet been sufficiently researched. The extent to which the natural adaptability of species influences the observable effects of climate change remains unclear in many areas. Furthermore, it is to be expected that, in certain cases, effects on habitats will only become apparent after a long time-lag. Therefore, no approach could be found to translate the effects of climate change on habitats, into a suitable indicator proposal.

- **Interaction of climatic effects with other influencing factors:** Overall, it has to be considered that climate-change-induced impacts on biological diversity interact with effects of other factors, such as land-use changes or the spread of alien species [42]. It should be noted, however, that these factors are also partly dependent on climate change, but have so far also essentially changed independently of it. For example, the general changes in land use that have prevailed for a long time, such as urbanization or agricultural intensification, result in massive changes in biological diversity, from which direct and indirect impacts of climate change can hardly be isolated. This is partly due to the fact that, in many cases, the indirect effects of climate change on biological diversity (e.g., through adaptation of land use to climate change), have so far been little pronounced and can, therefore, hardly be detected [43]. For these reasons, none of the indicator approaches discussed, fully meets the requirement to reflect changes in biological diversity that are predominantly and, above all, clearly attributable to land use adaptation measures to climate change or climate protection measures.

- **Difficulties in monitoring success:** At present, it is not possible to assess the success of adaptations to nature conservation strategies and measures to climate change, as such measures have hardly been implemented to date and it is very difficult to conduct a corresponding survey in terms of effectiveness monitoring. For this reason, no indicators have been implemented for this indication field, to date. However, considerations, such as balancing the decline in the vulnerability of climate-change-sensitive species or improving the conservation status of climate-change-sensitive habitats, are worthwhile approaches for developing indicators which, however, still require further elaboration and cannot be implemented directly. In particular, it should be clarified whether improvements in conservation statuses or the threat to climate-change-sensitive protected goods can actually be achieved through targeted adjustments and the implementation of appropriate nature conservation strategies and measures. Attention must be paid to the close relationship to other influencing factors, such as changes in land use.

5. Availability and Limits of Data Feeding Indicators

In order to report indicators, permanently, and provide policy advice, the requirements on monitoring programs and data mentioned in Section 2 have to be fulfilled, as far as possible. This is often not the case, especially in newly emerging policy and conservation fields—such as, climate change and biodiversity—in which no regular and systematic monitoring and data gathering could have been developed so far.

Even if suitable data exist, many other restrictions can appear. Heiland and Schliep discussed these data-related obstacles in indicator development [44]. Along with content-driven problems, the lack of appropriate data is a well-known problem in the development of indicators. This is also the case within the realm of climate-change impacts on biodiversity, for example, in connection with indicators relating to animal species [45]. Other problems include:

1. **Accessibility:** In some cases, appropriate data exist, but are not or are only partially provided by the data-holding institution.
2. **Quality:** Existing data are not sufficiently accurate (either in thematic or spatial accuracy) and, therefore, do not allow reliable statements.
3. **Scope:** Existing data are not comprehensive or representative, e.g., habitat maps are available only for some federal states.
4. **Heterogeneity:** Data of very different quality are collected regionally or with different methods and different classifications in the federal states and, therefore, cannot be compared nationwide. This is partly due to the federal structure of Germany, which refers not only to governmental structures, but also to NGOs and voluntary associations collecting data, e.g., on dragonflies, in our particular case. It was not possible to use those data as they were based on different, non-comparable data collection methods, at the federal state level, and as the continuity of data collection could not be ensured, due to lack of personnel.
5. **Frequency:** Data are collected, but at intervals that are too long, as is the case, e.g., with nation-wide floristic mapping.
6. **Time span:** Data are only available for a short period, which actually does not allow for showing trends. It would be ideal if the data were also available for past periods of time. This is often the case, e.g., with digital habitat or land use maps.
7. **Frame of reference:** Some indicators require the geometric and statistical intersection of different data sets. This causes further problems:

   - Several thematically-related data sets may have different spatial reference units (data set A e.g., habitat, data set B e.g., district). This means that they can no longer be sensibly blended together. Examples are official statistical data, which mostly refers to administrative units, and floristic data, which is captured in regular grids.
   - The datasets have different scales, e.g., nationwide data on climate and local floristic data.
   - The datasets have different time points of acquisition, e.g., datasets gathered by the federal states on the same thematic issues, but at different time points.

The mentioned problems can be illustrated by the example of habitat mapping. Habitats are of crucial importance in the field of climate change, e.g., in the case of shifting distribution areas of animal and plant species and in the need for networked corridors. For this reason, the data problem will be described in more detail, using this example. The main requirements of data are, a sufficiently high-resolution and a full area-coverage. If data are available, they are often not repeatedly updated or not comparable across the federal states of Germany. Only in some federal states, habitat maps, that are derived from aerial color-infrared photographs, cover the entire area [46]. These were collected in the 1990s, for all eastern German states and the federal state of Schleswig-Holstein. However, only a few states repeated the survey (e.g., Saxony [47] and Brandenburg [48]) after the year 2000. Another problem is that the mapping units differ from state to state, so that no uniform map can be produced. Almost all federal states record legally-protected biotopes in a separate mapping ("selective biotope mapping" [49]). Here, too, the problems are the comparability of the data between the different federal states and the regularity of the survey.

The only current, regularly updated source on habitats is the High Nature Value Farmland Monitoring [50], which maps valuable habitats in the agricultural landscape in randomly stratified sample plots of 1 km² size. It is representative for the entire agricultural landscape of Germany. A regular repetition of this survey is secured. At present, a much more comprehensive monitoring program is being developed and tested in a pilot study. It is carried out on the same sample plots as the High Nature Value Farmland Monitoring, but covers the whole range of habitat types that are both quantitatively and qualitatively surveyed. Habitat types and land use types of the entire landscape are recorded and assessed as basic units for future ecosystem monitoring. If the test was successful it could be a possible solution to obtain statistically accurate information on the basis of randomly stratified sampling if a coverage of the whole area is not possible due to financial constraints.

At the moment, the only valid, full area-coverage data basis for habitats, including all kind of land uses, are digital land-use data from the official land surveying [51,52]. Advantages are a very high accuracy of the data, a high topicality and the regular repetition of the recording. However, these data are not specifically collected for monitoring biological diversity, but for other purposes, such as land information, spatial, and urban planning, etc. Therefore, the data and information provided on habitats are not particularly in-depth. Against this background, it becomes clear that compromises have to be made in the development of indicators between the accuracy of the indicator and the availability of data, as the latter often have originally been collected for other purposes.

While developing the indicator system on climate-change impacts on biodiversity, we strived for reaching a balance between the requirements presented in Section 3. Indeed, there were cases where we could not calculate indicators because the needed data did not exist. This especially applies to indicators dealing with new and emerging trends, e.g., the effects of renewable energies on biodiversity. The challenge results from the fact that these trends have not been dealt with before. Consequently, they have not been monitored before, leading to a lack of appropriate data which can only be collected, from now on. An indicator on the subject necessarily depends on data which have been collected for other purposes, before the problem concerned had occurred, and, therefore, are not appropriate, or are only partly appropriate. To date, however, Germany does not have an established comprehensive biodiversity monitoring system at the federal level, nor does it have an indicator system regarding climate-change impacts on biodiversity. In Switzerland, for example, it was possible to analyze climate-change impacts on biodiversity, ex post [53], as the current Swiss biodiversity monitoring programs and projects are surveying all important components of biodiversity, at two different spatial levels [54]. It remains a challenging future task for German authorities, at the national level, to initiate a nationwide monitoring system that can meet this task.

To sum up, the requirements on indicators and indicator systems sketched in Section 3, turned out to be a rule of thumb during the development of an indicator system on climate-change impacts on biodiversity. In the light of only a few, long-term, time-series data, data availability certainly becomes a key criterion. In one case (community temperature index of breeding bird species communities) the indicator was taken up because data are available, although the algorithm for the calculation of the indicator values is quite complex. Other indicator prototypes were put on hold (e.g., Lusitanian fish species) because it was not possible to find an agreement between data holders and possible users (BfN), about the use of data. Another indicator prototype (changes in the flora of alpine summits) was put on hold because it was not clear for a certain period of time if the Global Observation Research Initiative in Alpine Environments (GLORIA) monitoring program [55], on which the indicator is based upon, will be continued.

6. Conclusions

Anthropogenic climate change causes substantial changes in biodiversity on the global scale, as well as in Germany. Indicators can help to illustrate this impact and make it easily comprehensible, beyond science, for the public and politicians. Worldwide, indicators at the interface between climate change and biodiversity are still underrepresented in indicator systems.

Thus, first appropriate indicators have been and, are being, developed. For Germany, six indicators are currently under development, to complement the existing set of five indicators, on the impacts of climate change on biodiversity, at the national level. However, data availability for indicator development is still insufficient. Therefore, an improved database is a goal to strive for, in the future.

When developing new indicators for policy advice two different approaches are usually combined. First, a data-driven bottom-up approach is determined by the availability of suitable data. Second,

Sustainability **2018**, *10*, 3959

a top-down approach is based on political fields of action and related normative goals, for which meaningful indicators and suitable data are sought. Both approaches have advantages, constraints, and shortcomings. The scientific accuracy of the indicators, the availability of data, and the purpose of policy advice have to be well-balanced while developing such indicator systems. As a matter of fact, in many cases, data have been collected for certain purposes and are ex post used for other purposes that have not been considered before.

Author Contributions: R.S., U.W., U.S. and S.H. have contributed substantially to the work reported.

funding: The research and development projects "Indikatorensystem zur Darstellung direkter und indirekter Auswirkungen des Klimawandels auf die biologische Vielfalt" (FKZ 3511 82 0400) and "Weiterentwicklung von Indikatoren zu Auswirkungen des Klimawandels auf die biologische Vielfalt" (FKZ 3517 81 1000) are funded by the German Federal Agency for Nature Conservation (BfN), on behalf of the German Federal Ministry for the Environment, Nature Conservation and Nuclear Safety (BMU).

Acknowledgments: The authors would like to thank the editor of the Special Edition—Joachim Spangenberg—for his kind invitation to write this paper and the three reviewers for their valuable comments on the draft version. This article would not have been possible without the contributions of many persons who have worked on the projects mentioned above: W. Ackermann, V. Aljes, C. Baierl, R. Bartz, E. Braeckevelt, R. Dröschmeister, F. Dziock, S. Dziock, D. Fuchs, I. Kowarik, S. Kretzschmar, A. Miller, L. Radtke, G. Rosenthal, S. Schäffler, S. Siedentop, C. Sudfeldt, S. Trautmann. We acknowledge support by the German Research Foundation and the Open Access Publication Funds of TU Berlin.

Conflicts of Interest: The authors declare no conflict of interest. The funding German Federal Ministry for the Environment, Nature Conservation and Nuclear Safety (BMU) had no role in the design of the study, in the collection, analyses, or interpretation of data, in the writing of the manuscript, or in the decision to publish the results.

References

1. Heink, U.; Kowarik, I. What are indicators? On the definition of indicators in ecology and environmental planning. *Ecol. Indic.* **2010**, *3*, 584–593. [CrossRef]
2. Sukopp, U. Indikatoren des Naturschutzes im Spannungsfeld von Politik und Wissenschaft [Indicators of nature conservation in the field of tension between politics and science]. In *Flächennutzungsmonitoring X*; Meinel, G., Schumacher, U., Behnisch, M., Krüger, T., Eds.; IÖR-Schriften 76; Rhombos: Berlin, Germany, 2018; pp. 273–281.
3. Sukopp, U. A tiered approach to develop indicator systems for biodiversity conservation. In *Second Sino-German Workshop on Biodiversity Conservation*; Kümper-Schlake, L., Ed.; BfN-Skripten 261; Bundesamt für Naturschutz [Federal Agency for Nature Conservation]: Bonn, Germany, 2009; pp. 38–40.
4. Dröschmeister, R.; Sukopp, U. Monitoring der Auswirkungen des Klimawandels auf die biologische Vielfalt in Deutschland [Monitoring the impacts of climate change on biodiversity in Germany]. *Natur und Landschaft* **2009**, *84*, 13–17.
5. Wiggering, H.; Müller, F. (Eds.) *Umweltziele und Indikatoren [Environmental Goals and Indicators]*; Springer: Berlin, Germany, 2004.
6. Hoffmann, A.; Penner, J.; Vohland, K.; Cramer, W.; Doubleday, R.; Henle, K.; Kõljalg, U.; Kühn, I.; Kunin, W.; Negro, J.J.; et al. The need for an integrated biodiversity policy support process—Building the European contribution to a global Biodiversity Observation Network (EU BON). *Nat. Conserv.* **2014**, *3*, 49–65. [CrossRef]
7. Pereira, H.M.; Ferrier, S.; Walters, M.; Geller, G.N.; Jongman, R.H.G.; Scholes, R.J.; Bruford, M.W.; Brummitt, N.; Butchart, S.H.M.; Cardoso, A.C.; et al. Essential biodiversity variables. *Science* **2013**, *339*, 277–278. [CrossRef] [PubMed]
8. Geijzendorffer, I.R.; Regan, E.C.; Pereira, H.M.; Brotons, L.; Brummitt, N.; Gavish, Y.; Haase, P.; Martin, C.S.; Mihoub, J.B.; Secades, C.; et al. Bridging the gap between biodiversity data and policy reporting needs: An Essential Biodiversity Variables perspective. *J. Appl. Ecol.* **2016**, *53*, 1341–1350. [CrossRef]
9. Proença, V.; Martin, L.J.; Pereira, H.M.; Fernandez, M.; McRae, L.; Belnap, J.; Böhm, M.; Brummitt, N.; García-Moreno, J.; Gregory, R.D.; et al. Global biodiversity monitoring: From data sources to Essential Biodiversity Variables. *Biol. Conserv.* **2017**, *213*, 256–263. [CrossRef]

10. Schmeller, D.S.; Mihoub, J.B.; Bowser, A.; Arvanitidis, C.; Costello, M.J.; Fernandez, M.; Geller, G.N.; Hobern, D.; Kissling, W.D.; Regan, E.; et al. An operational definition of essential biodiversity variables. *Biodivers. Conserv.* **2017**, *26*, 2967–2972. [CrossRef]

11. Sukopp, H.; Seidel, K.; Böcker, R. Bausteine zu einem Monitoring für den Naturschutz [Steps towards a monitoring for nature conservation]. *Berichte der Bayerischen Akademie für Naturschutz und Landschaftspflege (ANL)* **1986**, *10*, 27–39.

12. Dröschmeister, R. Ausgewählte Ansätze für den Aufbau von Monitoringprogrammen im Naturschutz—Möglichkeiten und Grenzen [Selected approaches for the development of monitoring programmes in nature conservation—possibilities and limitations]. In *Symposium Praktische Anwendungen des Biotopmonitoring in der Landschaftsökologie*; Fachsektion Freiberuflicher Biologen im Verband Deutscher Biologen, Ed.; Selbstverlag: Bochum, Germany, 1996; pp. 78–89.

13. Sukopp, U.; Weddeling, K. Fachliche Anforderungen an die Überwachung der Umweltwirkungen gentechnisch veränderter Organismen (GVO) bei Freisetzungen (Monitoring nach Teil B der RL 2001/18/ EG) [Technical requirements for monitoring the environmental effects of genetically modified organisms (GMOs) after deliberate releases (monitoring according to Part B of Directive 2001/18/EC)]. In *GVO-Monitoring vor der Umsetzung. Veröffentlichung zur Tagung vom 28. und 29. November 2006 im Bundesamt für Naturschutz*; Breckling, B., Dolek, M., Lang, A., Reuter, H., Verhoeven, R., Eds.; Naturschutz und Biologische Vielfalt 49; Bundesamt für Naturschutz [Federal Agency for Nature Conservation]: Bonn, Germany, 2007; pp. 185–206.

14. Biodiversity Indicators Partnership. *Guidance for National Biodiversity Indicator Development and Use*; UNEP World Conservation Monitoring Centre: Cambridge, UK, 2011.

15. Sukopp, U.; Neukirchen, M.; Ackermann, W.; Schweiger, M.; Fuchs, D. Die Indikatoren der Nationalen Strategie zur biologischen Vielfalt [The indicators of the National Strategy on Biological Diversity]. *Jahrbuch für Naturschutz und Landschaftspflege* **2011**, *58*, 12–33.

16. Ackermann, W.; Schweiger, M.; Sukopp, U.; Fuchs, D.; Sachteleben, J. *Indikatoren zur biologischen Vielfalt. Entwicklung und Bilanzierung [Biodiversity Indicators. Development and Accounting]*; Naturschutz und Biologische Vielfalt 132; Bundesamt für Naturschutz [Federal Agency for Nature Conservation]: Bonn, Germany, 2013; 229p.

17. Bubb, P.; Chenery, A.; Herkenrath, P.; Kapos, V.; Mapendembe, A.; Stanwell-Smith, D.; Walpole, M. *National Indicators, Monitoring and Reporting for the Strategy for Biodiversity. A Review of Experience and Recommendations in Support of the CBD Ad Hoc Technical Expert Group (AHTEG) on Indicators for the Strategic Plan 2011–2020*; UNEP-WCMC: Cambridge, UK, 2011.

18. Dale, V.H.; Beyeler, S.C. Challenges in the development and use of ecological indicators. *Ecol. Indic.* **2001**, *1*, 3–10. [CrossRef]

19. Heiland, S.; Tischer, M.; Döring, T.; Jessel, B. Kommunale Nachhaltigkeitsindikatorensysteme—Anspruch, Eignung, Wirksamkeit—Indikatoren zur Zielkonkretisierung und Erfolgskontrolle im Rahmen der Lokalen Agenda 21 [Municipal sustainability indicator systems—Claim, suitability, effectiveness—Indicators for target specification and success monitoring within the framework of Local Agenda 21]. *UVP Rep.* **2003**, *17*, 202–206.

20. Parr, T.W.; Jongman, R.H.G.; Külvik, M. *The Selection of Biodiversity Indicators for EBONE Development Work. Version 2.11*; European Biodiversity Observation Network: Wageningen, The Netherlands, 2010.

21. Schliep, R.; Bartz, R.; Dröschmeister, R.; Dziock, F.; Dziock, S.; Fina, S.; Kowarik, I.; Radtke, L.; Schäffler, L.; Siedentop, S.; et al. *Indikatorensystem zur Darstellung direkter und indirekter Auswirkungen des Klimawandels auf die biologische Vielfalt [Indicator System on the Direct and Indirect Impacts of Climate Change on Biodiversity]*; BfN-Skripten 470; Bundesamt für Naturschutz [Federal Agency for Nature Conservation]: Bonn, Germany, 2017; 249p.

22. Klotz, S.; Settele, J. Biodiversität [Biodiversity]. In *Klimawandel in Deutschland [Climate Change in Germany]*; Brasseur, G., Jacob, D., Schuck-Zöller, S., Eds.; Springer Spektrum: Berlin, Germany, 2017; pp. 151–160.

23. Parmesan, C. Ecological and evolutionary responses to recent climate change. *Ecol. Evol.* **2006**, *37*, 637–669. [CrossRef]

24. Campbell, A.; Kapos, V.; Scharlemann, J.P.W.; Bubb, P.; Chenery, A.; Coad, L.; Dickson, B.; Doswald, N.; Khan, M.S.I.; Kershaw, F.; et al. *Review of the Literature on the Links between Biodiversity and Climate Change: Impacts, Adaptation and Mitigation*; Technical Series 42; Secretariat of the Convention on Biological Diversity: Montreal, QC, Canada, 2009; 124p.

25. Dawson, T.P.; Jackson, S.T.; House, J.I.; Prentice, I.C.; Mace, G.M. Beyond predictions: Biodiversity conservation in a changing climate. *Science* **2011**, *332*, 53–58. [CrossRef] [PubMed]

26. Hannah, L.; Bird, A. Climate Change and Biodiversity: Impacts. In *Encyclopedia of the Anthropocene*; Dellasala, D.A., Goldstein, M.I., Eds.; Elsevier: Oxford, UK, 2017; pp. 249–258.

27. Bellard, C.; Bertelsmeier, C.; Leadley, P.; Thuiller, W.; Courchamp, F. Impacts of climate change on the future of biodiversity. *Ecol. Lett.* **2012**, *15*, 365–377. [CrossRef] [PubMed]

28. McMahon, S.M.; Harrison, S.P.; Armbruster, W.S.; Bartlein, P.J.; Beale, C.M.; Edwards, M.E.; Kattge, J.; Midgley, G.; Morin, X.; Prentice, I.C. Improving assessment and modeling of climate change impacts on global terrestrial biodiversity. *Trends Ecol. Evol.* **2011**, *26*, 249–259. [CrossRef] [PubMed]

29. Heiland, S.; Schliep, R.; Bartz, R.; Schäffler, L.; Dziock, S.; Radtke, L.; Trautmann, S.; Kowarik, I.; Dziock, F.; Sudfeldt, C.; et al. Indikatoren zur Darstellung von Auswirkungen des Klimawandels auf die biologische Vielfalt in Deutschland [Indicators for accounting impacts of climate change on biodiversity]. *Natur und Landschaft* **2018**, *93*, 2–13.

30. Bundesministerium für Umwelt, Naturschutz und Reaktorsicherheit. *National Strategy on Biological Diversity: Adopted by the Federal Cabinet on 7 November 2007*; Environmental Policy Series; Federal Ministry for the Environment, Nature Conservation and Nuclear Safety: Bonn, Germany, 2007; 178p.

31. Bundesregierung. *Deutsche Anpassungsstrategie an den Klimawandel [German Strategy for Adaptation to Climate Change]*; Federal Government: Berlin, Germany, 2008.

32. Schliep, R.; Bartz, R.; Dröschmeister, R.; Dziock, F.; Dziock, S.; Fina, S.; Kowarik, I.; Radtke, L.; Schäffler, L.; Siedentop, S.; et al. *Indikatorensystem zur Darstellung Direkter und Indirekter Auswirkungen des Klimawandels auf die biologische Vielfalt [Indicator System on the Direct and Indirect Impacts of Climate Change on Biodiversity]. BfN-Skripten 470. Online-Supplement: Anhänge A, B*; BfN-Skripten 470; Bundesamt für Naturschutz [Federal Agency for Nature Conservation]: Bonn, Germany, 2017; 80p.

33. Smeets, E.; Weterings, R. *Environmental Indicators: Typology and Overview*; Technical Report No 25; European Environment Agency (EEA): Kopenhagen, Denmark, 1999.

34. Umweltbundesamt. *Monitoringbericht 2015 zur Deutschen Anpassungsstrategie an den Klimawandel. Bericht der Interministeriellen Arbeitsgruppe Anpassungsstrategie der Bundesregierung [Monitoring Report 2015 on the German Adaptation Strategy to Climate Change. Report of the Federal Government's Interministerial Working Group on Adaptation Strategy]*; Federal Environment Agency: Dessau-Roßlau, Germany, 2015.

35. Bundesministerium für Umwelt, Naturschutz, Bau und Reaktorsicherheit. *Indikatorenbericht 2014 zur Nationalen Strategie zur biologischen Vielfalt [Indicator Report 2014 on the National Strategy on Biological Diversity]*; Federal Ministry of Environment, Construction and Nuclear Safety: Berlin, Germany, 2015.

36. Schäffler, L.; Schliep, R.; Ackermann, W. *Phänologische Veränderungen bei Wildpflanzenarten [Phenological Changes in Wild Plant Species]*; Indicator Factsheet prepared for the DAS Monitoring Report 2019; Bundesamt für Naturschutz [Federal Agency for Nature Conservation]: Bonn, Germany, 2018; unpublished.

37. Devictor, V.; Julliard, R.; Couvet, D.; Jiguet, F. Birds are tracking climate warming, but not fast enough. *Proc. R. Soc. Lond. B* **2008**, *275*, 2743–2748. [CrossRef] [PubMed]

38. Trautmann, S.; Sudfeldt, C. *Temperaturindex der Vogelartengemeinschaft [Temperature Index of the Bird Species Community]*; Indicator Factsheet prepared for the DAS Monitoring Report 2019; Bundesamt für Naturschutz [Federal Agency for Nature Conservation]: Bonn, Germany, 2018; unpublished.

39. Schliep, R.; Sukopp, U. *Rückgewinnung natürlicher Überflutungsflächen [Restoration of Natural Flood Plains]*; Indicator Factsheet prepared for the DAS Monitoring Report 2019; Bundesamt für Naturschutz [Federal Agency for Nature Conservation]: Bonn, Germany, 2018; unpublished.

40. Schliep, R.; Heiland, S.; Radtke, L.; Miller, A. *Berücksichtigung des Klimawandels in Landschaftsprogrammen und Landschaftsrahmenplänen [Consideration of Climate Change in Landscape Planning]*; Indicator Factsheet prepared for the DAS Monitoring Report 2019; Bundesamt für Naturschutz [Federal Agency for Nature Conservation]: Bonn, Germany, 2018; unpublished.

41. Schliep, R.; Sukopp, U. *Gebietsschutz [Protected Areas]*; Indicator Factsheet prepared for the DAS Monitoring Report 2019; Bundesamt für Naturschutz [Federal Agency for Nature Conservation]: Bonn, Germany, 2018; unpublished.

42. Thuiller, W. Climate Change and the ecologist. *Nature* **2007**, *448*, 550–552. [CrossRef] [PubMed]

43. Foden, W.B.; Mace, G.M.; Butchart, S.H.M. Indicators of Climate Change Impacts on Biodiversity. In *Biodiversity Monitoring and Conservation: Bridging the Gaps between Global Commitment and Local Action*; Collen, B., Pettorelli, N., Baillie, J.E., Durant, S.M., Eds.; Wiley-Blackwell: Hoboken, NJ, USA, 2013; pp. 120–137.

44. Heiland, S.; Schliep, R. Indikatorensystem zur Darstellung der Auswirkungen des Klimawandels auf die biologische Vielfalt—Anforderungen, Hemmnisse, Ergebnisse [Indicator system on the impacts of climate change on biodiversity—requirements, obstacles, results]. In *Flächennutzungsmonitoring VI. Innenentwicklung—Prognose—Datenschutz*; IÖR Schriften 65; Rhombos: Berlin, Germany, 2014.

45. Braeckevelt, E.; Heiland, S.; Schliep, R.; Sukopp, U.; Trautmann, S.; Züghart, W. Indikatoren zu Auswirkungen des Klimawandels auf die biologische Vielfalt—Stand und Perspektiven am Beispiel von Meereszooplankton und Vögeln in Deutschland [Indicators of climate change impacts on biodiversity—Status and perspectives using the example of marine zooplankton and birds in Germany]. *Natur und Landschaft* **2018**, *93*, 538–544.

46. Bundesamt für Naturschutz. *A System for the Survey of Biotope and Land Use Types (Survey Guide)*; Schriftenreihe für Landschaftspflege und Naturschutz 73; Bundesamt für Naturschutz [Federal Agency for Nature Conservation]: Bonn, Germany, 2002.

47. Sächsisches Landesamt für Umwelt, Landwirtschaft und Geologie. Kartiereinheiten der Biotoptypen- und Landnutzungskartierung Sachsen 2005 [Mapping Units of the Biotope Type and Land Use Mapping Saxony 2005]. Saxon State Agency of Environment, Agriculture and Geology, 2010. Available online: http://www.forsten.sachsen.de/umwelt/download/natur/Kartiereinheiten_BTLNK_2005.pdf (accessed on 17 March 2011).

48. Landesamt für Umwelt des Landes Brandenburg. Flächendeckende Biotop- und Landnutzungskartierung (BTLN) im Land Brandenburg—CIR-Biotoptypen 2009 [Full Area Biotope and Land Use Mapping (BTLN) in the State of Brandenburg—CIR Biotope Types 2009]. State Agency for the Environment in the Federal State of Brandenburg, 2009. Available online: https://lfu.brandenburg.de/cms/detail.php/bb1.c.359429.de (accessed on 17 March 2011).

49. Sächsisches Landesamt für Umwelt und Geologie. *Kartieranleitung: Biotopkartierung in Sachsen. Materialien zu Naturschutz und Landschaftspflege [Mapping Instructions: Biotope Mapping in Saxony. Materials on Nature Conservation and Landscape Management*; Saxon State Agency of Environment and Geology: Dresden, Germany, 2003.

50. Benzler, A.; Fuchs, D.; Hünig, C. Methodik und erste Ergebnisse des Monitorings der Landwirtschaftsflächen mit hohem Naturwert in Deutschland. Beleg für aktuelle Biodiversitätsverluste in der Agrarlandschaft [Methods and first results of High Nature Value Farmland Monitoring in Germany. Evidence of ongoing biodiversity loss within agricultural landscapes]. *Natur und Landschaft* **2015**, *90*, 309–316.

51. Bundesamt für Kartographie und Geodäsie. *Digital Base Landscape Model: Basis-DLM*; Federal Agency for Cartography and Geodesy: Frankfurt am Main, Germany, 2011.

52. Krüger, T.; Meinel, G.; Schumacher, U. Land-use monitoring by topographic data analysis. *Cartogr. Geogr. Inf. Sci.* **2013**, *40*, 220–228. [CrossRef]

53. Bundesamt für Umwelt. Klimawandel [Climate Change]. *BDM-Facts 4*; Federal Agency for the Environment: Bern, Switzerland, 2012. Available online: http://www.biodiversitymonitoring.ch/de/daten/berichte-und-publikationen.html (accessed on 9 May 2018).

54. Bundesamt für Umwelt. *Biodiversität: Monitoringprogramme [Biodiversity: Monitoring Programmes]*; Federal Agency for the Environment: Bern, Switzerland, 2018. Available online: https://www.bafu.admin.ch/bafu/de/home/themen/biodiversitaet/zustand/biodiversitaet--monitoringprogramme.html (accessed on 9 May 2018).

55. Pauli, H.; Gottfried, M.; Hohenwallner, D.; Reiter, K.; Casale, R.; Grabherr, G. *The GLORIA Field Manual—Multi-Summit Approach*; European Commission, Directorate-General for Research, Office for Official Publications of the European Communities: Luxembourg, 2004.

sustainability

MDPI

Article

Global SDGs Assessments: Helping or Confusing Indicators?

Svatava Janoušková [1,2], Tomáš Hák [2,*] and Bedřich Moldan [2]

[1] Faculty of Science, Charles University, Albertov 6, 128 43 Prague, Czech Republic;
    svatava.janouskova@natur.cuni.cz

[2] Environment Center, Charles University, José Martího 2/407, 162 00 Prague, Czech Republic;
    bedrich.moldan@czp.cuni.cz

*   Correspondence: tomas.hak@czp.cuni.cz; Tel.: +420-724698014

Received: 31 March 2018; Accepted: 9 May 2018; Published: 12 May 2018

Abstract: On 1 January 2016, the 17 Sustainable Development Goals (SDGs) of the 2030 Agenda for Sustainable Development—adopted by world leaders in 2015—came into force. They build on the Millennium Development Goals (MDGs) and call for action by all countries to promote prosperity while protecting the planet. Since the SDGs are not legally binding, governments are expected to take ownership and establish national frameworks for the achievement of the 17 Goals. Countries thus have the primary responsibility for follow-up and review of the progress made in implementing the Goals, which will require quality, accessible and timely data collection. This will be instrumental for both regional and global follow-up analyses and assessments—several such major global assessments have already appeared. It might be supposed that the SDGs framework, including indicators, is conceptually and methodologically well-designed and tested in order to function reliably and provide guidance for such assessments. However, while it seems that the current structure of the SDGs has provided a firm policy framework, the Goals and targets have been mostly operationalized by indicators. We demonstrate and argue that without a procedurally well-designed, conceptual indicator framework for selecting and/or designing indicators, the results of SDGs assessments may be ambiguous and confusing.

Keywords: sustainable development goals; Agenda 2030; global indicator framework; sustainability indicators; SDGs

---

1. Introduction

After thirty years of sustainable development summits, action plans, and reports, the major trends in the planetary environment, social equity, and economic sustainability are still going in the wrong direction, due to slow implementation, lack of public involvement, and inadequate information on progress. Indicators play an instrumental role in making the concept of sustainable development (SD) appealing to a wide spectrum of potential stakeholders as well as in assessing the progress [1–3].

Hundreds of different indicators are used in differing contexts for diverse purposes. It is difficult to assess the impact of these indicators on policymaking and progress towards sustainability since scientific information—such as that conveyed by indicators—is usually not sufficient to produce changes in either national decision-making or individual behavior. Thus the most significant effect of an indicator, particularly early in its adoption, can simply be communication—making a problem visible, sensitizing decision-makers and the public and expanding the basis for decision-making [4].

In 2015, a summit of heads of state adopted the Sustainable Development Goals (SDGs) [5]. The SDGs in their recent form are a universal set of Goals, targets, and indicators that UN member states will use to frame their agendas and policies over the next 15 years. Currently, they comprise 17 Goals, 169 targets, and 243 indicators [6]. It might be supposed that the SDGs framework—including indicators—is conceptually and methodologically well designed and tested in order to function reliably. However, it seems that the current structure and format of the proposed Goals and targets has laid "only" a policy framework. Being transparent and participatory in character, it is an appropriate way of designing it provided that Goals and targets would get through thorough expert and scientific follow up on their operationalization. Without a procedurally well-designed conceptual indicator framework for selecting and/or designing indicators, the results of SDGs assessment may be ambiguous and confusing [7].

The goal of this article is to critically review the state of the art in sustainability reporting by the application of SDG indicators and contribute to setting an appropriate approach in this regard. We have conducted a comprehensive review of the extensive body of work in this field—starting by reviewing the theoretical foundations for the operationalization of the sustainable development concept (there is more on this in the "Conceptualization and operationalization of sustainable development" section) and then looking into existing practice. We have chosen four major current SDGs assessments to examine how indicators have been used for the operationalization and communication of the SDGs. Our analysis focuses, in particular, on their relevance for the intended audience, interpretation of their results, and complexity of the assessment.

Our starting assumption is based on the original purpose of the SDGs—helping to further mainstream sustainable development at all levels, integrating economic, social, and environmental aspects and recognizing their interlinkages, so as to achieve sustainable development in all its dimensions [8]. Consequently, we have assumed that applying the SDG indicator framework inconsistently (by one) or uncoordinatedly (by many) in order to measure the same phenomenon, that is., progress towards the SDGs, may cause serious problems. Such assessments may convey very different messages that might raise doubts about the concept of SD or on the process of its operationalization. A worthy long-term global effort for communication of progress towards sustainability thus may be in vain or seriously undermined.

2. Indicator-Based Sustainability Communication

Despite recent scientific findings on many negative development trends [9], sustainability does not seem to have become a near-term priority for society [10–12]. In the process of changing this situation, an important role is given to sustainability communication. Its goal is to enable individuals and groups to develop the competences to adequately interpret the often contradictory and confusing scientific, technological, and economic information available to them and then be able to react to and cope with the resulting long-term and complex societal challenges [13].

Sustainable development, understood as a societal process of exploration, learning and shaping the future, necessarily involves communication. As global sustainability issues are characterized by high complexity and uncertainty, effective communication processes between the many actors involved are crucial to develop a mutual understanding of which actions to take [14]. In all three distinguished modes of communication—communication about sustainability, communication of sustainability, and communication for sustainability—sustainability indicators have an important role.

Indicators are by definition communication tools; indices, regardless of their many shortcomings, are particularly effective for communicating results to executives and the general public. Failure to communicate makes the indicators worthless. We may observe this in any context since knowledge production, having received an unprecedented boost in recent years, is no longer the privilege of an exclusive group of experts but takes place in a variety of constellations of actors. However, in these inter- and transdisciplinary work contexts, not enough attention has been paid to the problem of translating and communicating this knowledge in a way that is adequate to its target groups (e.g., the results of the European research projects POINT (Policy Influence of indicator (https://cordis.europa.eu/project/rcn/89898_en.html)) and BRAINPOol (BRinging Alternative INdicators into POLicy (https://cordis.europa.eu/project/rcn/100577_en.html)); or e.g., [15,16]).

Targeting sustainability communication is one of the most important steps toward making a problem visible, and hooking the interest and engagement of the target audience. It means identifying appropriate addressees and ensuring that the message reaches them. Since sustainable development is a multi-stakeholder process, indicators must be communicable to a variety of different participants. In general, sustainability communication moves in a special network of relationships among the three spheres of science, the public, and practice [17]. In more detail, some users need simple, structured information (voters—the public, non-specialist media, and decision makers), whereas others prefer an intermediate level of detail (local governments, policy implementers, non-government organizations, funding bodies, and industries), while technicians and academics may need more technical and specialized information. In targeting governments, it is useful to distinguish between politicians (ministers, political party members, parliamentarians etc.) who make decisions, and policy makers, implementers, and enforcers (mostly civil servants and experts in various positions with agenda areas such as economics, social affairs, transportation, environment, etc.) who design policy and regulatory portfolios, evaluate policy alternatives, analyze indicator results, and so on to provide the groundwork for decisions.

Indicators allow communication between scientists and policymakers, between policymakers and decision makers/politicians, between politicians and the public, even between scientists and the public, and so on. Communicating complex issues often presents difficulties since a large number of indicators complicates communication and imposes a great demand on users' knowledge capabilities because of the multidimensional character of sustainable development. Moreover, the problem is not trivial, it is not just understanding figures and charts (presented indicator results), but people have to grasp numerous underlying concepts that they are not necessarily familiar with.

A key challenge for sustainability indicators producers and/or promoters is to deliver easily communicable messages on the progress towards sustainable development and hence to ease the use, and enable implementation of indicators in the policy process and by citizens [18]. Regardless of the use and users, we claim the need for the selection and design only of such indicators that fall into a given measurement concept (a policy goal or objective, a policy measure, etc.) and contribute to its appropriate operationalization.

3. Conceptualization and Operationalization of Sustainable Development

Before proceeding to the conceptualization and operationalization of SDGs, let us look briefly at the sustainable development concept. Sustainability is a concept understood intuitively by all but very difficult to express in concrete, operational terms [19–22]. Brundtland's seminal definition [23] serves as a springboard for a variety of interpretations that emphasize the issues of needs, limits on development, futurity, inter- and intra-generational equity and the simultaneous fulfillment of economic efficiency, environmental protection, and social justice goals. Although the term is accompanied by imprecision, ambiguity, and, at times, contradictions, there is a generally accepted understanding of what sustainable development means.

The pragmatic way to SD definition relates to its "measurement" and includes indicators, as from the inception of the SD concept it has been clear that information and namely quantitative indicators will play an important role [24]. Nowadays, there are many SD indicators and indices already developed and new ones certainly have yet to appear, for example, [25,26]. Regardless of the truth—whether there is an obsession with numbers stimulating an indicator explosion, or a lack of indicators limiting humankind's competence to embark on a sustainable path—many serious efforts seeking reliable SD metrics have been made so far (the European Commission's 'Beyond GDP', OECD's 'Measuring the Progress of Societies', etc.). This line of thinking was emphasized and supported in the main Outcome document of the Rio+20 Summit: "We recognize that progress towards the achievement of the Goals needs to be assessed and accompanied by targets and indicators, while taking into account different national circumstances, capacities and levels of development" [8].

One basic idea behind the development of indicators for monitoring and performance evaluation of SD policies is evidence-based policymaking—indicators being viewed as knowledge-agents serving the simplification and communication of evidence in a form suited for policy- and decision-makers. Besides this rationalistic conception of the instrumental role of knowledge for decision-making, indicator influence has also conceptual and political dimensions (helping to diffuse ideas, alternative thinking and new concepts rather that leading to political action). There are often trade-offs between different types of influence and between the roles that indicators play in policymaking. Indicator providers and promoters should therefore seek clarification for themselves concerning the types of influence that indicators are expected to achieve in a given policy situation (is the indicator-based report to consciously influence decision-makers, or is it to influence how policy-makers think, define problems, or provide new perspectives on problems? Or to provide ammunition to support the pre-determined position of a user? [18]). Thus, the purpose of the assessment predetermines the indicator selection to the same extent as the concepts behind the Goals and targets. We claim that concepts of SD as well as the SDGs and their targets cannot be solely defined by a pack of statistics and indicators, regardless of how relevant they are and regardless of their use. Employing indicators on the availability principle is methodologically incorrect and might lead to distortions in development of policy agendas.

4. The Sustainable Development Goals

In 2015, a summit attended by heads of state adopted the Sustainable Development Goals (SDGs) [5]. The SDGs, also known as the Global Goals, are a universal call to action to end poverty, protect the planet, and ensure that peace and prosperity will be enjoyed by all. They are structured in 17 general themes (Goals), 169 more specific tasks (targets), and 244 indicators (Since nine indicators repeat under two or three different targets, the actual total number of individual indicators in the Framework is 232), that is, there are 5–19 targets and 6–27 indicators per Goal (Table 1). Despite the endorsed Global indicator framework, the work on the entire reporting mechanism is still in progress—data for the global SDG indicator database must be checked for availability and quality, and storylines for SDG global reports must be further developed [6]. The major identified weaknesses were the poor alignment of targets and Goals with existing international agreements and political processes; lack of effective implementation; conflicts between Goals and targets, non-quantified targets, lack of and/or low quality data for indicators [27]. And most of all—lack of operationalization of the targets [7].

Table 1. Global indicator framework structure [6].

Goal	Number of Targets	Number of Indicators
SDG 1	7	14
SDG 2	8	13
SDG 3	13	27
SDG 4	10	11
SDG 5	9	14
SDG 6	8	11
SDG 7	5	6
SDG 8	12	17
SDG 9	8	12
SDG 10	10	11
SDG 11	10	15
SDG 12	11	13
SDG 13	5	8
SDG 14	10	10
SDG 15	12	14
SDG 16	12	23
SDG 17	19	25
Total	169	244

We agree with Holden et al. [28] that formulating the 2030 Agenda and defining the SDGs would have been much easier if the world community had already reached a consensus on how to define and operationalize the concept of SD. We insist that it is still necessary to define each target, specify the concept behind each target, and describe what is and what is not part of that concept, and so on. This step will be important particularly for the targets which have a broad, multi-theme definition (there are majority such defined targets). This is to be followed by elaboration of clear-cut and detailed formulations of working hypotheses on the measurement of particular facts (phenomena, objects, processes) [29]. Only proper conceptualization and operationalization of the targets will transform them from broad, vague, and mostly political/theoretical concepts to tools which are clearly understandable in terms of empirical observations measurable or describable by appropriate indicators. It is an urgent task—since the first SDGs reports have already been published—to apply relevant and reliable indicators communicating global progress towards the Goals. A task of the same importance is at national level. Each country should seriously pursue the global SDGs concepts and methodologies and adapt them to national circumstances and conditions. What does, for example, "equitable and quality primary and secondary education" mean in each particular country and what policy implications does the underlying concept bring about? Is the proposed global indicator (Proportion of children and young people at certain grades achieving at least a minimum proficiency level in reading and mathematics) relevant and capable of capturing both as a global phenomenon and nation-specific? Do values play any role in it? [30]. Such questions should be laid and answered before publishing official SDGs reports.

5. Analysis of the SDG Reports

Several major reports monitoring the implementation of the SDGs emerged during the period 2015–2017. For the analysis we identified and selected four SDGs indicator-based assessments at global or supra-national/regional scales:

- The Sustainable Development Goals Report 2017 [31];
- SDGs: Are the rich countries ready? [32];
- SDG Index and Dashboards Report 2017: International spillovers in achieving the Goals [33]
- Sustainable development in the European Union. Monitoring report on progress towards the SDGs in an EU context [34].

We used Google Scholar (a widely-used web search engine indexing scholarly literature across an array of publishing formats and disciplines) that generated these reports based on several searching criteria. We searched for publicly available documents written in English, which were comprehensive assessment reports (not journal articles), legitimate (in terms of mandate of the report's producer or its capability to conduct transparent high-quality analytical work), and at a supra-national or global scale (not national reports), that included a combination of keywords "report" and "Sustainable Development Goals". It may be that the resulting list of major SDGs reports (November 2018) is not fully comprehensive but it is very likely they will have an impact on the politicians and policy-makers—and other users—they target. The reports' main characteristics are in Table 2.

Table 2. Key characteristics of the analyzed SDGs assessments.

	The Sustainable Development Goals Report 2017	Sustainable Development in the European Union	SDGs: Are the Rich Countries Ready?	SDG Index and Dashboards Report 2017
Developer/author	UN (Department of Economic and Social Affairs—DESA)	European Commission (Eurostat)	Bertelsmann Stiftung	Bertelsmann Stiftung and SDSN
Date of publication	2017	November 2017	September 2015	July 2017
Report extent	64 pp.	353/20 pp.*	106 pp.	122 pp.

Table 2. *Cont.*

	The Sustainable Development Goals Report 2017	Sustainable Development in the European Union	SDGs: Are the Rich Countries Ready?	SDG Index and Dashboards Report 2017
Country coverage	Global (Results per UN regions)	28 (EU member states)	34 (OECD member states)	Global (Results per 157 countries and geopolitical regions)
Number of indicators	100	100/100 *	34	83 (OECD member states—99)
Headline indicators	Yes (Overview indicators; 2–4 per Goal)	No	Yes (Entire assessment is based on "snapshot indicators"— 2 per Goal)	No
Link to global indicator Framework	Yes (exclusive)	No	Yes	Yes
Interpretation	Goal thresholds, description of state and development (trends)	Policy objectives, benchmarking, trends	Benchmarking against the top countries	Goal thresholds, benchmarking, trends
User	Not specified	Not specified	Policy makers, businesses, civil society	Governments, academia, civil society, businesses
Supplementary information (on data and indicators)	Available separately (at unstat.un.org/sdgs)	A loose link to the Eurostat statistical portal	Reference to the data source for each indicator	No

Note: * denotes a separately published Overview.

In terms of our methodological approach, we applied a comparative analysis. We started with a description that provided an informative comparison about the reports concerned (the summary results are in the Table 2). The key feature defining comparative analysis, as understood here, was an interest in the explanatory question of why the observed similarities and differences between cases exist. In particular, we tried to find out why the level of SDGs implementation in the same subject (a country) is assessed differently by each report. The analysis was based on collection of data on all cases included in the reports. The data was analyzed according to a designed common framework comprising additional explanatory variables: relevance for the intended audience, interpretation of the indicators results, and complexity of the assessment.

The relevance of the report—that is, relevance of the contained information—for the intended audience is a key factor of success. If the Goals are important to and understandable by people, they will ask their governments to act. Civil society must be able to put pressure on governments to hold them to account for what they pledge at world summits [32]. However, the main Outcome Documents on SDGs (The future we want (A/RES/66/288*) and Transforming our world: the 2030 Agenda for Sustainable Development (UN A/RES/70/1)) are not very specific about the target audience—all countries and all stakeholders, acting in collaborative partnership, are to implement the Goals. So it's a whole society enterprise, with governments in the broadest sense (ministers, elected politicians, policy makers—state and regional administration officials, administrators, bureaucrats …) on one hand and civic society components on another hand (civic society organizations including business and entrepreneurs). A crucial factor for enhancing particularly the instrumental role and direct utilization of indicators in policy is setting a proper communication mode for the SDGs. Communication science has already developed to the extent that there are specific types of communication, and thematically-defined communication mechanisms (sustainability communication, climate change communication, risk communication etc.); see for example, [35,36].

Here, we focus on indicator-based communication on sustainable development. Based on the indicator's characteristics, the communicated information may be either highly composed/aggregated or detailed; just proxies for main topics or exhaustive; technical or lay-focused, and so on. The typology of indicators, types of use (instrumental, conceptual, political), and users may be seen in [37–39]. In general, the public requires relatively simple, condensed, and easy to interpret information; it seems that just a limited number of indicators are sufficient. By contrast, professionals—policy makers, statisticians, and administrators need more detailed, disaggregated data and indicators suitable for further analyses. Politicians are somewhere in between: in terms of what they might be expected to do with indicators, they are closer to policy-makers (professionals) but in terms of the level of detail they might be expected to process, they are probably closer to the public. Specific users such as the business community, media, teachers, and so on then usually require thematically targeted information meeting their specific needs. Many major reports and assessments therefore publish special overviews and summaries for politicians, business, NGOs etc. Hence first we explore whether the format—namely number and type—of reported indicators may affect the intended audience.

The second variable is defined on the assumption that every assessment should have a clearly specified use (purpose) and audience. Interpretation of indicators results is an important part of indicator use: alongside their instrumental role, indicators can play a useful role in fostering social learning, for example, by helping to structure policy problems, build indicator frameworks, and clarify the various interpretations concerning the information indicators convey. An important aspect is the use of target values—policy objectives, legislative limits and standards, sustainability reference values etc. Thus SDGs may be assessed according to a desirable development in time (trend analysis) or according to relevant target values (distance to target approach) (See more in [40–42]). Since SDGs reports also employ compound indicators—indices—it is important to keep in mind both the pros and cons of their usage [43–45]. Lastly, it is necessary to distinguish the statistical use of information the purpose of which is to describe reality without any interpretation. With indicators the purpose is, specifically, to evaluate the development of policies and their impact on the state of affairs [34,46].

The last variable—complexity—regards selection of the indicators. Indicators always make the measured concept (more) complete but it in the case of the SDGs this criterion is of the utmost importance because of the low level of conceptualization of Goals and targets. To explore this variable, we look into the link between the employed indicators in each report and the Global indicator framework [6]. Although the Framework is a dynamic structure that will be probably be refined and specified to some extent building on experience and new indicator methodologies, we may assume it will provide firm guidance for both global assessments as well as for conducting national and thematic reviews of the Agenda 2030 [47]. Therefore, this variable shows to what extent the analyzed reports employ the framework (i.e., its indicators) assuming that it would secure some consistency among assessments conducted by different actors and/or at different times. Ideally, metadata of all used indicators (definitions, data sources, uncertainties, etc.) would be checked across all analyzed documents to identify sources of differences in results—different data, different indicators, methodologies, or just different terminology. Despite the importance of such information, it exceeds the scope of this article; however, we checked consistency among all indicators employed in the four analyzed reports and in the framework (name and rationale of indicators) (Table 3) as inexplicable differences in results might raise doubts among statisticians and experts.

Table 3. Consistency check of indicators in the four analyzed reports and the Global indicator framework (An example of the Goal 11, selected targets 11.1, 11.2, 11.6 and 11.7).

Goal 11 Make Cities and Human Settlements Inclusive, Safe, reSilient and Sustainable				
Global indicator framework (IAEG-SDGs)	The Sustainable Development Goals Report 2017	Sustainable development in the European Union	SDGs: Are the rich countries ready?	SDG Index and Dashboards Report 2017
Target 11.1 By 2030, ensure access for all to adequate, safe and affordable housing and basic services and upgrade slums				
11.1.1 Proportion of urban population living in slums, informal settlements or inadequate housing	Proportion of urban population living in slums	Poor dwelling conditions	n.a.	n.a.
Target 11.2 By 2030, provide access to safe, affordable, accessible and sustainable transport systems for all, improving road safety, notably by expanding public transport, with special attention to the needs of those in vulnerable situations, women, children, persons with disabilities and older persons				

Table 3. *Cont.*

Goal 11 Make Cities and Human Settlements Inclusive, Safe, reSilient and Sustainable				
11.2.1 Proportion of population that has convenient access to public transport, by sex, age and persons with disabilities	n.a.	Access to public transport	n.a.	n.a.
Target 11.6. By 2030, reduce the adverse per capita environmental impact of cities, including by paying special attention to air quality and municipal and other waste management				
11.6.2 Annual mean levels of PM2.5 and PM10 in cities	Proportion of urban population living in areas meeting WHO air quality PM2.5 standard	Concentration of particulate matter	Particulate matter, share of population exposed to >15 μg/cbm	PM2.5 in urban areas (μg/m^3)
11.7 By 2030, provide universal access to safe, inclusive and accessible, green and public spaces, in particular for women and children, older persons and persons with disabilities				
11.7.2 Proportion of persons victim of physical or sexual harassment, in the previous 12 months	n.a.	n.a.	n.a.	n.a.
Indicators used in the assessments not linked to the Global indicator framework				
n.a.	n.a.	Population living in households suffering from noise	Rooms per person	Rent burden (% disposable income)

6. Results

This section provides an overview of the main findings based on the three variables defined in the research framework.

Report: The Sustainable Development Goals Report 2017

The Sustainable Development Goals Report 2017 published by the UN Department of Economic and Social Affairs (UNDESA) reviews progress towards the 17 Goals in the second year of implementation of Agenda 2030. It employs 100 indicators to monitor the achievement of SDGs that are fully based on the Global indicator framework. Selection of indicators is not intended to represent the SDG targets according to their importance as all Goals and targets are equally important and will need to be addressed by the appropriate indicators [31]. The first part of the report—an Overview—emphasizes key global results in all 17 Goals. Clear short messages are accompanied by simple graphics (symbols, charts, maps). The analytical part of the report then presents more detailed information in various formats based on data availability—global results or figures disaggregated by the standard UN country groupings (Sub-Saharan Africa, Oceania, Northern Africa and Western Asia, Central and Southern Asia, Europe and Northern America, Latin America and the Caribbean, Australia and New Zealand, and Eastern and South-Eastern Asia). The indicators mostly show trend developments or only the last available year.

Several findings may be drawn from the report analysis: The first regards its communication power. The report is not very voluminous as it contains concise and condensed information. The 8-page Overview part is appropriately designed for politicians and the general public (and perhaps specific groups such as educators etc.). The analytical part seems to be more appropriate for professionals—policy makers, experts, specialized NGOs etc.). Indicators provide a statistical description of the state of affairs and a trend analysis over several years or just a simple visualization of the time development between two times in both global and regional scope. Global objectives for the Goals are used for the results interpretation when available. Thus, the report is appropriate for a broad audience interested in global development issues.

Report: Sustainable development in the European Union: Monitoring report on progress towards the SDGs in an EU context

The European Commission—or *sensu stricto* Eurostat, the statistical agency of the EU—monitors in this report the "next steps for a sustainable European future and European action for sustainability" [34].

Progress in all 28 EU member states is assessed by 100 indicators; each Goal has six indicators primarily attributed to it (Goals 14 and 17 have only five). Forty-one out of the 100 indicators are multi-purpose, that is, they are used to monitor more than one SDG. The indicators are not based on the Global indicator framework (despite there are many overlaps) but with a few exceptions they stem from already existing indicator sets used for monitoring long-term EU policies, such as the EU Sustainable Development Indicators, the Europe 2020 headline indicators, performance and impact indicators of the Strategic Plan 2016–2020, and so on. Like the above UN report, the EU Monitoring report offers an overall picture of the EU's development (aggregated EU-28 level) but it also looks into disaggregated data for all member states. Whenever possible (in 16 cases), the calculation of indicator trends takes into account concrete objectives set in relevant EU policies and strategies. All indicators are interpreted also by trend—towards or from the objective or desirable path (even for indicators without quantitative objectives Eurostat has developed a method showing the pace and direction of indicator development). Besides the main bulky document, a 20-page "Overview of progress towards the SDGs in an EU context" published separately presents a first statistical overview of short-term trends (five years) relating to the SDGs in the EU by easy-to-grasp symbols for the same indicators as the main report.

The main report is quite extensive (372 pages) and it is likely to be assigned to policy makers and professionals. Although the abridged Overview is just a brochure it is still an information-rich document—the number of indicators is quite large to be read and understood as a whole. In both publications, figures, charts and symbols create a false impression of even more indicators, orientation and correct understanding of which is not easy, in particular for lay people. This makes not only complicated reading but also obscures understanding of the SDGs operationalization. In addition, some indicators (e.g., agricultural factor income, low work intensity, relative median at-risk-of-poverty gap) are not intuitively understandable in terms of meaning, interpretation, or relation to other indicators and objectives.

The EU SDG indicator set is the result of the official/political initiative involving a wide consultation process among Member States' statistical authorities, European Council Committees, Commission services, the European Statistical Advisory Committee, members of academia and various international and non-governmental organizations. Thus, a thorough discussion on all Goals and targets may be assumed. Despite the EU having its own legitimate priorities for both domestic and international agendas, differences in operationalization (demonstrated by different indicators and their interpretation) may be viewed as (i) an inability or unwillingness to come to conclusions on the definitions of Goals and targets and/or (ii) taking into account "policy relevance from an EU perspective, availability, country coverage, data freshness and quality". Policy relevance from an EU perspective may denote that the employed indicators are related exclusively to the objectives of the European policies. Then in fact, they would measure only what has been measured in the EU anyway, meaning unclear. However, the "SDGs implementation" in terms of measurement is supposed to help to identify the role of European countries in a global effort for sustainability as well as to contribute to SDGs operationalization by bringing well-elaborated and justified regional perspectives

Report: SDGs: Are the rich countries ready?

This report [34] examines how exclusively high-income countries are currently performing in SDGs achievement. In total 34 "snapshot indicators", two per Goal, were selected based on the following three criteria: (i) Feasibility: Data must be available today in good quality at least for OECD countries; (ii) Suitability: The indicator should represent the—often multifaceted—Goal in a broad sense like a headline indicator; there should be a close conceptual fit between Goal and indicator; the indicators should be appropriate for the particular challenges of economically advanced nations; (iii) Relevance: The indicator should stand a good chance of becoming an actual part of the SDG monitoring system as currently being discussed by the Inter-Agency Expert Group for SDGs (In 2015 the United Nations Statistical Commission created the IAEG-SDGs and tasked it with developing and implementing the Global indicator framework for the Goals and targets of the 2030 Agenda) (IAEG-SDGs).

The 34 reported indicators have a plausible potential for communication on sustainability provided there is a thoughtful process of indicators selection. Such "headline indicators" would, by definition, capture the most important aspects of each Goal but they could not express their full operationalization. The indicators passing the above criteria (feasibility, suitability and relevance) were selected from a broad pool of global indicators—the Global indicator framework [6], SDGs monitoring indicators [48], and Sustainable Governance Indicators (a framework with 136 indicators) [49]. The report offers an overall "country league" ranking based on each indicator and SDG index (calculated as an unweighted average of all 34 indicators). The former benchmarks countries' performance to the five best performing countries and thus compares each country with the realistically achievable results of their peers. The latter provides results of the first attempt for an integrated view of countries' SDGs performance. Lucid visualization by radial charts for country profiles and bar charts for country rankings provide an evidence base for policymakers, businesses, and civil society to act.

An indicator selection—although based on three robust criteria—is inevitably an arbitrary decision always raising conceptual and methodological concerns. Other indicators would likely provide different rankings, different interpretation, different uncertainties, and so on. Another prerequisite of the credible indicator-based assessment is full comparability of data and indicators (in terms of sources, definitions, methodology, and interpretation), in particular for such a scientifically and politically sensitive task as country ranking (naming and faming—or shaming, is still the usual interpretation of results). In that regard, some indicators are not methodologically comparable or have low information value on/for some countries (secondary school attainment), are irrelevant (ocean health), or are not unambiguously interpretable (indicators using GDP ratio). The resulting numerical ladders look nice and scientific but they may not be justified by correct numbers.

Report: SDG Index and Dashboards Report 2017

This report was prepared by a team of independent experts of the Sustainable Development Solutions Network (Sustainable Development Solutions Network is an independent global network of research centers, universities and technical institutions aiming to mobilize scientific and technical expertise for problem-solving in relation to sustainable development. It was initiated by the UN in 2012) and Bertelsmann Stiftung (Bertelsmann Stiftung is a German private operating foundation). For 83, or 99 resp. (OECD countries have more accurate and better data available across a wide range of indicators, so 16 additional variables created an Augmented SDG Index for the OECD countries), of the used indicators, the official SDG indicators proposed by the Global indicator framework are employed where possible. New data and improvements in methodology are major changes from the previous year's report. It strengthens the legitimacy and credibility of the SDGs operationalization; however, it is not a global multi-stakeholder consensus on SDGs assessment but an expert-based effort. It seeks to assess in particular the adverse "spillovers" (Positive and negative spillover effects are called "externalities" in economic literature)—development patterns of the rich countries that may hinder the ability of poorer countries' to achieve the SDGs (e.g., high consumption levels, banking secrecy and tax havens, weapons exports, etc.). The underlying assumption is that traditional SDG indicators mostly ignore these spillover effects and therefore favor the high-income countries tending to generate them to a significant extent. Thus, the report identifies and measures three groups of the most important SDG-related spillovers and misuses of the global commons: environmental spillovers; spillovers related to the economy, finance, and governance, and security spillovers. Both the SDG index and dashboard use the same indicators.

The geographical coverage is 157 (out of the 193) UN member states. They can benchmark themselves against their peers—individual countries or relevant geopolitical regions (OECD countries, Eastern Europe and Central Asia, Latin America and the Caribbean, East and South Asia, Middle East and North Africa, Sub-Saharan Africa)—as well as against the Goal thresholds (absolute quantitative thresholds are used when possible, for example, zero poverty, universal school completion, full gender equality). These thresholds are derived from the SDGs and their targets or other official sources; when no such thresholds exist, an average of the top five performers is used. The importance (relevance) of the assessment is emphasized by comparing the country's performance on the SDG Index to other common development metrics: GDP per capita, subjective wellbeing, Human Development Index, Environmental Performance Index, Global Competitiveness Index and Global Peace Index. The key users of the report results are governments; besides them, it explicitly aims at other SDG stakeholders such as businesses, civil society organizations, foundations, universities, media, and others who "have a vital role in turning the SDGs into practical tools for explaining sustainable development" [33].

7. Conclusions

The current UN Sustainable Development Goals will frame global action until 2030. The SDGs are already firmly embedded in a policy framework: during the course of their development they went through a political process and broad political negotiations. For monitoring and assessment of global sustainability an agreed set of global indicators was designed [6]. If this framework is used inconsistently, for example, if only arbitrarily selected indicators, additional indicators to some targets, compounds (indices) created from some indicators, and so on are used, the results will be commensurately inconsistent, incomprehensible, or even dubious. Despite the fact that SDG assessments are not intended to replace or compete with other SDG monitoring and indicators, in fact they do. If they motivated intergovernmental or/and national agencies to develop a suite of monitoring systems supporting the SDG indicators, such testing and experimenting with various indicators and indices would be well justified. However, the current inconsistent messages conveyed by the four analyzed SDGs assessments may be interpreted not as a call for better data and full conceptualization of all targets but as a rash exercise of researchers and experts almost randomly quantifying any SDG metric at hand. It is needless to say that it may open room for skepticism concerning the role of indicators as policy support instruments.

A flagrant example of inconsistent results is the SDG index. Regardless of the fact that the SDGs indicators have not been primarily designed for this purpose (therefore their authors have not handled issues of their substitutability, doublecounting, autocorrelations etc.), the SDG index is an attractive idea. Aggregated indicators, composites, indices and so on have always drawn attention due to their main advantage—simplifying communication of even complex issues. The real problem occurs when two similar indices show very different results. In particular, when the indices are named the same, or similarly assess the same facts or phenomena, they show remarkably distinct results. Only experts are, in fact, usually aware of the conceptual and/or methodological differences and therefore they understand the ensuing differences in results. While some results show good consistency of ranking (e.g., Sweden—1st place, Germany—6th place, etc.), the Czech Republic may serve as a country where inconsistent results may be politically harmful: One SDG index [32] ranks it in 24th place in country ranking (out of 34 assessed OECD countries)—that is, among the worst third—while a similar SDG index [33] places the same country at a very positive fifth place in the global competition (among 157 assessed countries). Unlike the Czech improvement—or more precisely "positive difference" of 19 places—the US lost 13 places (29. vs. 42.), Mexico 24 places (24. vs. 58.), and Turkey 34 places (33. vs. 67.). These differences are not caused just by different country samples—countries are placed differently since the indices are different. After getting such unclear overall information, assessment of particular targets also requires careful reading and some knowledge of interpretation. For example, a Czech reader interested in the topic of poverty (Goal 1), finds out that the global number of people living in extreme poverty fell significantly while people at risk of poverty in Europe are still numerous and thus it is moving away from sustainability objectives; however, while the Czech Republic is currently doing best at this indicator (much better than more affluent Germany or UK) it does not tell us anything about whether this is at a sustainable rate. Every assessment thus provides an important piece of the SDG puzzle; however, putting them together and seeing the whole picture it not a trivial enterprise.

Sustainability assessment is a tremendously difficult task, see for example, [50,51]. Besides developing new scenarios, models, and indicators it is necessary to assess the existing ones and account for their strengths and weaknesses, in particular in their role as policy support instruments—systematic research into that must continue, in particular in scientific journals. Experimenting with various SDGs rankings and indices may have a clear and acceptable rationale in terms of context analysis, correlation calculations, sensitivity analysis, and other numerical testing. We argue that different and inconsistent results published publicly and mostly channeled to the same audience (mostly politicians and policy makers) may cause serious misunderstanding or doubts on the capability to assess SDGs implementation: Have countries' performances improved or worsened suddenly and inexplicably? Has the methodology changed and measured the same phenomenon differently? Have the indicators evinced big errors/uncertainties? Etc.

As mentioned above, the SDGs (i.e., Goals and targets) are firmly embedded in a policy framework and their operationalization has been mostly done by indicators. Because such an approach generates many caveats [7,52], it is absolutely necessary that the expert community reach full consensus on the indicator framework and its use. As emerging needs show, the global set of individual indicators should be complemented by a set of key (headline) indicators while an SDG index raises more doubts than gains so far (similarly to other sustainability indices mostly having negligible use in policy making). An instrumental role in this process belongs to the IAEG-SDGs. The UN Statistical Commission foresees the possibility of yearly refinements to the Framework and of two comprehensive reviews in 2020 and in 2025 [53]. Such a clear work plan with the strong leadership of the UN gives a chance to replace the "survival of the fittest" approach (very appropriate in the context of research published in scientific journals) and effectively make progress in the understanding of the SDGs at global level. In parallel, due to national adaptations of the Goals, targets, and related indicators many complementary data sets and indicators for national and regional SDGs assessment will emerge over time.

Author Contributions: The paper has resulted from cooperation of all authors. They delivered equal shares of work.

Acknowledgments: This work has been supported by the research program "Progres Q16" funded by Charles University.

Conflicts of Interest: The authors declare no conflict of interest. The founding sponsors had no role in the design of the study; in the collection, analyses, or interpretation of data; in the writing of the manuscript, and in the decision to publish the results.

References

1. Fernando, J.L. The power of unsustainable development: What is to be done? *ANNALS Am. Acad. Political Soc. Sci.* **2003**, *590*, 6–34. [CrossRef]
2. Mastny, L. (Ed.) *State of the World 2015: Confronting Hidden Threats to Sustainability*; Island Press: New York, NY, USA, 2015.
3. Hák, T.; Janoušková, S.; Moldan, B. Closing the sustainability gap: 30 years after "Our Common Future", society lacks meaningful stories and relevant indicators to make the right decisions and build public support. *Ecol. Indic.* **2018**, *87*, 193–195. [CrossRef]
4. Dahl, A.L. Achievements and gaps in indicators for sustainability. *Ecol. Indic.* **2012**, *17*, 14–19. [CrossRef]
5. United Nations. Transforming our world: The 2030 agenda for sustainable development. In *Resolution Adopted by the General Assembly on 25 September 2015*; RES/70/1; UN: New York, NY, USA, 2015.
6. United Nations. Work of the Statistical Commission pertaining to the 2030 Agenda for Sustainable Development. In *Resolution Adopted by the General Assembly on 6 July 2017*; A/RES/71/313; UN: New York, NY, USA, 2017.
7. Hák, T.; Janoušková, S.; Moldan, B. Sustainable Development Goals: A need for relevant indicators. *Ecol. Indic.* **2016**, *60*, 565–573. [CrossRef]
8. United Nations. The future we want. In *Resolution Adopted by the General Assembly on 27 July 2012*; A/RES/66/288; UN: New York, NY, USA, 2012.

9. Ribeiro, T.; Volkery, A.; Pirc Velkavrh, A.; Vos, H.; Hoogeveen, Y. Assessment of Global Megatrends. The European Environment–State and Outlook 2010. EFP Brief No. 227. 2012. Available online: http://www.foresight-platform. eu/wp-content/uploads/2012/11/EFP-Brief-No.-227_Assessment-of-Global-Megatrends.pdf (accessed on 25 March 2018).
10. Harcourt, W. Sustainable Development: Who cares? *Development* **2002**, *45*, 3–5.
11. Sen, A. The ends and means of sustainability. *J. Hum. Dev. Capab.* **2013**, *14*, 6–20. [CrossRef]
12. Thompson, R.; Green, W. When sustainability is not a priority: An analysis of trends and strategies. *Int. J. Sustain. Higher Educ.* **2005**, *6*, 7–17. [CrossRef]
13. Adomßent, M.; Godemann, J. Sustainability communication: An integrative approach. In *Sustainability Communication*; Springer: Dordrecht, The Netherlands, 2011; pp. 27–37.
14. Newig, J.; Schulz, D.; Fischer, D.; Hetze, K.; Laws, N.; Lüdecke, G.; Rieckmann, M. Communication regarding sustainability: Conceptual perspectives and exploration of societal subsystems. *Sustainability* **2013**, *5*, 2976–2990. [CrossRef]
15. Lyytimäki, J.; Rosenström, U. Skeletons out of the closet: Effectiveness of conceptual frameworks for communicating sustainable development indicators. *Sustain. Dev.* **2008**, *16*, 301–313. [CrossRef]
16. Wardekker, J.A.; de Boer, J.; Kolkman, M.J.; van der Sluijs, J.P.; Buchanan, K.S.; de Jong, A.; van der Veen, A. *Tool Caloque Frame-Based Information Tools*; Klimaat voor Ruimte, Group Science, Technology and Society, Copernicus Institute: Utrecht, The Netherlands, 2009.
17. Godemann, J.; Michelsen, G. Sustainability Communication—An Introduction. In *Sustainability Communication*; Springer: Dordrecht, The Netherlands, 2011; pp. 3–11.
18. Sébastien, L.; Bauler, T.; Lehtonen, M. Can indicators bridge the gap between science and policy? An exploration into the (non) use and (non) influence of indicators in EU and UK policy making. *Nat. Cult.* **2014**, *9*, 316–343. [CrossRef]
19. Buckingham-Hatfield, S.; Evans, B. Achieving sustainability through environmental planning. In *Environmental Planning and Sustainability*; John Wiley & Sons: Chichester, UK, 1996; pp. 1–18.
20. Zaccai, E. Over two decades in pursuit of sustainable development: Influence, transformations, limits. *Environ. Dev.* **2012**, *1*, 79–90. [CrossRef]
21. De Vries, B.J.; Petersen, A.C. Conceptualizing sustainable development: An assessment methodology connecting values, knowledge, worldviews and scenarios. *Ecol. Econ.* **2009**, *68*, 1006–1019. [CrossRef]
22. Kuhlman, T.; Farrington, J. What is sustainability? *Sustainability* **2010**, *2*, 3436–3448. [CrossRef]
23. Brundtland, G.H. *Report of the World Commission on Environment and Development: "Our Common Future"*; United Nations: New York, NY, USA, 1987.
24. Waas, T.; Hugé, J.; Block, T.; Wright, T.; Benitez-Capistros, F.; Verbruggen, A. Sustainability Assessment and Indicators: Tools in a Decision-Making Strategy for Sustainable Development. *Sustainability* **2014**, *6*, 5512–5534. [CrossRef]
25. Tasaki, T.; Kameyama, Y.; Hashimoto, S.; Moriguchi, Y.; Harasawa, H. A survey of national sustainable development indicators. *Int. J. Sustain. Dev.* **2010**, *13*, 337–361. [CrossRef]
26. Böhringer, C.; Jochem, P.E. Measuring the immeasurable—A survey of sustainability indices. *Ecol. Econ.* **2007**, *63*, 1–8. [CrossRef]
27. Stokstad, E. Sustainable goals from UN under fire. *Science* **2015**, *347*, 702–703. [CrossRef] [PubMed]
28. Holden, E.; Linnerud, K.; Banister, D.; Schwanitz, V.J.; Wierling, A. *The Imperatives of Sustainable Development: Needs, Justice, Limits*; Routledge: London, UK, 2017.
29. Bunge, M. What is a quality of life indicator? *Soc. Indic. Res.* **1975**, *2*, 65–79. [CrossRef]
30. Burford, G.; Tamás, P.; Harder, M.K. Can We Improve Indicator Design for Complex Sustainable Development Goals? A Comparison of a Values-Based and Conventional Approach. *Sustainability* **2016**, *8*, 861. [CrossRef]
31. United Nations. *The Sustainable Development Goals Report 2017*; UN: New York, NY, USA, 2017.
32. Kroll, C. *SDGs: Are the Rich Countries Ready?* Bertelsmann Stiftung: Gütersloh, Germany, 2015.
33. Sachs, J.; Schmidt-Traub, G.; Kroll, C.; Durand-Delacre, D.; Teksoz, K. *SDG Index and Dashboards Report 2017: International Spillovers in Achieving the Goals*; Bertelsmann Stiftung and Sustainable Development Solutions Network: Paris, France; New York, NY, USA, 2017.
34. Eurostat. *Sustainable Development in the European Union—Monitoring Report on Progress towards the SDGs in an EU Context*; Eurostat: Luxembourg, 2017.

35. Fischer, D.; Lüdecke, G.; Godemann, J.; Michelsen, G.; Newig, J.; Rieckmann, M.; Schulz, D. Sustainability Communication. In *Sustainability Science*; Heinrichs, H., Martens, P., Michelsen, G., Wiek, A., Eds.; Springer: Dordrecht, The Netherlands, 2016.

36. McGreavy, B. Addressing the Complexities of Boundary Work in Sustainability Science through Communication. *Sustainability* **2013**, *5*, 4195–4221. [CrossRef]

37. Gudmundsson, H.; Hall, R.P.; Marsden, G.; Zietsman, J. *Sustainable Transportation: Indicators, Frameworks, and Performance Management*; Springer: Berlin/Heidelberg, Germany, 2016.

38. European Environmental Agency. *Environmental Indicators: Typology and Overview*; Technical report No 25; EEA: Copenhagen, Denmark, 1999.

39. Hák, T.; Moldan, B.; Dahl, A. *Sustainability Indicators: A Scientific Assessment*; Island Press: Washington, DC, USA, 2007.

40. Moldan, B.; Janoušková, S.; Hák, T. How to understand and measure environmental sustainability: Indicators and targets. *Ecol. Indic.* **2012**, *17*, 4–13. [CrossRef]

41. Eurostat. *Getting Messages across Using Indicators—A Handbook Based on Experiences from Assessing Sustainable Development Indicators*; Eurostat: Luxembourg, 2014.

42. Castellani, V.; Benini, L.; Sala, S.; Pant, R. A distance-to-target weighting method for Europe 2020. *Int. J. Life Cycle Assess.* **2016**, *21*, 1159–1169. [CrossRef]

43. Nardo, M.; Saisana, M.; Saltelli, A.; Tarantola, S.; Hoffman, A.; Giovannini, E. Handbook on Constructing Composite Indicators. OECD Statistics Working Papers. 2005. Available online: http://www.oecd-ilibrary.org/docserver/download/533411815016.pdf?expires=1521999211&id=id& accname=guest&checksum=71C6B39D88794FDA8445133A5073781A (accessed on 25 March 2018).

44. Mayer, A.L. Strengths and weaknesses of common sustainability indices for multidimensional systems. *Environ. Int.* **2008**, *34*, 277–291. [CrossRef] [PubMed]

45. Mori, K.; Christodoulou, A. Review of sustainability indices and indicators: Towards a new City Sustainability Index (CSI). *Environ. Impact Assess. Rev.* **2012**, *32*, 94–106. [CrossRef]

46. Yli-Viikari, A. Confusing messages of sustainability indicators. *Local Environ.* **2009**, *14*, 891–903. [CrossRef]

47. Adams, B.; Karen, J. 2030 Agenda and the SDGs: Indicator Framework, Monitoring and Reportng. Global Policy Watch 10. 2016. Available online: http://osthailand.nic.go.th/files/image/sdgs/GPW10_2016_03_18.pdf (accessed on 25 March 2015).

48. SDSN. *Indicators and a Monitoring Framework the Sustainable Development Goals: Launching a Data Revolution*; Sustainable Development Solutions Network: New York, NY, USA, 2015; Available online: http://unsdsn.org/resources/publications/indicators/ (accessed on 25 March 2015).

49. Bertelsmann Stiftung. Policy Performance and Governance Capacities in the OECD and EU: Sustainable Governance Indicators 2017. Bertelsmann Stiftung, 2017. Available online: http://www.sgi-network.org/docs/2017/basics/SGI2017_Overview.pdf. (accessed on 25 March 2015).

50. Dizdaroglu, D. The role of indicator-based sustainability assessment in policy and the decision-making process: A review and outlook. *Sustainability* **2017**, *9*, 1018. [CrossRef]

51. Konys, A. An Ontology-Based Knowledge Modelling for a Sustainability Assessment Domain. *Sustainability* **2018**, *10*, 300. [CrossRef]

52. Yonehara, A.; Saito, O.; Hayashi, K.; Nagao, M.; Yanagisawa, R.; Matsuyama, K. The role of evaluation in achieving the SDGs. *Sustain. Sci.* **2017**, *12*, 969–973. [CrossRef]

53. United Nations. Report of the Inter-Agency and Expert Group on SDG Indicators. In Proceedings of the Economic and Social Council, New York, NY, USA, 6–9 March 2018; E/CN.3/2018/2.

sustainability

MDPI

Article

Measure or Management?—Resource Use Indicators for Policymakers Based on Microdata by Households

Johannes Buhl [1], Christa Liedtke [1,2], Jens Teubler [1,*], Katrin Bienge [1] and Nicholas Schmidt [3]

[1] Wuppertal Institut fuer Klima, Umwelt, Energie gGmbH, Division Sustainable Production and Consumption, Doeppersberg 19, 42103 Wuppertal, Germany; johannesbuhlsonthofen@gmail.com (J.B.); christa.liedtke@wupperinst.org (C.L.); katrin.bienge@wupperinst.org (K.B.)

[2] Industrial Design, Folkwang University of the Arts, Klemensborn 39, 45239 Essen, Germany

[3] Faculty of Management and Economics, Ruhr University Bochum, Universitätsstraße 150, 44801 Bochum, Germany; nicholas.schmidt1995@gmail.com

* Correspondence: jens.teubler@wupperinst.org

Received: 28 September 2018; Accepted: 16 November 2018; Published: 28 November 2018

Abstract: Sustainable Development Goal 12 (SDG 12) requires sustainable production and consumption. One indicator named in the SDG for resource use is the (national) material footprint. A method and disaggregated data basis that differentiates the material footprint for production and consumption according to, e.g., sectors, fields of consumption as well as socioeconomic criteria does not yet exist. We present two methods and its results for analyzing resource the consumption of private households based on microdata: (1) an indicator based on representative expenditure data in Germany and (2) an indicator based on survey data from a web tool. By these means, we aim to contribute to monitoring the Sustainable Development Goals, especially the sustainable management and efficient use of natural resources. Indicators based on microdata ensure that indicators can be disaggregated by socioeconomic characteristics like age, sex, income, or geographic location. Results from both methods show a right-skewed distribution of the Material Footprint in Germany and, for instance, an increasing Material Footprint with increasing household income. The methods enable researchers and policymakers to evaluate trends in resource use and to differentiate between lifestyles and along socioeconomic characteristics. This, in turn, would allow us to tailor sustainable consumption policies to household needs and restrictions.

Keywords: sustainable production and consumption; resource indicator; sustainable development goals; material footprint; household consumption; microdata

1. Introduction

Meeting the resource demand of a growing global consumer class increasingly affects the environment and places a burden on climate and ecosystems [1]. Since household consumption and production for consumer goods are at the core of the present resource-intensive lifestyles, it is important to analyze the behavior of private households and assist them in transforming their routines into more sustainable ones. This means providing new technologies, products, and services that enable, perhaps even stimulate, a resource-friendly life. Production and consumption in this sense form an interlaced system that can only be thought and developed in an integrated way.

Resource efficiency in the context of sustainable production and consumption is currently gaining attention on a national and international level. The current trend towards Product Service Systems (PSS) as an approach for increasing sustainability can contribute to a sustainable way of linking consumption and production [2–5]. Several attempts have been made to support the development of low-resource and socially accepted approaches of integrating production and consumption. Examples for this are the Consumer Information Program of the 10 Year Framework of Programmes on Sustainable Consumption and Production (10YFP) as well as the European Union with its Ecodesign Directive [6,7].

The Sustainable Development Goal 12 (SDG 12) "Ensure sustainable production and consumption patterns" integrates a wide range of stakeholders into the process of increasing sustainability in consumption and production [8]. However, the ambitious SDGs and their subgoals require appropriate indicators for measuring the status quo and the progress until 2030. There is a lack of indicators which are able to provide the necessary differentiation for socioeconomic characteristics like sex, age, or income [9] and fields of consumption like housing or mobility that hampers the process of providing improved assistance for producers and consumers in implementing more sustainable product-service systems and production and consumption patterns [10] as advocated by SDG 12.

Germany published its first sustainability strategy in 2002 and reports the progress towards its goals every four years [11]. This strategy includes different indicators for measuring the development of sustainability in Germany. The latest update from 2016 adopts the framework of the Sustainable Development Goals (SDGs). Besides this strategy, Germany implemented a National Program on Sustainable Consumption that aims to identify the relevant fields of action and adequate measures [12]. It gives five guiding principles for a sustainable consumption policy, for example enabling consumers to implement a sustainable way of consumption. In this respect, the German Program on Resource Efficiency (Progress II) demands the implementation of a National Program on Sustainable Consumption in order to promote resource efficiency in consumption [13]. Therefore the program strives to develop and improve its set of indicators for a better measurement of the effects of changes in consumption. Behavioral changes in favor of more resource efficient consumption are still hampered by obstacles such as a lack of information and personalized feedback applications. The National Program on Sustainable Consumption suggests providing such information by the use of assisting carbon and resource calculators [12].

Certain routines and social practices in consumption, as well as patterns in production and existing business models, complicate a change towards a more sustainable behavior [14]. Sustainable consumption requires sustainably designed product service systems and infrastructures [15]. It is only possible to shape both together and step by step. Progress or regression, as well as rebound effects, must be visible and therefore demonstrable. Indicators play a crucial role in setting up goals and measuring progress in this regard. They simplify the complex cause-effect chains within our societies, economies, and with our environment. On a national level, indicators can be used to develop pathways for sustainability or to identify trends. Scenario developers usually use these goals and indicators to define a target corridor in comparison to a status quo or business-as-usual. They are but a tool for aggregated measurement of impacts and not their management.

However, indicators can potentially also be a tool to evaluate and inform in a differentiated way by depicting and sometimes explaining the differences—with the means of modern societies almost in real time. This would make them relevant not only politically (programmes and measures), but also in everyday decision-making situations, whether in a company (products, infrastructures) or in a household (lifestyles). This can be achieved using microdata (e.g., from online surveys) and combining it with already existing methods.

Recent research has managed to quantify some levels of sustainable resource use. While the global material extraction has drastically increased over the last four decades (from 26.7 billion tonnes in 1970 to 75.6 billion tonnes in 2010) [16], material consumption levels in Europe already reached 40 tonnes per capita and more at the beginning of the century [17]. By comparison, Lettenmeier et al. calculated a sustainable level of only 8 tonnes of a Material Footprint (per person and year) [18], using the MIPS concept (Material Input Per unit of Service) This means a reduction by the factor five, which requires an appropriate consumer policy and education for sustainable consumption patterns [19]. MIPS (developed by Schmidt-Bleek in the 1990s [20]) provides micro-economic indicators for the resource use of households that include the extraction of materials with and without economic use (e.g., overburden from mining). Its methodology is based on Material-Flow-Accounting and compatible with similar input indicators such as cumulated energy demand (ced) or cumulated raw material demand (KRA). Its indicator Material Footprint can also be adapted to the currently suggested SDG 12 indicator with the same name. Recent methodological developments make use of improved LCA data [21–25].

Further research in the field also allowed us to differentiate between different household types (milieus) and their resource use, although limited to small samples of selected households using a diary approach. It could also be shown that the calculation of Material Footprints for households is compatible with methods for the calculation of Carbon Footprints, thus allowing us to compare lifestyles with high resource use but low carbon intensity and vice versa [21,26].

Two tools have developed that aim at supporting consumers in transforming their consumption patterns and are supposed to develop synergy effects by combining them. Buhl et al. [10] developed a Material Footprint (MF) indicator based on the MIPS concept and microeconomic expenditure data in Germany. This indicator was already used to analyze the behavior of households in Germany and the German federal state of North Rhine-Westphalia (NRW) and allows for differentiation between regions (here, the federal states of Germany and Germany itself), socioeconomic characteristics of households and between categories of consumption. The other method is based on microdata that is directly obtained from an online tool. The "Resource Calculator" [27] is a free online application that enables consumers to examine their consumption patterns by calculating their own Material Footprint. Consumers can also supply information about their socioeconomic characteristics on a voluntary and anonymous basis (such as age or years of schooling). Thus, the Resource Calculator provides an anonymized dataset for analyzing the resource use of private households that—in future—could provide a representative basis for a new indicator of consumption in the future using a consumer panel. The calculator itself could also be developed further as an interactive tool for real-time decision making in all-day routines and practices.

The aim of this paper is to contribute to the process of examining the consumption patterns of households and to provide the means for micro-economic SDG indicators. Using the example of natural resource use, the authors show how environmental indicators can be differentiated for private household types and categories of consumption. We posit that using microdata is a viable solution to distinguish between the age, sex, income, ethnicity, geographic location, and other characteristics as required by national policies in Germany [28–30]. We propose to enhance the present highly aggregated macro-oriented indicator system for SDG 12 with the help of disaggregating microeconomic data and indicators.

We hypothesize that a micro-based Resource Consumption Indicator could be an adequate tool to monitor consumer's Material Footprint and target achievement (measurement but also management). Differentiating indicators between arrays of consumption and different consumer groups reveal shifts and changes between arrays and groups that may otherwise stay undetected and camouflaged by aggregated macro indicators. Additionally, the online tool based Resource Lifestyle Footprint could help to facilitate achieving the given targets and address the different types of households and lifestyles appropriately in this process.

We start by introducing the data and methods that we used in Section 2: the Resource Consumption Indicator (R_{CI}) and the Resource Lifestyle Footprint (R_{LF}). The results are presented in Section 3, followed by a discussion of limitations and the derived implications in Section 3. In Section 5 (conclusion), we put the results into the context of research and consumer policies.

2. Methodology

The following section describes briefly the methods and data used for calculating the Material Footprints of both Resource Consumption Indicator and Resource Lifestyle Footprint. The Resource Consumption Indicator (1) relates top-down resource-intensities of consumption in a country to expenditures of consumers. The Resource Lifestyle Footprint (2) models the resources of product-services and their use bottom up. Both approaches account for the amount of extracted abiotic and biotic materials from nature and relate them annually on a per person or per capita basis.

2.1. The Resource Consumption Indicator (R_{CI})

The first approach is based on tables on international trade (see Reference [31] on multi-regional footprint analysis). These multi-regional Input-/Output tables (MRIO) allow for the accounting of globally extracted raw materials (alongside other indicators) for goods consumed within a country (including imports but excluding exports of an economy). By allocating these goods to the consumption of households, country-specific resource-intensities are that can be directly linked to country-specific household expenditures calculated (see also References [32,33]). This top-down model converts traded monetary value into the physical material use of households, thus linking the macro-economy with microdata on the level of households. It provides a holistic view of resource consumption and is consistent when comparing countries with each other. Thus, it can be used to generate representative data on the resource use of households in countries and to differentiate levels of resource consumption depending on socioeconomic characteristics in the microdata. Buhl et al. (2016) [10] successfully applied the resource intensities to household expenditure data for Germany in order to describe the Material Footprint (sum of globally induced resource extractions) of different households in the federal state of North-Rhine-Westphalia in Germany itself.

The weakness of this top-down approach is its inability to explain the differences between household types and their resource consumption sufficiently. The highly aggregated data with respect to resource intensities based on MRIO tables also does not allow the identification of specific product and service options for more sustainable measures by households or policies catering towards a more resource-efficient lifestyle. This is where bottom-up models can help to fill data gaps by focusing on the most relevant areas of consumption and disaggregating further into different services and products.

To measure private household consumption for the approach of the Resource Consumption Indicator, data from the German Survey of Household Income and Consumption (EVS) for the years 2003, 2008 and 2013 were used. The EVS is conducted by the Federal Statistical Office, using household expenditure as a proxy for consumption. The data are structured into eleven main categories and 152 subcategories according to the Classification of Individual Consumption per Purpose (COICOP). The analysis described here focuses on the eleven main categories. Furthermore, the EVS includes socioeconomic data and enables a differentiation between different groups of households or individuals, clustered by characteristics such as age or household net income [10].

Table 1 shows the summary statistics for the yearly expenditures of the main categories between 2003 and 2013 in Germany.

Table 1. The overview of selected variables and descriptive statistics of the EVS.

Variables	N (Sample Size)			Mean			Std.Dev. (Standard Deviation)		
	2003	2008	2013	2003	2008	2013	2003	2008	2013
Food and beverages	42,744	44,088	42,792	3634.7	3831.69	3825.74	1933.35	2060.8	2100.27
Clothing	42,744	44,088	42,792	1646.34	1514.8	1577.43	1572.12	1569.62	1665.11
Housing	42,744	44,088	42,792	9449.24	9642.25	10,746.5	6337.31	4900.78	5129.06
Furnishing	42,744	44,088	42,792	1900.51	1624.52	1671.71	4191.31	3805.17	3702.8
Health	42,744	44,088	42,792	1332.44	1438.11	1552.15	3822.46	3694.82	4232.48
Transport	42,744	44,088	42,792	4610.35	4687.23	4628.17	11,824.1	10,489.9	11,369.6
Communication	42,744	44,088	42,792	896.51	833.13	821.45	668.83	527.96	554.92
Recreation and Culture	42,744	44,088	42,792	3807.11	3701.09	3575.99	4002.47	4512.23	4743.77
Education	42,744	44,088	42,792	298.38	292.53	272.98	865.56	1046.73	1070.36
Hotels	42,744	44,088	42,792	1477.48	1654.37	1782.77	1890.12	2143.4	2316.07
Miscellaneous	42,744	44,088	42,792	1379.76	1351.69	1297.62	1892.59	2103.99	1948.51
Household size	42,744	44,088	42,792	2.43	2.28	2.10	1.23	1.17	1.09
NRW	9223	7708	7823	1	1	1	0	0	0

Data: German Survey of Household Income and Consumption, 2003, 2008, 2013. Expenditure data in Euro. "Household size" and "NRW" (i.e., living in the federal state of NRW in Germany) represent socio-demographics of the sample.

The expenditures of households in the EVS were related to so-called resource intensity factors (household resource use per Euro). These factors stem from multi-regional input-output analyses

(MRIO) of economy-wide material flow accounts and the continuous household budget surveys for Germany in the year 2005. Table 2 provides an overview of the average resource intensities in the main consumption categories [34].

Resource intensities allow the measurement of the impact of private consumption on the environment and can be used to calculate the Material Footprint of consumption. The calculation of the Material Footprint based on microdata on expenditure (EVS) and respective resource intensities of the main COICOP categories are described in Appendix A.

The further analysis is based on the differentiation between the main COICOP categories from "Food and beverages" to "Miscellaneous". However, Buhl et al. (2016) show an application of the method that further differentiates within the main COICOP category "Transport" by calculating resource intensities for specific transport services like local and long distance trains, air travel, or the use of second-hand cars [10].

Table 2. The resource intensities of private household consumption in Germany.

Consumption Categories	Resource Intensity (kg/€)
Food and beverages	5.09
Housing etc.	3.18
Furnishings etc.	2.99
Transport	1.50
Restaurants and hotels	1.40
Health	0.60
Education	0.48
Recreation and culture	0.41
Communication	0.37
Clothing	0.19
Miscellaneous	0.19

Based on Buhl et al., 2016 [10]. Data: Buhl and Acosta 2015 [32].

2.2. The Resource Lifestyle Footprint (R_{LF})

The "Resource Calculator" tool (see https://www.ressourcen-rechner.de/) provides a footprint of a household's lifestyles. It calculates the Material Footprint of products, their services, and usage directly and over the whole lifecycle of their production, use, and end-of-life (including material extractions in other countries). It combines quantitative (and often physical) survey data on household consumption with survey data on socioeconomic characteristics and household attitudes in order to calculate an individual or lifestyle footprint. This approach allows us to identify drivers and barriers of resource use and matches socio-demographic characteristics, lifestyle decisions, subjective attitudes or assessments, social norms, and individual preferences as well as budget restrictions to the individual footprint or ecological backpack (see References [35,36] on the concept). Resource use can thus be reduced not only by consuming resource efficient products, but also by improving the service these products provide. This bottom-up model has been successfully tested in several studies ([18,21,26]) and is compliant with the Material Flow Accounting (MFA) and Life Cycle Assessment (LCA) methodology. It is also compatible with generic databases for lifecycle inventories as well as assessments of output indicators such as carbon footprints (as shown by References [22,23]).

The calculator generates a growing database because of its permanent online accessibility. Besides questions regarding the most important fields of consumption like housing and mobility, users can voluntarily and anonymously provide data concerning their socioeconomic characteristics. This was surveyed alongside other subjective attitudes and norms such as relative household income in comparison, subjective health or subjective well-being. Table 3 lists the different areas of private consumption in the Resource Calculator.

Table 3. The description of consumption categories in the Resource Calculator.

Groups of Consumption in Resource Calculator	Description of Category
Nutrition	diets, food waste, and consumption of foodstuffs and drinks
Housing	buildings, heat, and electricity use
Consumer Goods	appliances, clothes, furniture
Mobility	day-to-day travel with cars, bikes, public transport
Leisure	hobbies, sports, cultural activities
Vacation	vacation travel and accommodation

The Resource Calculator application was advertised via different channels such as the website of the Wuppertal Institute, online blogs on sustainable living, and reviews of product testing magazines. Between the launch on 25 February 2015 and 13 February 2017, 49,037 persons participated without any incentives. Data preparation and the removal of invalid and implausible responses left a database of 44,514 being analyzed. For a more detailed description, necessary transformations and underlying assumptions see Buhl et al., 2017 [27]. Table 4 comprehends the most relevant dimensions and variables surveyed by the Resource Calculator. Socioeconomic, personal, and household characteristics, as well as subjective assessments and other lifestyle features, complement disaggregated information on the Material Footprint.

Table 4. The overview of variables and descriptive statistics of the Resource Calculator.

Statistic	N	Mean	Std. Dev.	Min	Max
Personal characteristics					
Female	26,103	0.62	0.49	0	1
Age	24,596	36.00	12.00	18	71
Schooling years	26,118	14.00	3.20	9	21
Occupational status	18,463	3.00	1.10	1	4
Unemployed	18,463	0.14	0.35	0	1
Household characteristics					
Household size	44,238	2.20	1.00	1.00	6.00
Number of children	9119	1.60	0.71	1	4
Size of dwelling (m^2)	30,482	95.00	47.00	7.00	300.00
Subjective assessments					
Subjective health	17,297	1.30	0.57	−1	2
Relative income	22,125	−0.41	1.00	−2	2
Life satisfaction	26,041	7.30	1.80	1	10
Social ties satisfaction	17,690	1.00	0.71	−2	2
Lifestyle					
Diet	44,317	2.20	0.84	1	4
Vegetarian	44,317	0.33	0.47	0	1
Hobby hours	44,091	8.00	12.00	0.00	75.00
Days on vacation	44,056	15.00	13.00	0	81
Trips (in km)	44,086	220.00	327.00	0.00	1,800.00
Material Footprints (kg)					
Housing	44,068	8722.00	4059.00	45	26,804
Consumer goods	44,068	2859.00	1161.00	2	6936
Nutrition	44,068	5160.00	1323.00	82	9145
Leisure	44,069	446.00	639.00	0	5113
Mobility	43,456	6682.00	6407.00	1	39,447
Vacations	44,068	1525.00	1532.00	0	10,200
Overall Material Footprint	44,068	25,897.00	10,041.00	2.711	76,570

Note: Descriptive statistics include the number of observations (N), mean, standard deviation (Std.Dev.), minimum (Min.) and maximum (Max.) of observations. "Trips" is the distance in km for trips and events during the past month. "Days on vacation" are days on vacation overall in the past year. "Hobby hour" are the hours overall spent on hobbies on average per month. "Social ties satisfaction" is the personal evaluation on how often social relations are perceived as satisfying (as the Likert scale). "Relative income" is the assessment of the household net income in comparison (as the Likert scale).

3. Results

The following section shows original results as well as results from recent studies on the Resource Calculator using the methods and data sets described in Section 2.

3.1. Resource Consumption Indicator Based on Microdata EVS and Resource Intensities

The R_{CF} was used to monitor the resource use of private households in the sustainability report of the Ministry for Environment, Agriculture, Conservation, and Consumer Protection of the State of North Rhine-Westphalia (NRW). One aim was to examine if and to which extent the Resource Indicator can contribute to the goals and indicators of SDG 12 and how it could be improved. For this purpose, the EVS data and the resource intensity data described in Section 2.1. were used as a database.

The Material Footprint of private households in NRW accounted for 31 t per capita in 2013. Using microdata enabled the researchers to further analyze the distribution of the Material Footprint among households. Figure 1 shows a right-skewed distribution although the 99th percentile was removed. This implies a relatively strong bias of the average Material Footprint due to relatively few households being responsible for relatively high amounts of resource use.

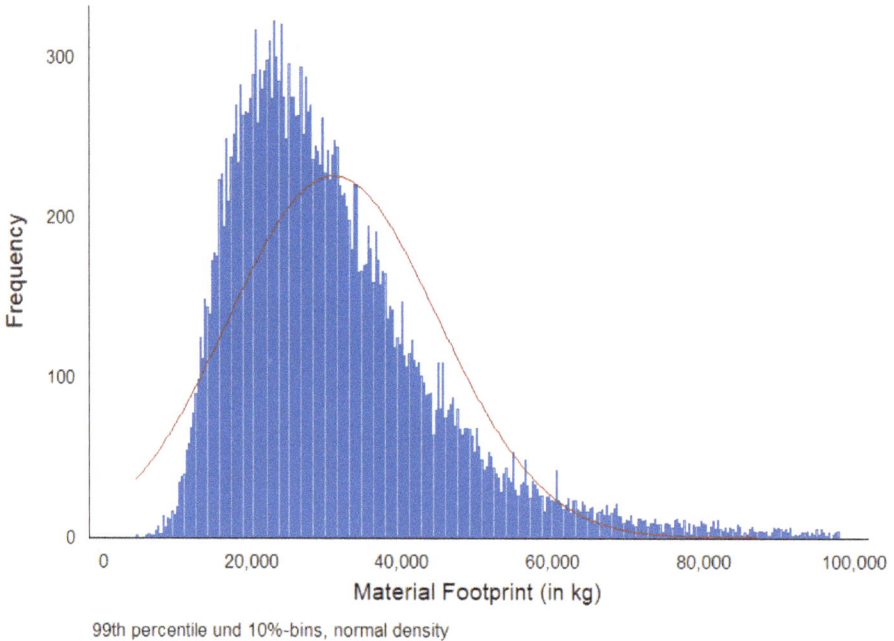

99th percentile und 10%-bins, normal density

Figure 1. The distribution of Material Footprint (years 2003, 2008, 2013) according to Buhl et al., 2016 [10].

The application of the indicator of private household data from NRW revealed three categories that accounted for the highest shares in resource consumption: housing, food, and transport [32,37]. However, smaller shares on household expenditure do not necessarily lead to lower Material Footprints, as resource intensities can be very different between categories of consumption.

Figure 2 shows the overall change in resource use of private households in NRW between 2003 and 2013. The environmental impact of these relative changes in resource consumption depends on the share of the categories in the overall Material Footprint. On the one hand, Communication, for example, exhibits a strong increase of more than 30%, which might come from rapid innovations in information and communication technologies. On the other hand, transport, for example, exhibits a decrease in the Material Footprint. Buhl et al. (2017) differentiate resource intensities in "Transport" and show that a decrease in its Material Footprint comes from, e.g., a reduction of gas consumption, reduced car ownership, and "other" reasons. Due to the relatively high resource intensity of transport, a small decrease in expenditure for transport cancels out a larger increase in expenditure for communication services and technologies between 2003 and 2013.

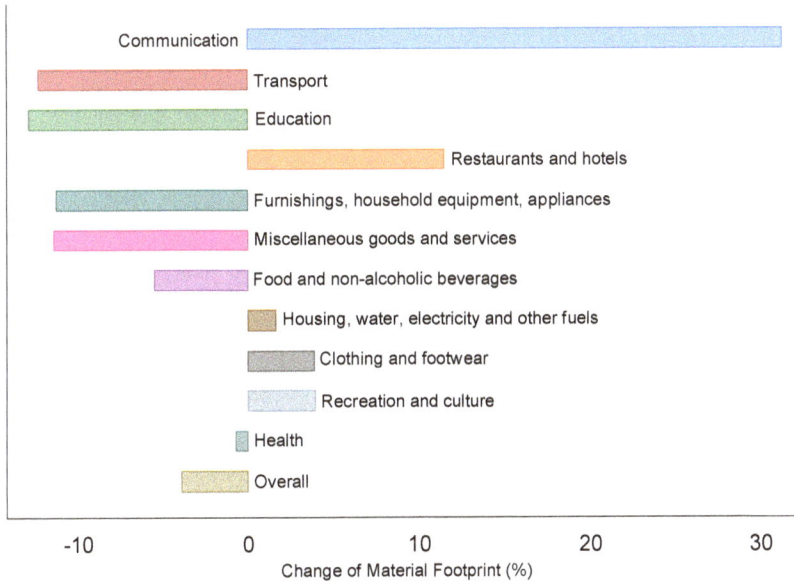

Figure 2. The change in the Material Footprint in NRW 2003–2013 according to Buhl et al., 2016 [16]. Data: Buhl and Acosta 2015 [32].

In sum, the total resource use in NRW remained almost unchanged over the three reporting periods with a reduction of 3.9% between 2003 and 2013 on a comparable high level of resource use. It is interesting to note that this small change in total is a result of significant shifts between the different fields of consumption. This implies that consumption patterns in NRW changed, even though the overall resource use did not by a large margin [16].

3.2. Resource Lifestyle Footprint Based on Survey Data from an Online Web Tool

The overall Material Footprint of users of the Resource Calculator accounts for 26 t per user (and year). The distribution of the Material Footprint shows a similar right-skewed distribution as revealed by the Resource Indicator. This corroborates our findings that the Material Footprint of private households is strongly biased by high resource use of relatively few households.

Figure 3 shows the six categories presented in Table 3 and their shares in the respective Material Footprints of the deciles. It is notable that some shares, such as food and vacation, remain nearly constant from the first to the tenth decile while others, such as housing and mobility, increase strongly. This allows us to conclude that the potential main drivers of a high Material Footprint appear to be these categories.

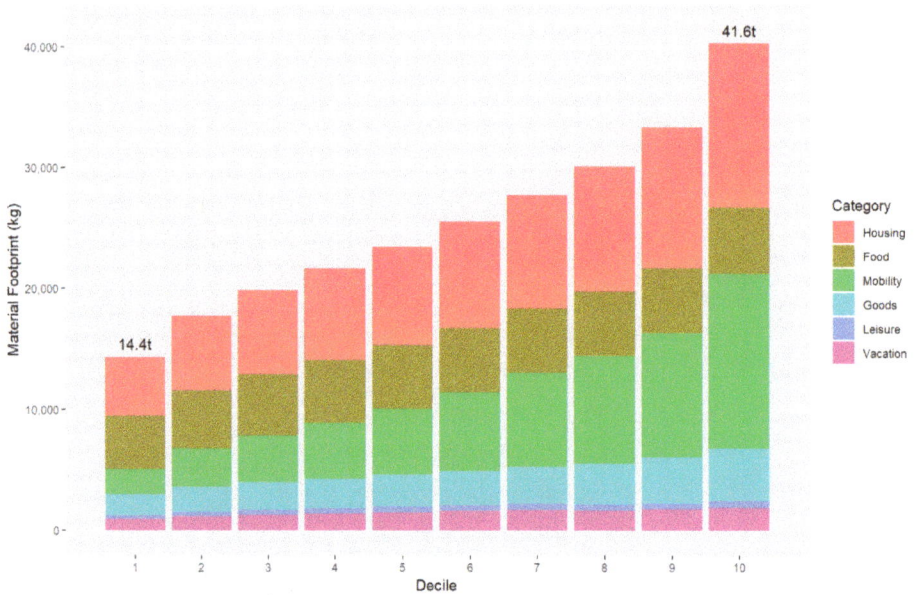

Figure 3. The Material Footprints for deciles and category shares.

Users have been asked to classify their income in respect to the average household net income on a symmetric scale from clearly below average to clearly above average. Surveying the relative household net income makes it easier for users of the calculator to state their net income and to prevent non-response of users. Again, the results reveal an increasing Material Footprint with increasing household net income (see Figure 4).

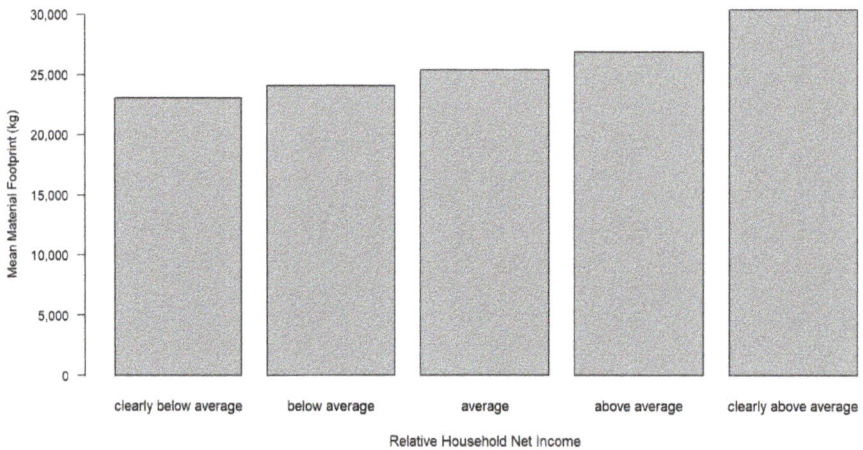

Figure 4. The relative household net income categories and related mean Material Footprint.

The data was also used by Buhl et al., 2017 [27] to examine the relationship between the Material Footprint and life satisfaction. As postulated by Buhl et al., 2017, the use of natural resources is not clearly linked to users subjective well-being (see Figure 5).

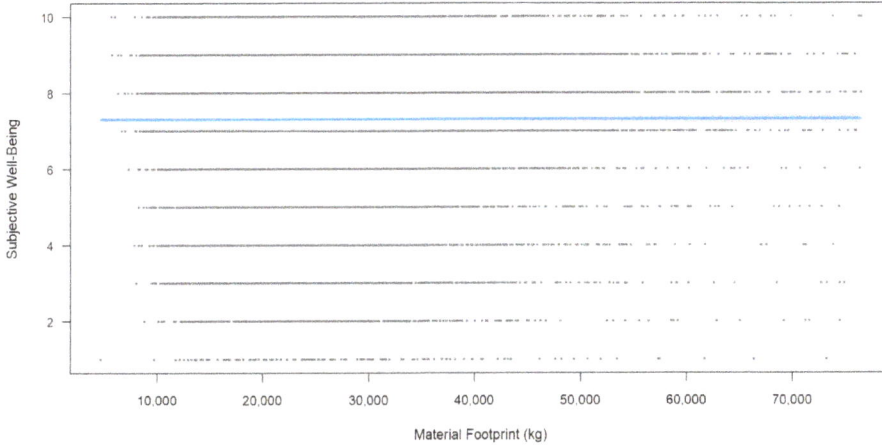

Figure 5. The scatter and line prediction plot of the Material Footprint (in kg) vs. life satisfaction (10-point scale). Confidence band with $a = 0.01$. Buhl et al., 2017 [27].

To test their hypothesis, Buhl et al., 2017 conducted a stepwise multivariate regression analysis. They found that the strongest impacts on life satisfaction are measured for subjective health and for satisfaction with social ties. Real income and gender reveal smaller, but still notable effects. The influence of age, vacation days, and the Material Footprint is rather weak. Subjective assessments and norms appear to have the strongest impact on subjective well-being, followed by socio-demographic characteristics that seem to have less relevance in this context. The Material Footprint has the smallest impact with a slightly negative effect on life satisfaction [27].

Data from the Resource Calculator allows for the disaggregation of Material Footprints and the analysis of complex research questions in the realms of empirical consumer research regarding the link between socioeconomic features and the Material Footprint. In addition, the online web tool approach allows for a quick and flexible alteration of the variables surveyed and a constant flow of survey data.

4. Discussion

The results presented in the previous sections are based on two methods to analyze the Material Footprint of private households according to the requirements of SDG 12. Both concepts have certain strengths as well as potential weaknesses or limitations.

4.1. Resource Consumption Indicator

Regarding the R_{CI}, limitations are the relatively high data aggregation of the main categories and the restriction to consumption expenditure as a proxy for consumption.

Using aggregated data limits the differentiation ability in regard to the consumption of products and services. For instance, one euro invested in the construction of a private house cannot be differentiated from another one invested in maintaining heating. Both are equally subsumed under "housing". Due to this, the depth of analysis of resource use related to certain consumption patterns is restricted. Lifecycle data could be used to extend the current database by disaggregating resource intensities for specific products and services. Such an improved disaggregation of data was successfully conducted by Buhl et al., 2017 for transport and mobility services [37].

Additionally, expenditure data are used as a proxy for consumption. Expenditure data are available in internationally harmonized, official and representative household statistics, which ensure continuous surveys and high data quality. There is a proven correlation between expenditure, consumption and hence resource use. However, there are other factors influencing the measurable impact on the environment. Disregarding those factors can cause bias. Examples of such factors are the households' repairing behavior, their willingness to decide on second-hand goods, and the way and intensity of using a certain good. Value conceptions may also lead a household to opt for goods that are more expensive than comparable alternatives, but cause a similar resource use [16].

4.2. Resource Lifestyle Footprint

The method and data limitations of the R_{LF} stem from non-representative sampling on the one hand and the necessary time efficiency of the survey on the other hand.

Even though the Resource Calculator provides a large amount of user data due to the high usability and, thus, the acceptance of the calculator tool, the sample includes some bias due to the voluntary sampling. The share of young female users, vegetarians, and vegans, for example, is disproportionally high, which indicates a self-selection of pro-environmental users [27]. Future studies should aim for a more representative sampling when using the Resource Calculator as a survey tool. Adding more detailed questions regarding personal information about the users themselves could increase the informative value and the representativeness of the database.

The second limitation of the Resource Calculator relates to the requirement to conduct a survey within a certain amount of time. This results in a limited set of questions that do not allow us to analyze every aspect of consumer's consumption patterns. Many products and services were omitted from the survey (e.g., compared to the "diary" approach in Reference [26]), because they would not contribute much to a higher footprint. Other questions were simplified, aiming at helping the households to complete the survey rather than asking for precise physical values. Finally, even the most comprehensive bottom-up survey would exclude certain products and could not account for every variation of the product types. So there is always some part of the Material Footprint that cannot be related to households individually. Further analysis of the available footprint data could help to identify the essential questions, e.g., by means of unsupervised learning and by using an average pedestal of resource consumption for areas of a low importance (e.g., durable goods such as jewelry or the use of non-living space).

5. Conclusions

5.1. Summary

We introduced two methods for analyzing the Material Footprint of private households based on microdata. The first method (resulting in the Resource Consumption Indicator) is based on expenditure data according to internationally harmonized COICOP. The second method (resulting in the Resource Lifestyle Footprint) is based on survey data from a web tool called Resource Calculator. Both methods allow us to differentiate the Material Footprint along arrays of consumption like housing and mobility as well as socioeconomic characteristics like age or income and thus meet the disaggregation requirement to SDG indicators. The results from applying the two methods in Germany shows that the Material Footprint ranges between 26 t and 31 t per capita in Germany and its distribution is right-skewed. The most relevant categories are housing, mobility, and nutrition. When it comes to disaggregating the Material Footprint along socioeconomic characteristics, we showed that an increasing household net income leads to an increasing Material Footprint.

5.2. Methods

Using microdata from the statistical offices for a Resource Indicator offers three main benefits [32].

- First, it enables a representative depiction of private household consumption.
- Second, private household consumption can be examined by looking at differentiated consumption categories such as energy or food and its shifts and changes for the past decades.
- Third, private household consumption can be examined by looking at differentiated population groups (disaggregated for example by income or age).

Analyzing consumption by using resource intensities offers a possibility to evaluate its environmental impact. The concept relies on a representative, internationally harmonized and thus comparable data according to COICOP that is available in different countries.

The method used for the Resource Lifestyle Footprint (based on the Resource Calculator) provides new options for consumers to receive real-time feedback and for researchers to collect and gather data quickly, flexibly, and constantly over time [27]. Further research regarding the impact of socioeconomic characteristics on resource use could help us to identify appropriate reduction strategies for different groups of consumers as Lettenmeier 2018 successfully showed [38]. Moreover, we strive to collect more data from users abroad in order to compare the Material Footprints internationally (e.g., in a current project on sustainable lifestyles in 7 different countries). So far, the sample of users from abroad is too small to conduct a proper comparative analysis.

Despite some weaknesses, the presented Resource Consumption Indicator appears to be a good and expandable method for measuring the resource use of private households according to SDG 12. However, an improved database is crucial for increased reliability. This issue could be addressed by collecting lifecycle data.

The Resource Lifestyle Footprint is a promising attempt but should be improved regarding the aforementioned limitations. Especially, it will be important to focus on improving the database to receive a more representative sample while condensing the questions about resource use to the most essential ones. In this regard, the survey instrument that indicates the Material Footprint of private households could be incorporated into existing representative surveys like the Socioeconomic Panel (SOEP) or GESIS Panel in Germany or equivalent panels on a European level, e.g., the European Community Household Panel (ECHB). This way, environmental policy evaluation and research on sustainable consumption would benefit from the longitudinal design of the surveys and link environmental issues with an extensive set of socioeconomic predictors efficiently. In any case, it would be helpful to gather more detailed personal and household information to facilitate differentiation between them.

Combining the presented tools could address some of the aforementioned limitations and further improve the usability of microdata for measuring progress towards achieving SDG 12. The Resource Consumption Indicator offers a possibility to measure this progress over time and the status quo. The Resource Lifestyle Footprint can provide a new and more differentiated micro-level database for analyzing consumption-related resource use. The combination of both methods (or similar methods with microdata for that matter) would also enhance scenario building. As the majority of environmental scenarios currently focus on technological and economic feasibility, there is a lack of scenario models that also investigate the social and cultural drivers and barriers of sustainable development [39].

5.3. Policy Making

The Resource Consumption Indicator and the Resource Lifestyle Footprint appear to be promising tools for deepening the understanding of private household consumption, the interaction of production and consumption patterns, and detecting unused potentials to increase its sustainability according to the SDGs. First results from applying the tools already revealed insights about the structure of the resource use of private households. We conclude that microeconomic data offers an important enhancement of the present macro data-based indicator system. Indicators based on microdata are able to evaluate and inform in a differentiated and disaggregated way, in perspective even in real time. As such the methods reveal shifts in resource use between different arrays of consumption and consumer groups that would otherwise stay undetected and camouflaged by highly aggregated macro indicators. Policy evaluations benefit from a disaggregated perspective on the Material Footprint of private household instead of evaluating the overall trend in the Material Footprint. Policymakers may wonder why efforts to reduce the natural resource in mobility does not show a decreasing overall Material Footprint, e.g., due to indirect rebound effects and shifts of consumption patterns. For instance, differentiating the Material Footprint along arrays of consumption allows us to evaluate whether a reduction of the Material Footprint in mobility is offset by an increase in natural resource use by housing or communications. As such, policymakers may identify which policies in specific arrays of consumption may be more effective in reducing the Material Footprint since rebound effects and shifts of consumption are less pronounced.

A more differentiating approach to indicators is not relevant politically (for (inter)national policies and programs like the indicator framework of SDGs and national programmes striving to implement them), but also in everyday decision-making situations, whether in the company (products, infrastructures) or in the household (lifestyles). In fact, the households themselves may evaluate whether changes in one array of consumption are offset by shifts of their consumption into other arrays. For instance, private households may reduce their resource use by foregoing resource-intensive vacations abroad. At the same time, they may become aware that their savings are offset due to intensified leisure activities.

Indicators based on microdata (or indicator set for different goals) are fundamental for the implementation of national policies such as the National Program on Sustainable Consumption in Germany. They allow us to combine efforts for sustainable lifestyles by companies, households and policymakers alike. Does a product or service contribute to achieving an SDG? Are certain production and consumption patterns sustainable and to what extent? Which rebounds can be anticipated? Which trends evolve and do we leave certain groups behind in doing so? Does a policy instrument support sustainable development or not? This type of evaluation system would—in the long run and combined with real-time tools—help to manage and measure sustainable development.

Author Contributions: J.B. and C.L. drafted the thesis. J.B., C.L., J.T. and K.B. conceptualized the paper. J.B. and J.T. analyzed the data and wrote the paper. K.B. and N.S. contributed research and reviewed the paper. All authors draw the conclusions.

funding: This research received no external funding.

Acknowledgments: No funding was received in support of this paper. The original research and discussion on the resource use of households was partly funded by the federal Ministry for the Environment in North Rhine-Westphalia, Germany (Ministerium für Umwelt, Landwirtschaft, Natur-und Verbraucherschutz des Landes Nordrhein-Westfalen).

Conflicts of Interest: The authors declare no conflict of interest.

Appendix A. Calculating the Material Footprint Based on Resource Intensities

The Resource Indicator is calculated as the Material Footprint of the consumption of private households. This Material Footprint is the product resulting from the multiplication of the consumption expenditure c by the resource intensity r.

$$\text{Material Footprint} = c \times r \tag{A1}$$

The consumption expenditure for the jth consumption category of k consumption categories in total is calculated as the arithmetic mean of the consumption expenditure of the ith household out of n households in total in time t (measured in years).

$$c_j = \frac{1}{n} \sum_i^n c_{ij}^t \tag{A2}$$

The consumption expenditure is then adjusted for inflation to the base year t by considering the inflation rate π of the subsequent years in the respective consumption category j. This prevents a bias resulting from inflation.

$$c_j = \frac{1}{n} \left[\sum_i^n c_{ij}^t - \left(c_{ij}^{t+1} \times \pi_j^{t+1} \right) \right] \tag{A3}$$

The consumption expenditure of the ith household is put into the context of the household size h to obtain a per capita result instead of a per household result.

$$c_j = \frac{1}{n} \left[\sum_i^n [(c_{ij}^t - (c_{ij}^{t+1} \times \pi_j^{t+1})) / h_i^t] \right] \tag{A4}$$

To enable a differentiation by different subgroups, Buhl et al. introduce a dimension X, representing socioeconomic characteristics like household income.

$$c_j = \frac{1}{n} \left[\sum_i^n [(c_{ijX}^t - (c_{ijX}^{t+1} \times \pi_j^{t+1})) / h_{iX}^t] \right] \tag{A5}$$

The resource intensity is calculated by dividing the total resource use (indicated by household consumption) R_j^t by the associated consumption expenditure in category j in year t (Equation (A3)).

$$r_j = \frac{R_j^t}{\sum_i^n c_{ij}^t} \tag{A6}$$

The Material Footprint can be expressed as the arithmetic mean of the respective Material Footprints of the jth consumption category out of k consumption categories in total by inserting Equations (A5) and (A6) into Equation (A1):

$$\text{Material Footprint} = \frac{1}{k_x} \frac{1}{n_x} \frac{\sum_j^k \sum_i^n [(c_{ijX}^t - (c_{ijX}^{t+1} \times \pi_j^{t+1})) / h_{iX}^t] \times R_j^t}{\sum_i^n c_{ij}^t} \tag{A7}$$

References

1. Steffen, W.; Rockström, J.; Richardson, K.; Lenton, T.M.; Folke, C.; Liverman, D.; Summerhayes, C.P.; Barnosky, A.D.; Cornell, S.E.; Crucifix, M.; et al. Trajectories of the Earth System in the Anthropocene. *Proc. Natl. Acad. Sci. USA* **2018**, *115*, 8252–8259. [CrossRef] [PubMed]
2. Van Beers, D.; Grossi, F.; Brüggemann, N.; CRI, N.K.; CRI, D.W.; Mont, O.; Voytenko, Y.; UBA, C.L.; Robey, M.; Jones, M.; et al. *Reflections and Lessons Learnt from EEA's Work on Innovative Business Models for Sustainable Lifestyles*; Working Paper for the European Topic Centre on Waste and Materials in a Green Economy; ETC/WMGE: Boeretang, Belgium, 2014.
3. Reim, W.; Parida, V.; Örtqvist, D. Product–Service Systems (PSS) business models and tactics—A systematic literature review. *J. Clean. Prod.* **2015**, *97*, 61–75. [CrossRef]
4. Lewis, M. Product-Service Systems. In *Wiley Encyclopedia of Management*; Cooper, C.L., Ed.; John Wiley & Sons, Ltd.: Chichester, UK, 2015; p. 1. ISBN 978-1-118-78531-7.
5. Hankammer, S.; Steiner, F. Leveraging the sustainability potential of mass customization through product service systems in the consumer electronics industry. *Procedia CIRP* **2015**, *30*, 504–509. [CrossRef]

6. European Parliament; Council of the European Union. *Directive 2009/125/EC of The European Parliament and of the Council of 21 October 2009 Establishing a Framework for the Setting of Ecodesign Requirements for Energy-Related Products (Recast)*; Publications Office of the European Union: Brussels, Belgium, 2009.
7. UNEP. *International Trading Center 10YFP Consumer Information Programme for Sustainable Consumption and Production (CI-SCP)—Guidelines for Providing Product Sustainability Information*; UNEP: Nairobi, Kenya, 2016.
8. German Federal Government. *Die Deutsche Nachhaltigkeitsstrategie 2016—der Weg in eine enkelgerechte Zukunft*; German Federal Government: Berlin, Germany, 2016.
9. UN. *General Assembly Work of the Statistical Commission pertaining to the 2030 Agenda for Sustainable Development: Resolution*; UN: New York, NY, USA, 2017; 25p.
10. Buhl, J.; Teubler, J.; Liedtke, C.; Stadler, K. *Ressourcenverbrauch private Haushalte NRW—Explorative Analyse. Final Report of the Funded Project "Konzeptionelle Analysen und Überlegungen zur Ausgestaltung einer Nachhaltigkeitsstrategie aus wissenschaftlicher Sicht" for the State Agency for Nature, Environment and Consumer Protection NRW (LANUV)*; Wuppertal Institute for Climate, Environment and Energy: Wuppertal, Germany, 2016.
11. German Federal Government. *Perspektiven für Deutschland: Fortschrittsbericht...; unsere Strategie für eine nachhaltige Entwicklung*; Presse-und Informationsamt der Bundesregierung: Berlin, Germany, 2002.
12. German Federal Government. *Nationales Programm für nachhaltigen Konsum. Gesellschaftlicher Wandel durch einen nachhaltigen Lebensstil*; German Federal Ministry for the Environment, Nature Conservation and Nuclear Safety: Berlin, Germany, 2017. Available online: https://www.bmu.de/fileadmin/Daten_BMU/Download_PDF/Produkte_und_Umwelt/nat_programm_konsum_bf.pdf (accessed on 20 November 2018).
13. *Bundesministerium für Umwelt, Naturschutz, Bau und Reaktorsicherheit (BMUB) Deutsches Ressourceneffizienzprogramm II Programm zur nachhaltigen Nutzung und zum Schutz der natürlichen Ressourcen*; BMUB: Berlin, Germany, 2016.
14. Hölsgens, R.; Lübke, S.; Hasselkuß, M. Social innovations in the German energy transition: An attempt to use the heuristics of the multi-level perspective of transitions to analyze the diffusion process of social innovations. *Energy Sustain. Soc.* **2018**, *8*, 8. [CrossRef]
15. Spangenberg, J.H. Design for Sustainability (DfS): Interface of Sustainable Production and Consumption. In *Handbook of Sustainable Engineering*; Kauffman, J., Lee, K.-M., Eds.; Springer: Dordrecht, The Netherlands, 2013; pp. 575–595. ISBN 978-1-4020-8938-1.
16. Bringezu, S.; Ramaswami, A.; Schandl, H.; O'Brien, M.; Pelton, R.; Acquatella, J.; Ayuk, E.T.; Chiu, A.S.F.; Flanegin, R.; Fry, J.; et al. *Assessing Global Resource Use: A Systems Approach to Resource Efficiency and Pollution Reduction*; United Nations Environment Programme: Nairobi, Kenya, 2017; p. 99.
17. Bringezu, S.; Schütz, H.; Saurat, M.; Moll, S.; Acosta-Fernández, J.; Steger, S. Europe's resource use. Basic trends, global and sectoral patterns and environmental and socioeconomic impacts. In *Sustainable Resource Management: Global Trends, Visions and Policies*; Bringezu, S., Bleischwitz, R., Eds.; Greenleaf Publishing: Sheffield, UK, 2009; pp. 52–154.
18. Lettenmeier, M.; Liedtke, C.; Rohn, H. Eight Tons of Material Footprint—Suggestion for a Resource Cap for Household Consumption in Finland. *Resources* **2014**, *3*, 488–515. [CrossRef]
19. Speck, M.; Liedtke, C. *Chancen und Grenzen nachhaltigen Konsums in einer ressourcenleichten Gesellschaft. Jahrbuch Nachhaltige Ökonomie 2016/2017: im Brennpunkt: Ressourcen-Wende*; Metropolis-Verl: Marburg, Germany, 2016; pp. 255–269.
20. Schmidt-Bleek, F. *Das MIPS-Konzept: Weniger Naturverbrauch—mehr Lebensqualität durch Faktor 10*; Droemer Knaur: München, Germany, 2000; ISBN 3-426-77475-5.
21. Teubler, J.; Buhl, J.; Lettenmeier, M.; Greiff, K.; Liedtke, C. A Household's Burden—The Embodied Resource Use of Household Equipment in Germany. *Ecol. Econ.* **2018**, *146*, 96–105. [CrossRef]
22. Wiesen, K.; Saurat, M. Michael Lettenmeier Calculating the Material Input per Service Unit using the Ecoinvent Database. *Int. J. Perform. Eng.* **2014**, *10*, 357–366.
23. Wiesen, K.; Wirges, M. From cumulated energy demand to cumulated raw material demand: The material footprint as a sum parameter in life cycle assessment. *Energy Sustain. Soc.* **2017**, *7*, 13. [CrossRef]
24. Teubler, J.; Kiefer, S.; Liedtke, C. Metals for Fuels? The Raw Material Shift by Energy-Efficient Transport Systems in Europe. *Resources* **2018**, *7*, 49. [CrossRef]
25. Saurat, M.; Ritthoff, M. Calculating MIPS 2.0. *Resources* **2013**, *2*, 581–607. [CrossRef]
26. Greiff, K.; Teubler, J.; Baedeker, C.; Liedtke, C.; Rohn, H. Material and Carbon Footprint of Household Activities. In *Living Labs: Design and Assessment of Sustainable Living*; Keyson, D.V.,

Guerra-Santin, O., Lockton, D., Eds.; Springer International Publishing: Cham, Switzerland, 2017; pp. 259–275. ISBN 978-3-319-33527-8.

27. Buhl, J.; Liedtke, C.; Bienge, K. How Much Environment Do Humans Need? Evidence from an Integrated Online User Application Linking Natural Resource Use and Subjective Well-Being in Germany. *Resources* **2017**, *6*, 67. [CrossRef]

28. United Nations High Commissioner for Human Rights (OHCHR). *A Human Rights Based Approach to Data—Leaving No One Behind in the 2030 Development Agenda*; United Nations High Commissioner for Human Rights (OHCHR): Geneva, Switzerland, 2018.

29. United Nations System Chief Executives Board for Coordination (CEB). *Leaving No One Behind: Equality and Non-Discrimination at the Heart of Sustainable Development*; United Nations: New York, NY, USA, 2017.

30. United Nations. *The Road to Dignity by 2030: Ending Poverty, Transforming All Lives and Protecting the Planet*; United Nations: New York, NY, USA, 2014.

31. Wood, R.; Stadler, K.; Bulavskaya, T.; Lutter, S.; Giljum, S.; de Koning, A.; Kuenen, J.; Schütz, H.; Acosta-Fernández, J.; Usubiaga, A.; et al. Global sustainability accounting—Developing EXIOBASE for multi-regional footprint analysis. *Sustainability* **2014**, *7*, 138–163. [CrossRef]

32. Buhl, J.; Acosta, J. Work Less, Do Less? Working Time Reductions and Rebound Effects. *Sustain. Sci.* **2016**, *11*, 261–276. [CrossRef]

33. Watson, D.; Acosta Fernandez, J.; Wittmer, D.; Pedersen, O.G. *Environmental Pressures from European Consumption and Production: A Study in Integrated Environmental and Economic Analysis*; Publications Office of the European Union: Luxembourg, 2013.

34. Buhl, J. Revisiting Rebound Effects from Material Resource Use. Indications for Germany Considering Social Heterogeneity. *Resources* **2014**, *3*, 106–122. [CrossRef]

35. Schmidt-Bleek, F. *Der ökologische Rucksack. Wirtschaft für eine Zukunft mit Zukunft*; Schmidt-Bleek, F., Ed.; Hirzel: Stuttgart, Germany, 2004.

36. Liedtke, C.; Bienge, K.; Wiesen, K.; Teubler, J.; Greiff, K.; Lettenmeier, M.; Rohn, H. Resource Use in the Production and Consumption System—The MIPS Approach. *Resources* **2014**, *3*, 544–574. [CrossRef]

37. Buhl, J.; Teubler, J.; Liedtke, C.; Stadler, K. Der Ressourcenverbrauch privater Haushalte in NRW. *Uwf UmweltWirtschaftsForum Sustain. Manag. Forum* **2017**, *25*, 255–264.

38. Lettenmeier, M. *A Sustainable Level of Material Footprint—Benchmark for Designing One-Planet Lifestyles Materiaalijalanjäljen kestävä taso—Mittapuu Yhden Planeetan EläMäNtapojen Toteuttamiseen*; Aalto University: Espoo, Finland, 2018.

39. Kirby, P.; O'Mahony, T. Planning Future Pathways: Implications and Outcomes of Scenario Studies. In *The Political Economy of the Low-Carbon Transition*; Springer: New York, NY, USA, 2018; pp. 115–141.

sustainability

MDPI

Article

An Assessment of the Implementation of the European Tourism Indicator System for Sustainable Destinations in Italy

Patrizia Modica [1], Alessandro Capocchi [2,*], Ilaria Foroni [3] and Mariangela Zenga [3]

[1] Department of Economics and Business, University of Cagliari, Via Sant'Ignazio da Laconi, 70, 09123 Cagliari, Italy; modica@unica.it

[2] Department of Business Economics and Law-DiSEADE, University of Milano Bicocca, Via Bicocca degli Arcimboldi, 8, 20126 Milano, Italy

[3] Department of Statistics and Quantitative Methods, University of Milano-Bicocca, Via Bicocca degli Arcimboldi, 8, 20126 Milano, Italy; ilaria.foroni@unimib.it (I.F.); mariangela.zenga@unimib.it (M.Z.)

* Correspondence: alessandro.capocchi@unimib.it; Tel.: +39-0264483191

Received: 21 June 2018; Accepted: 27 August 2018; Published: 4 September 2018

Abstract: The European Tourism Indicators System (ETIS) is a product of the European Union (EU) Sustainable Development Strategy, which was formulated with the objectives of promoting economic prosperity, social equity, cohesion, and environmental protection. In this paper, we present an analysis of the results of the implementation of the ETIS during the period 2013–2016, in the Italian tourist destination of South Sardinia. While the implementation of ETIS constitutes a significant advancement in Italy, and more widely in Europe, our findings reveal that an adaptive management approach is necessary for achieving the anticipated objectives and adapting these standardized indicators to different territorial contexts. Difficulties were encountered in both data collection and stakeholders' involvement in the implementation process. Insufficient knowledge, and familiarity with the complex technical aspects of the indicator toolkit among primary stakeholders, was another constraint associated with its implementation. We believe that the findings of this analysis can provide guidelines and inputs for other European countries and tourist destinations that are currently in the process of implementing the ETIS toolkit or similar methodologies. In particular, the pioneering sustainable tourism performance measurement system (STPMS) can be adapted to meet local needs.

Keywords: tourist destination; sustainable tourism; indicators; European Tourism Indicator System (ETIS); Visit South Sardinia

1. Introduction

In recent decades, sustainability has emerged as a primary goal in tourism-related decision making [1]. Stakeholders in the tourism sector, including tourists and host communities, are now considerably more aware of the importance of sustainable development in tourism than they were in the past [2]. Nonetheless, the concept and nature of sustainability remain vague, especially in the absence of their operationalization using tools that enable the planning, management, and monitoring of the impacts of tourism on the target destinations [3–5]. Apart from the necessity of formulating quantitative measures for sustainable tourism relating to its social, economic, and environmental dimensions (i.e., indicator systems), a methodology is required for implementing these operational tools. There have been relatively few studies on indicator systems and associated methodologies for their implementation. This study, which was aimed at developing a procedure for operationalizing indicator systems to measure sustainability, seeks to address this gap. In general, the process of selecting an indicator system entails multiple stages. Firstly, a literature review is conducted to analyze potentially suitable indicator systems developed by international organizations. Secondly, in light of the findings of this review, a specific indicator system is selected. Thirdly, individual indicators are chosen and working groups are established to discuss these indicators with tourism stakeholders. Fourth an implementation process is developed at the municipal level. Lastly, the results are presented and discussed in the tourist destination with concerned stakeholders in tourism and related sectors.

We conducted a case study to assess the process of implementing the European Tourism Indicator System (ETIS) for sustainable destinations designed by the European Commission (EC) [6]. The selected case was the project of "Visit South Sardinia" (VSS) destination management organization (DMO) in Italy. This project has been promoted by public sector stakeholders in Southern Sardinia, with the aim of managing and marketing the above destination in collaboration with the private sector and other primary stakeholders in tourism. The project was developed to assess and implement a pioneering sustainable tourism performance measurement system (STPMS) in collaboration with the University of Cagliari, with the subsequent involvement, too, of the University of Milano-Bicocca.

In 2013, VSS became an early adopter of the Global Sustainable Tourism Council (GSTC) criteria and indicators program). The GSTC is an international organization endorsed by the United Nations (UN), the United Nations World Tourism Organization (UNWTO), and the United Nations Environment Programme (UNEP). As the acknowledged global authority in this field, its sustainability standards relating to the travel and tourism industry are definitive. VSS was one of 10 international destinations selected to demonstrate pioneering initiatives, and progress in sustainable management. During 2013 and 2014, it participated in the first pilot phase of implementing the ETIS, the objective of which was to define a comprehensive tourism monitoring system for European destinations, with the objective of maintaining Europe's standing as "the world's number one tourist destination" [7]. Whereas implementation of both programs, GSTC and ETIS, in Southern Sardinia demonstrated high levels of sustainability relating to communities and the environment. They also highlighted the need to improve methods of managing and monitoring tourism impacts. Lessons learned from implementing the STPMS were applied in policy making and management by organizations in the public and private sectors. Their enhanced awareness of sustainable development of tourism served as a strategic lever, motivating their decision-making processes. For example, since 1998, Capo Carbonara, which is situated in the municipality of Villasimius on the east coast of the VSS site, has been designated as a marine protected area. In 2018, a new marine protected area, Capo Spartivento, located within the municipality of Domus de Maria, was established on the west coast. Through its recognition by VSS primary stakeholders, STPMS evidently contributed to the development of environmental policies and practices in the destination area.

This paper is organized as follows. Further details on the background of VSS are provided in the Section 2, and a review of the literature on sustainable tourism indicators is presented in the Section 3. The study methods and results are discussed in the Sections 4 and 5, respectively, and conclusions are offered in the Section 6 of the paper.

2. Background on the Case Study Destination

The case study examined in this paper is the VSS project, under which the Gulf of Angels destination in Southern Sardinia, including the city of Cagliari, Sardinia's capital, is managed (see Figure 1). The project also encompasses four coastal municipalities, while private sector interests are represented by four consortia.

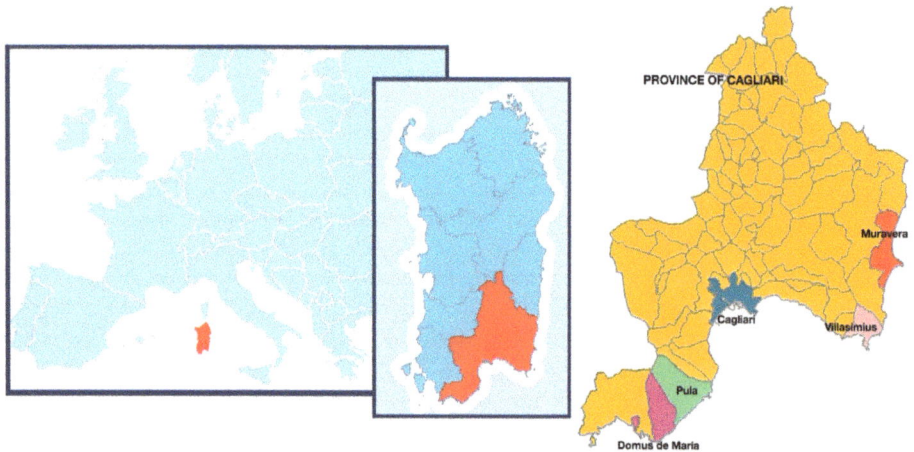

Figure 1. Map of the Province of Cagliari in Sardinia, including Cagliari and the other four municipalities included in the "Visit South Sardinia" (VSS) project.

The island of Sardinia is a well-known Mediterranean tourist destination that receives more than 3,100,000 tourists annually, with a recorded figure in 2017 of 14,386,000 tourist nights and an average length of stay of 4.59 nights [8]. The island's official accommodation comprises a total of 212,751 beds. In 2017, Cagliari Province received 758,487 tourists, and figures for tourist nights and the average length of stay were 3,308,011 and 4.36 nights, respectively. The total number of beds available for tourists during this year was 43,717. The Sistema Informativo di Raccolta ed Elaborazione Dati (SIRED) [8] of the Region of Sardinia reported that the five municipalities included in the VSS project received a total of 572,372 tourists in 2017, and recorded 2,453,641 tourist nights and an average length of stay of 4.28 nights.

VSS is actively engaged in sustainable tourism initiatives, and its progress over time can be tracked using internationally recognized standards. In the spring and summer of 2013, VSS was included in the GSTC international program for assessing sustainable tourism. An on-site evaluation was conducted by a third-party organization, Sustainable Travel International. The assessment was based on 40 criteria and 81 indicators related to the four pillars of tourism sustainability: (1) Destination management, (2) social and economic benefits, (3) cultural heritage, and (4) environmental protection.

Following its launch in early 2013, VSS also took up the challenge of implementing the ETIS for sustainable destinations [6]. Accordingly, VSS participated in the first pilot phase of ETIS implementation and remained involved in the initiative from 2013 to 2016. The initial ETIS pilot project implemented by VSS in 2013 included 27 core and 40 optional indicators relating to four domains: (1) Destination management, (2) economic value, (3) social and cultural impact, and (4) environmental impact. In 2016, based on the findings of the two pilot phases (in 2013 and 2014) in destinations across Europe, the ETIS was revised, with inputs provided by the ETIS pool of experts (PoE) [9]. The principal difference between the ETIS and the GSTC program is that the former monitors ongoing developments relating to sustainability, whereas the latter measures the current status of sustainable tourism management.

In 2016, VSS was awarded the European Sustainable Destination prize associated with the first joint ETIS and Accessible Tourism Awards disbursed by the EC. This prize was awarded to the VSS project in recognition of its effective combination of UN and EU indicators of sustainable tourism in destination management and monitoring resulting from its involvement in the GSTC assessment and in the ETIS pilot phase.

3. Literature Review

In recent decades, the literature on sustainable tourism has largely focused on: Clarifying the evolving meaning of sustainability in the context of tourism; identifying the methods and tools deemed valid for measuring sustainability; verifying the models proposed; and scrutinizing the indicators whose implementation has progressively advanced at international, national, regional, and local levels. A brief overview of the sustainability literature relating to the purpose of this study is presented below.

According to Reference [10] and other authors, key issues in the interpretation of sustainable development are the role of economic growth in promoting human well-being, the impacts of human population growth, the existence of environmental limits to growth, the substitutability of natural resources, the role of new technologies, the degree to which a systems (ecosystems) perspective should be adopted, and the importance of maintaining the functional integrity of ecosystems [11–13]. Some studies focusing on the sustainability of the tourism sector have highlighted initiatives aimed at satisfying current needs without compromising the ability of future generations to meet their own needs [14,15]. From this perspective, balancing economic growth, conservation of environmental resources, and development is critical at local destination levels [16–26]. However, several examples of tourism destination management, discussed in the literature, have fallen short of adhering to the principles of sustainability [27–29]. The following topics are highlighted in this literature: The relationship between residents and tourists [30]; the environmental implications of tourism; the development and preservation of the culture, inheritance, and artistic values of local communities [31,32]; support for the local economy; engagement of local communities in discussions between stakeholders and residents; and managing tourism development through the creation of clear and transparent policies for involving all local players, increasing tourism education and training, and improving the services offered [33–35].

Following the above clarification of the meaning of sustainability in the context of the tourism sector, determining whether sustainability can be measured at the local systemic level in the destination becomes an important task. Measurement of sustainability first requires the identification of its dimensions, followed by the determination of tools capable of measuring these dimensions [36]. According to Reference [37], three integrated dimensions, namely, economic growth, environmental sustainability, and social equity constitute the basis for the measurement process [38].

Several sets of indicators have been proposed for measuring sustainability in relation to tourism [39–41], with the aim of operationalizing "sustainable tourism" and facilitating its implementation [42–46]. Most indicator sets refer to criteria such as involvement of local communities, sustainable use of resources, tourism planning, and promoting information and research [36,47].

Indicators are considered the best tools for controlling and measuring progress toward sustainable tourism [14,48–52]. In one study, indicators were defined as the biophysical, social, managerial, or other conditions that concern people in a given situation [3]. Conversely, Reference [3] suggested that indicators are helpful for measuring and framing management objectives in quantitative terms and for specifying appropriate levels or acceptable limits for tourism's impacts. According to Reference [53], a longstanding objective has been to develop quantitative indicators of sustainability for the tourism sector [14,16]. The most difficult aspect entails establishing environmental accounting measures, so this remains a research priority. The measurement and management of all types of tourism impacts are growing in importance.

In addition to discussions of indicator sets, there have also been some attempts to measure the interconnections among different dimensions of sustainability and to conduct cross-analyses, as revealed in the literature. One such attempt is the "prism of sustainability" developed in [53] as a holistic framework entailing four interrelated dimensions of sustainability: Environmental, economic, sociocultural, and institutional. This holistic model has been adopted by several researchers as its indicators are suitable for dynamic modeling. Consequently, it is suitable for assessing the sustainability of different policies and strategies. The use of indicator sets for controlling and measuring the multiple dimensions of sustainability within the tourism sector has become widespread, although not all researchers agree on their importance and effectiveness [4,53–55].

In 2003, the EC adopted guidelines that focused entirely on sustainable development in the field of tourism, titled "Basic orientations for the sustainability of European tourism." Three years after its inception in 2004, the Tourism Sustainability Group adopted the "Action for More Sustainable European Tourism, 2007." In the same year, the EC approved an "Agenda for a sustainable and competitive European tourism." In 2010, the EC defined four strategic priorities: (1) Encouraging competitiveness within the tourism sector; (2) promoting sustainable, high-quality tourism; (3) strengthening Europe's image as a tourism destination; and (4) improving EU financial policies and instruments.

The EC's continued focus on the sustainability issue culminated, in 2013, in the formulation of a European system of indicators [6] for the EU's sustainable development strategy, based on the objectives of achieving economic prosperity, social equity, cohesion, and environmental protection. Twenty-one actions were derived from the four priorities, including the ETIS for sustainable tourism. The ETIS was launched in Brussels on 22 February 2013. It was designed, on behalf of the EC, by a consortium of organizations led by the University of Surrey, and tested in a selected number of European destinations, including Saint Tropez in France, Florence in Italy, Alqueva in Portugal, and Brasov in Romania. Two pilot phases, implemented across Europe in 2013 and 2014, led to the updating of the ETIS and related tools in 2016. As noted by [56], the ETIS "is designed as a locally owned and led process for monitoring, managing, and enhancing the sustainability of a tourism destination," and "it has been developed as a result of lessons learned from previously existing indicator system initiatives." The ETIS provides all of the specific tools necessary for developing local-level tourism impact monitoring mechanisms at the tourist destination.

Seven steps are required for facilitating the implementation of the ETIS toolkit, which is aligned with the most commonly applied international standards, such as those of the UNWTO and GSTC. The first step of raising awareness is particularly important for advancing understanding of sustainability among stakeholders. The second step defines and creates a profile of the destination. In the third step, a working group comprising stakeholders is formed, which plays a fundamental role in tourism destination management. The fourth step entails assigning roles and responsibilities within the working group during its consultations. Data collection and analysis are key aspects constituting the fifth and sixth steps of the ETIS. The final step entails the formulation of an action plan and strategic management for long-term improvement.

There are few applications of the ETIS reported in the tourism literature. Examples include "ATL del Cuneese" in Italy [57]; Malta [58]; and Brasov County in the Romanian Carpathians [59]. However, only the Brasov case study provides details relating to the challenges and difficulties encountered in the implementation of the ETIS in a tourist destination. The development of an innovative decision-making support system for tourist destination management based on the ETIS has been proposed [60]. In this context, the present case study of VSS, considered as a successful model of sustainably developing an island destination in the absence of conflict between tourists and residents [61], is in line with recent studies focusing on municipalities [5].

4. Materials and Methods

The VSS project is the only example entailing the testing of two international systems relating to the impacts of tourism, namely the GSTC program and the ETIS in the Mediterranean region. Several other destinations in Italy, such as Cuneo Alps, Abano Terme, and Terrae Anio Iubensanae, and within Europe, such as Broceliande (France), the province of Barcelona (Spain), Podgorica (Montenegro), Ljubljana (Slovenia), Birmingham (UK), Dark Sky Alqueva (Portugal), and Uzundure (Turkey), have been involved in the ETIS testing phases. However, none of these destinations participated in the GSTC Early Adopter Program.

In Sardinia the pioneering STPMS was the outcome of a step-wise procedure, coordinated by the University of Cagliari. First, the primary stakeholders group (PSG), comprising key stakeholders was established and a VSS sustainability team (ST) was subsequently formed. The next step comprised tourism data collection, followed by an assessment of indicators through PSG discussions. A software survey platform (SSP) was used to store tourism data. The final three steps entailed quantifying the selected indicators, analyzing the results, and presenting and discussing lessons learned with the PSG.

The VSS project commenced in February 2013 and continues to be operational. The main project partners include the University of Cagliari, which coordinates activities in the destination areas and is the project's liaison; the municipality of Cagliari, which leads the project; the municipalities of Domus de Maria, Muravera, Pula, and Villasimius; the Area Marina Protetta Capo Carbonara; the consortia of tourism enterprises, namely Consorzio Costa Sud, Consorzio Turistico di Villasimius, Azienda di Promozione Turistica, Muravera, and Consorzio Costiera Sulcitana; and the Regione Autonoma della Sardegna, which supervises the project.

The PSG that was initially formed comprised mayors and tourism councilors from the five municipalities. During the second phase, it was expanded to include the presidents of the tourism enterprises consortia. One of the objectives of the VSS project was to combine public and private sector representatives, which proved to be a strategic lever for the initiative's success. Moreover, the PSG was responsible for relating to the university coordinator and for implementing the STPMS. In the third phase, the group was further expanded to include key representatives of public organizations (e.g., the port authority and labor agency), associations, single enterprises, media representatives, and other representatives from the private sector. Most members of the expanded PSG owned or had access to data that was relevant for developing the STPMS.

The ST, coordinated by research assistants under the supervision of the University of Cagliari, was established following the PSG's creation. Initially comprising four student interns from a professional graduate program in tourism, its composition subsequently changed with the addition of 20 student trainees from a university undergraduate program in tourism. The two primary responsibilities of the ST are to identify all tourism stakeholders possessing relevant data in the destination area and to collect these data through ETIS surveys. The PSG was involved in the implementation of the STPMS and in the assessment and discussions on which indicators should be included for each of the four aspects of sustainability.

In our project, data were collected through face-to-face interviews and self-completed questionnaires. LimeSurvey software version 2.55.2 (LimeSurvey GmbH, Hamburg, Germany) was used to set up an SPSS v. 25 for the data analysis.

By the end of 2014, the VSS project had implemented the entire ETIS toolkit. The principal aim was to evaluate all of the indicators suggested in the EC toolkit, published in 2013. The 27 core indicators and 40 optional indicators (the complete list of indicators is listed in Table A1 of Appendix A) were aggregated into the following four categories: (1) Destination management, (2) social and cultural impacts, (3) economic value, and (4) environmental impacts.

During the first phase of the investigation, to prevent duplication of efforts, the ST explored the main available statistical information sources providing relevant data on ETIS indicators at the local level in Italy. Table 1 shows the results of this first phase. The data sources that the ST decided to use to calculate all of the indicators in VSS are listed in this table, which indicates a lack of statistical data sources, especially at the municipal level. To bridge this gap, we conducted four separate surveys covering the principal stakeholders of VSS: Residents, tourists and daily visitors, enterprises, and local public actors. We decided to employ the questionnaires contained in the ETIS toolkit produced in 2013 [62].

Table 1. Data sources used to calculate the European Tourism Indicator System (ETIS) during the implementation of the VSS project.

Data Sources Classification	Source	Reference Number of ETIS Indicators
Publicly available data from official sources	"Occupancy of tourist accommodation establishments" and "Capacity of collective tourist accommodation" ISTAT census surveys	B.1.1; B.2.1; B.2.2; C.1.1; C.1.1.2
	Italian Institute for Environmental Protection and Research and Italian Ministry of the Environment, Land and Sea (http://www.minambiente.it/).	D.3.1; D.3.1.1; D.9.1
Ad hoc surveys realized by VSS	Residents survey	A.1.1.1 C.1.1.1; C.4.1.1.
	Tourists and same day visitors survey	A.3.1; A.3.1.1; A.4.1; B.1.1.3; B.1.2; B.2.1.1; C.3.2.1; D.1.1.1; D.1.2; D.1.2.1
	Enterprises survey	A.2.1; A.2.2.1; A.4.1.1; B.2.2.1; B.3.1.1; B.3.1.2; B.4.1; B.5.1; B.5.1.2; C.2.1; C.2.1.1; C.2.1.2; C.3.1; D.2.1; D.3.1.1; D.4.1.1; D.5.1; D.5.1.1; D.5.1.2; D.6.1; D.6.1.1; D.6.1.2; D.7.1.1
	Local public actors survey	A.1.1; A.1.1.2; B.1.1; B.1.1.2; B.2.1.1; C.1.1.3; C.3.1.1; D.7.1; D.7.1.2; D.8.1.

The ETIS questionnaire, which was administered to a sample comprising 590 residents from the five municipalities included in the VSS project, was aimed at evaluating the indicators for measuring the impacts of tourism on the local community. Random sampling was performed to recruit representative participants from the resident population. Respondents were selected through random quota sampling according to sex and age as well as the population size of the municipality. We set the sample size at 1% of the target population that we evaluated based on information furnished by the Italian Statistics Institute (ISTAT) in 2014. Questionnaires were completed through face-to-face interactions conducted in public areas (e.g., on the street and at public events) from May to September 2015.

A survey of tourists and same-day visitors was also conducted from May to September 2015. Again, the questionnaire was administered directly, face-to-face, among Italian and foreign tourists who were present in the VSS territory. In determining the survey sample, we applied time location sampling (TLS) in light of the particular characteristics of the population. The specific TLS for tourism-focused surveys entailed a two-stage stratified sampling design with unequal selection probabilities for first-stage units and constant selection probabilities for second-stage units. The first-stage units comprised a combination of places, days, and hours (i.e., venue-day-time units). The second-stage units comprised (non-resident) Italian and foreign tourists visiting the VSS municipalities. Our aim was to collect relevant direct information for the entire period spent in the tourist destination. Following the approach, described in Reference [63], and using the ISTAT official data on tourist arrivals, we selected a random sample characterized by unequal probabilities (proportional to the estimated tourism flows for each combined unit comprising the month, place, and tourist typology). The final dataset comprised 514 units.

The survey of enterprises was conducted from July 2015 to February 2016, using the computer-assisted web interviewing technique. Given the low response rate for this survey, companies were solicited through emails and direct phone calls. Ultimately, even though a large number of enterprises visited the website on which the questionnaire was posted, only 25 of them partially or fully answered the questionnaire.

In addition, the ETIS toolkit contained a questionnaire tailored for local administrators and aimed at gathering information concerning the 10 indicators listed in Table 1. Questionnaires were provided to the boards of the five municipalities involved in VSS: Cagliari, Villasimius, Pula, Domus De Maria, and Muravera.

5. Results

In light of our objective of assessing the implementation of the ETIS, in this section we identify the main problems that we encountered during the phase of evaluating the indicators. In some cases, missing data affected the reliability of the indicators and in others, it was difficult to contact the respondents who had not completed the entire questionnaire. Below, we elaborate on our experiences in collecting the data that we used for calculating the indicators.

5.1. Official Relevant Statistics for the Evaluation of ETIS Indicators

ISTAT, which conducts two monthly surveys on tourist accommodation capacity and occupancy, respectively, is the official and principal source of tourism data in Italy. Data on numbers of tourists who stay in registered accommodation, obtained from this source, were used to calculate the following four indicators in the system: Number of tourist nights per month (B.1.1); occupancy rate in commercial accommodation per month and the average for the year (B.2.2.), number of beds available in commercial visitor accommodation per 100 residents (C.1.1.2), and the average length of stay of tourists (nights) in commercial accommodation per month (B.2.1). In addition, access to databases created and managed by the Italian Institute for Environmental Protection and Research (the Italian Institute for Environmental Protection and Research is part of the national system for environmental protection network; comporising of 21 territorial environmental protection agencies established in accordance with regional laws), enabled the calculation of the following indicators: Waste volume produced in the destination (D.3.1), level of contamination per 100 mL (fecal coliforms, campylobacter (D.9.1), and number of days beach/shore closed due to contamination (D.9.1.1).) Because the separation of different types of waste is mandatory in Italy, it was possible to estimate an optional indicator: Percentage of tourism enterprises separating different types of waste (D.3.1.1). Accessibility to official data ensured that the information obtained for these indicators was complete, reliable, and valid for the analysis.

Table 2 shows the values of the eight indicators that we estimated for the year 2015. These values clearly reveal the strengths of the DMO in terms of sustainability. This DMO has one of the highest values for the tourism dimension in Italy (about 174 miles of tourist nights per month, and an occupancy rate of 50% of the available beds, that is, 15.1 per 100 residents' beds in the area for commercial accommodation), and the high quality of the surrounding sea is remarkable.

Table 2. Indicator values estimated on the basis of publicly available data from official sources (* yearly average).

Indicator Code	Indicator Value
B.1.1	173,426.58 tourist nights per month
B.2.1 *	6 days
B.2.2 *	49.4%
C.1.1.2	15.1 per 100 residents
D.3.1	104,798.3 tonnes
D.3.1.1	100%
D.9.1	0.0%
D.9.1.1	0

5.2. Survey of Residents

The face-to-face modality of survey administration that we selected for the residents in the DMO proved to be highly effective. The number of surveyed residents corresponded to the preset sample size and respondents answered all of the questions. The data in the collected questionnaires enabled us to calculate the following ETIS indicators: Percentage of residents satisfied with their involvement and their influence in the planning and development of tourism (A.1.1.1), percentage of residents who have positive views on the impacts of tourism on destination identity (C.4.1.1), and percentage of residents who are satisfied with tourism in the destination per season (C.1.1.1). Given the comprehensiveness of the information obtained through the residents' survey, the calculated values of these indicators, which were assessed in the analysis, were considered reliable and valid. Table 3 shows the values of the indicators estimated using data collected through the residents' survey. The results indicate that seasonality affected the satisfaction level relating to tourism among residents in VSS. Specifically, we found that respondents were highly satisfied in the peak season but were highly dissatisfied in the off-season. Moreover, although most residents felt that tourism helps to strengthen the distinctiveness of the VSS destination, and to enhance its local identity, culture, and heritage, they felt that their involvement in tourism planning and development was minimal.

Table 3. Values of indicators estimated from data obtained in the residents' survey.

Indicator Code	Indicator Value
A.1.1.1	35.6%
C.1.1.1 (in summer)	75.5%
C.1.1.1 (in winter)	25.9%
C.1.1.1 (in autumn)	30.7%
C.1.1.1 (in spring)	60.9%
C.4.1.1	60.8%

5.3. Survey of Tourists and Same-Day Visitors

We administered the questionnaire to tourists and same-day visitors, applying the face-to-face modality, and did not experience any particular difficulties in collecting the preset number of questionnaires. Nonetheless, contrasting with respondents in the residents' survey, some of the respondents in this survey did not answer all the questions. Table 4 shows the indicators that we calculated using the responses obtained from surveyed tourists and daily visitors and the percentage of missing data affecting the corresponding answers. On average, missing data in the responses amounted to 4.4%. Specifically, missing data for questions on the core questions averaged 2.6%, whereas missing data for optional indicators averaged 6%. Given the low percentage of non-responses for individual questions, we overcame the problem using the donor technique, which entails replacing missing values with values obtained from a "similar" responding unit. After applying the abovementioned correctional procedure, we obtained estimates of the indicators, listed in Table 4. The compiled responses revealed that almost all tourists and same-day visitors (92.2%) were very satisfied with their overall experience at the VSS destination, and more than a half of the respondents (56.2%) had visited it at least once during the last previous 5 years. Considering the lack of data on the local economic impacts of tourism, the average daily spending of same-day visitors (37 €) and that of tourists (56 €) were considered two of the most important evaluated indicators. It is noteworthy that with reference to the indicators that most related to the degree of sustainable development, only 39% of the surveyed respondents were aware of efforts to promote sustainable destinations (indicator A.4.1), and slightly more than 50% of the tourists were satisfied with the destination's accessibility for those with disabilities or specific access requirements (indicator C.3.2.1). The assessment of indicators relating to the environmental dimension revealed that 44.8% of respondents used different modes of transport to reach the destination (indicator D.1.1), but only 40.1% used local/"soft" mobility/public transport services to travel around the destination site (indicator D.1.1.1). On average, tourists traveled

1,160 km to and from home (indicator D.1.2), whereas same-day visitors traveled 90 km to and from the destination (indicator D.1.2.1).

Table 4. ETIS indicators evaluated on the basis of data obtained from the survey of tourists/same-day visitors.

Indicator Code	Missing Data (%) for the Question Generating the Indicator	Indicator Value
A.3.1	4.5	92.2%
A.3.1.1	4.9	56.2%
A.4.1	6.5	38.8%
B.1.1.3	10.5	37.38 €
B.1.2	1.9	56.02 €
B.2.1.1	7.0	7.34 h
C.3.2.1	1.7	58.3%
D.1.1	0	44.8%
D.1.1.1	0	40.1%
D.1.2	0	1160 km
D.1.2.1	11.4	90 km

5.4. Survey of Enterprises

As discussed in Section 4, because of the high number of enterprises and their dispersion across the VSS territory, we applied a computer-assisted web interviewing technique for surveying the enterprises. Only a very small percentage of the contacted subjects answered the questionnaire, resulting in invalidation of the sample randomness. Moreover, because of the incompleteness of some of the answers, we were unable to obtain a stable and reliable estimate for the indicators listed in Table 5. This table shows the percentage of missing data affecting the corresponding answers for each indicator. Evidently, the percentages of missing data range from a minimum of 12% (for the D.6.1.1 and D.3.1.1 indicators) to a maximum of 52% (for the core indicator, C.2.1), with an average value of 30.13%. In this case, it was not possible to apply any technique to overcome the issue of missing data. Therefore, we did not calculate this group of indicators. The lack of data received from enterprises was discussed during PSG meetings, with the objective of increasing awareness among tourism enterprises on the importance of sustainability practices relating to their customers, and of strengthening the involvement of the private sector in implementing the STPMS.

Table 5. Evaluation of ETIS indicators based on data from the surveyed enterprises.

Indicator Code	Missing Data (%) for the Item Generating the Indicator
A.2.1	44.0
A.2.2.1	40.0
A.4.1.1	40.0
B.2.2.1	40.0
B.3.1.1	36.0
B.3.1.2	20.0
B.4.1	36.0
B.5.1	20.0
B.5.1.2	28.0
C.2.1	52.0
C.2.1.1	20.0
C.2.1.2	32.0
C.3.1	28.0
D.2.1	32.0
D.3.1.1	12.0
D.4.1.1	24.0
D.5.1	50.0
D.5.1.1	24.0
D.5.1.2	24.0
D.6.1	17.0
D.6.1.1	12.0
D.6.1.2	32.0
D.7.1.1	17.0

5.5. Survey of Local Public Actors

The ETIS toolkit included a questionnaire that was tailored to local administrators, with the aim of gathering information relating to the 10 indicators listed in the last row of Table 1. Questionnaires were provided to the boards of the five municipalities involved in the VSS project: Cagliari, Villasimius, Pula, Domus De Maria, and Muravera.

Table 6 shows the estimated values of the indicators. The local administrators evidently demonstrated different degrees of interest in realizing the system of indicators. For instance, repeated requests elicited a limited response from the local administration of Cagliari. This is partly attributable to the fact that data for the capital city are distributed across a large number of locations. Moreover, the attitude and involvement of the PSG in the implementation of indicator systems can change over time. Some of the indicators showed strongly contrasting values for the municipalities. Although all of the municipalities confirmed that they had implemented a public policy for sustainable tourism management (A.1.1. and A.1.1.2), their situations relating to accessibility (C.3.1.1) and landscape and biodiversity protection (D.7.1 and D.7.1.2) differed.

Table 6. ETIS evaluation based on data obtained from surveyed local administrators.

Indicator Code	Indicators Values for Each Municipality of the Destination Management Organization (DMO)				
	Pula	Domus de Maria	Villasimius	Cagliari	Muravera
A.1.1	100%	100%	100%	100%	100%
A.1.1.2	100%	100%	100%	100%	100%
B.1.1.1	-	-	90%	-	50%
B.1.1.2	-	-	It is not possible to know	-	It is not possible to know
B.2.1.1	-	-	12 h	-	It is not possible to know
C.1.1.3	206.9%	181.0%	120.2%	-	150.6%
C.3.1.1	21.6%	100%	100%	-	21.4%
D.7.1	94%	96%	100%	-	27%
D.7.1.2	16%	6.4%	58%	-	23%
D.8.1	Yes	Yes	Yes	Yes	Yes

5.6. An Overview of the ETIS in VSS

Table 7 shows the percentages of indicators that VSS estimated for each category of the ETIS. For the categories of destination management, social and cultural impacts, and economic value, the calculated indicators were more than 50% of the complete list of indicators. Only 35% of the indicators of environmental impact were calculated, with the majority of these indicators associated with the enterprise survey that reflected serious problems relating to missing data and sample representativeness.

Table 7. Percentages of ETIS indicators calculated in the VSS project for each category of the ETIS.

Category	%
Destination management	67
Social and cultural impacts	50
Economic value	50
Environmental impact	35

The overall analysis of the ETIS showed that VSS could be considered a sustainable destination. Despite the extensive tourism in this area, residents did not perceive tourism as an intrusion into their personal lives; on the contrary, they believed that tourism helps to enhance the distinctiveness of the destination, strengthening its local identity, culture, and heritage. The tourists were very satisfied with their experiences in this destination, with more than a half of them returning within a 5-year period. In general, the high quality of the sea and territorial environments was confirmed using each of the environmental indicators.

Several insights emerge from the implementation of the ETIS in the VSS tourist destination. The first is that the different sources used to calculate the ETIS complement each other. For example, the official statistics did not reveal unregistered tourism supply, which could be explored using information provided by the municipalities on second/rental homes. Moreover, some indicators were objectively difficult to calculate in relation to missing data (e.g., when queried on the distance traveled in kilometers to and from a destination, a visitor would need to respond, and could decide whether or not to answer to the question). In addition, the surveying technique applied influenced the availability of respondents; whereas a survey administered personally allows for direct contact with respondents, it entails high costs and covers a limited area.

5.7. Conclusion of the Process of Implementing Indicators

A final sequence of PSG meetings, which was aimed at critically analyzing best practices in sustainable management and identifying areas for improvement, marked the conclusion of the VSS project. The GSTC indicators were first employed, followed by the ETIS indicators for assessing best practices relating to the environmental and social dimensions of sustainability. An environmental concern relating to the indiscriminate use of plastic bottles in the destination area was highlighted and discussed. The lack of tourism data on the economic dimension of sustainability (e.g., the contribution of tourism to the GDP) was also considered. Last, the PSG recognized that while the ETIS and similar methodologies promote responsible management, monitoring, and marketing of the tourism industry at the sub-national level, the key role of the destination coordinator in implementing the indicator systems cannot be neglected.

5.8. Highlights

From the onset of the implementation of the ETIS across Europe, the VSS PSG demonstrated an enduring commitment to pursue the EC initiative under the coordination of the University of Cagliari. Active and fully-fledged engagement within the ETIS entailed participation in events, meetings, and working groups, as shown in Table 8. The objective of this paragraph is to first demonstrate and subsequently explain the most important events in terms of outcomes that can be useful for strengthening awareness of the level of involvement that is needed for replication of the STPMS in other destinations.

Table 8. VSS events, meetings, and working groups associated with implementation of the ETIS.

Event	Place	Date	Content	Results
1	Bruxelles	22 February 2013	Launch of the ETIS	Knowledge on the ETIS
2	Cagliari	13 March 2013	Sustainable Tourism conference	PSG decision to start with international and European indicator systems implementation (GSTC and ETIS)
3	Bruxelles	19 April 2013	Expert Meeting	First discussions at the EU level on the problems that destinations encountered with the ETIS toolkit and its first implementation
4	Cagliari, Domus de Maria, Muravera, Pula and Villasimius	24 July–5 August 2013	PSG working group discussion	Discussion on the utility and availability of environmental, social and economic indicators based on GSTC criteria and indicators Early Adopters program
5	Cagliari	30 November 2013	Press release organized by PSG and University of Cagliari	Presentation of GSTC implementation and results
6	Rome	25 June 2014	Info day-European Tourism Indicator System. ETIS implementation in Italian Destinations. Conference organized by Lazio Region, Italian ETIS PoE in collaboration with the EC	EC ETIS implementation across Europe. Results from VSS and Cuneo Alps ETIS first pilot phase

Table 8. *Cont.*

Event	Place	Date	Content	Results
7	Bruxelles	4 July 2014	WORKSHOP—European Tourism Indicator System. The results of the first pilot testing phase: Exchanges of experiences	Presentation of the results of the 1 ETIS pilot phase from 6 selected destinations and presentation of the document of the overall results from the EC and ETIS PoE
8	Oristano	9 March 2015	Presentation of VSS project and STPMS	Involvement of PSG and students in ETIS data collection through 2015 surveys
9	Villasimius	29 April 2015	VSS DMO promotion with the participation of tourism enterprises	Presentation of ETIS surveys to PSG and distribution of the ETIS enterprise survey: Request of collaboration
10	Bruxelles (videoconference)	25 June 2015	ETIS pilot phases	Discussion between EC, ETIS PoE and destination representatives
11	Bruxelles (videoconference)	29 October 2015	ETIS pilot phases	Discussion between EC, ETIS PoE and destination representatives
12	Bruxelles	28 January 2016	ETIS and Accessible Tourism conference. Managing and promoting sustainable and accessible tourism destinations	EC release of the ETIS toolkit 2016. Presentation of VSS implementation of GSTC and ETIS indicators, difficulties and challenges.
13	Bruxelles	22 April 2016	ETIS Award	ETIS ceremony. Decision of the ETIS winners to continue their experience and share results through the establishment of the ETIS Destinations Network (EDN) leaded by VSS

More than 350 delegates from European countries participated in Event 1, which was organized by the EC. The ETIS was launched by the EC on 22 February 2013, and this initiative concluded on 22 April 2016 with the bestowal of the ETIS award. Whereas the 2016 ETIS toolkit has been implemented in specific destinations in Croatia, the UK, Italy, Spain, France, and other countries, without the coordination of the EC, its implementation at the level of Europe as a whole is still pending.

Event 2 can be considered as foundational for the VSS STPMS. International standards and indicators, such as GSTC and ETIS, were introduced to VSS mayors participating in the event. Tourism indicators were considered a means for acquiring and/or systematizing tourism data required for decision making. The plan was for the VSS project to be included in the GSTC Early Adopter initiative. However, at that time, fragmented modalities were being applied by VSS municipalities in an uncoordinated manner to compile tourism data.

Event 3 was the first to include exchanges among representatives of the EC and agencies at the tourist destination interested in ETIS implementation. At the inception of the ETIS, the system and toolkit were only available in the English language. This was emphatically viewed as a strong limitation, given that not all stakeholders at local levels may be conversant in English. Two key questions concerned the costs of ETIS implementation. The first concerned financial support provided by the EC and the second related to the implementation cost incurred at the destination. These questions were motivated by the generally limited resources available to municipalities for collecting tourism data. The ETIS pilot phases were developed on a voluntary basis in the selected destinations, with costs dependent on the implementation level of the ETIS system.

Event 4 was at the core of the overall STPMS. The focus of PSG meetings was contingent on the locations and special features within each municipality. Discussions held on economic indicators in the Cagliari municipality revealed a lack of relevant economic data related to tourism, which was also confirmed by the representative from the statistics office of the region of Sardinia. The PSG highlighted the need for collection of economic data at the municipal level and the use of indicator systems to achieve this objective. In the municipalities of Domus de Maria and Muravera, the meetings of the PSG focused on enterprises based on tourism and related sectors, and on the public sector.

The importance of utilizing indicators from the perspective of tourism enterprises was discussed. Enterprises acknowledged the need for data compilation, but in some cases, they observed that the implementation of sustainability practices constrained their business development. Discussions in the municipality of Pula focused on the social aspect of sustainability and related indicators, whereas those in the municipality of Villasimius focused on environmental indicators and their utility for the marine protected area. During PSG meetings held in 2013, primary stakeholders suggested new indicators that better fitted with the information needed for the management of the tourist destination and more accurately reflected its characteristics.

Event 5 involved the Sardinian media and press, whose attendance was required for broadcasting the results of the STPMS derived from the GSTC assessment. The EC produced a video highlighting the importance of the ETIS for sustainable destinations and the implementation of the Visit South Sardinia project.

Events 6 and 7 enabled sharing of the methodology for implementing the VSS project used during the first year (2013–2014) of ETIS implementation. In the absence of a dedicated office in the destination area for gathering tourism data relating to the construction of indicators, it was proposed, first of all, to restrict the level of implementation selectively to a limited number of geographical areas at the destination. Second, it was recommended that the number of indicators collected should be limited, starting with those that were easily available. After a period of testing the usefulness of the compiled indicators, it would then be possible to gradually extend the number of indicators collected and the areas of collection at the destination.

Events 8 and 9 were aimed at strengthening the PSG's awareness regarding a new 2015 ETIS phase, termed EC GROW ETIS (The term GROW derives from the name of the EC Directorate General (DG) GROWTH for Internal Market, Industries, Entrepreneurship and SMEs that was responsible for the ETIS in 2015) to enable collection of all data related to ETIS indicators through the administration of the ETIS surveys provided in the ETIS toolkit.

During Events 10 and 11, the EC and agencies at the destination site shared their experiences and suggested improvements relating to the indicators and the toolkit. Destinations that had not established a ST requested overall simplification of the system and a reduction in the number of indicators. VSS, following the implementation of the 2015 ETIS surveys, shared the finding that administration of the ETIS survey of residents took just 5 min per respondent, while surveying each tourist required 10 min. Nonetheless, in the absence of a ST, and insufficient human resources and knowledge of indicators at local levels, it is not possible for destinations to administer the preset number of questionnaires for achieving the objective of compiling the impacts of tourism impacts for decision making.

Considering the results of events 7, 10, and 11, and in light of the inputs of the pool of experts, the EC released the new ETIS 2016 toolkit at Event 12.

Event 13 marked the conclusion of the EC's commitment to the ETIS. During the award-giving ceremony, the EC representatives encouraged the VSS project to assume a leading position as an ETIS destination. Following the EC encouragement, the ETIS Destination Network (EDN) was established as an informal network in 2016 with the following two objectives: (1) To promote exchanges and augment experiences of measuring and monitoring sustainable tourism performances at the destination level through the use of a common methodology and tools, such as ETIS and/or other recognized European and/or international schemes; and (2) to benchmark and compare destinations. A final EDN-facilitated meeting was held at the University of Cagliari on 28 June 2018 in collaboration with the University of Surrey.

6. Conclusions and Discussion

The experience of implementing the ETIS in the VSS project within an Italian tourism destination provides insights on several critical issues. Firstly, it is objectively difficult to obtain statistical data at local levels in Italy. Statistical data are often not collected, and when they are, the methodologies usually differ, even for geographically proximate destinations. There is no codification of the methods used to collect statistical data at local levels. Another important constraint concerns the time taken to collect data. The delay in collecting statistical data concerning tourism performance, such as occupancy rate, the average daily rate, and the yield rate, is usually at least six months, and sometimes longer. For management purposes, this is a significant limitation that reduces the efficiency of the system. In sum, statistical data are not collected by following codified methodologies, which means that they are often not comparable, and they are not generated in a timely manner. The main consequence at the local level is the high cost of collecting statistical data, both in terms of time and financial resources. Such data should be collected periodically, but this requires an efficient system that has not yet been established in Italy, as demonstrated in the VSS case study.

Secondly, only a few of the surveyed enterprises completed the questionnaire (partially or fully). This finding suggests the need within future investigations for strengthening the involvement of the private sector in implementing the STPMS. Similarly, local administrators demonstrated different degrees of interest in realizing the system of indicators, revealing another area for future research.

Thirdly, as a consequence of the above two limitations, it was not possible for the VSS project to develop a governance system at the local level to promote more sustainable destination management using only the ETIS indicators toolkit. To achieve this aim, it proved necessary to implement the pioneering STPMS. This is an important finding, indicating that the ETIS should not be perceived merely as a statistical instrument. It should be an important driver for reducing gaps among different stakeholders, particularly at the local level, to create a shared vision of sustainable tourism. This requires the creation of a system for regulating destination management. In the case of the VSS project, the ETIS fulfilled its scope as an instrument with the capacity to bring and keep together different tourism stakeholders, but this was only possible through the use of the STPMS to ensure their cooperation.

Fourthly, the VSS experience highlights the key role of the destination coordinator, for the success of the project. The destination coordinator must perform more activities than those foreseen by ETIS. Because local stakeholders do not have the tools, not even the organizational ones, to continue the project independently. This represents a great weakness of the whole ETIS system. For this reason, it is important that ETIS projects are supported by institutions (such as universities, research centers, etc.), that they are able to raise funds, train staff, etc., as local stakeholders cannot implement indicator systems independently.

The above findings reveal the importance of working with stakeholders within a territory to simplify the indicators toolkit and improve the statistical culture and implementation of joint procedures, supported by new technologies that facilitate the collection of statistical data.

At the EU level, it is necessary to facilitate the implementation of standard indicator systems to increase sustainability policies and facilitate planning processes. The indicator systems must also encourage the development of practical methodologies that support the simple use of indicators. Only through the development of appropriate methodologies it is possible to optimize the results obtained from the implementation of indicator systems. We recommend simplifying the ETIS in consideration of the organizational characteristics of local stakeholders.

The use of recognized and relatively simple indicator systems allows comparability between different local experiences. Comparability is an essential prerequisite for the adoption of best practice at local, regional, national and international levels. The implementation of best practice, through evaluation of indicator systems, can be a significant support for both public and private planning processes.

The VSS experience shows that the lack of reliability and timeliness in the collected data may undermine the quality of some indicators. This is important in ETIS, having been conceived as a tool to implement and monitor sustainable policies at local level with respect to the objectives proposed by the EU.

To be effective in planning policies at the local level, it is essential to have reliable and accurate indicators. This requires the investment of considerable resources for data collection which are not often available locally. The lack of resources therefore makes the indicators less reliable and consequently less used, which may be to the detriment of local planning policies

In an area where data gathering can be problematic, indicator systems can still afford significant insight into public and private planning, although in the absence of sufficient hard data, caution must be exercised in the interpretation of these indicators. We recommend the continuity of the project so that, at the local level, both public and private actors can obtain valid insights into the local planning processes via the evaluation of indicator systems.

In summary, when implementing the ETIS, the VSS project relied on the STPMS to achieve the expected results. Following the revisions made to the ETIS in 2016, it would be advantageous for the EC to improve the indicator toolkit in light of the results of the implementation of new voluntary pilots in destinations across Europe. However, it is essential to first improve data collection techniques and procedures.

Any destination seeking to implement the ETIS toolkit or a similar methodology should be cognizant of the associated challenges. The lessons from this case study are of particular relevance at the municipal level. Our findings contribute to a better understanding of the ETIS as a globally recognized standard for developing best practices in monitoring the impacts of tourism. Though it clearly has great potential, this instrument is not yet sufficiently developed to achieve tangible outcomes reflecting the enhancement of sustainable cultures at local levels.

Author Contributions: The authors have contributed equally to research design and development, data analysis, and writing the paper. The authors have read and approved the final manuscript.

funding: This research received no external funding.

Acknowledgments: The project presented in this paper has been supported by the municipalities of VSS, Area Marina Protetta Capo Carbonara, Università di Cagliari and Fondazione Banco di Sardegna. We also thank the academic editor and the two anonymous reviewers for their constructive comments.

Conflicts of Interest: The authors declare no conflict of interest.

Appendix A

Table A1. ETIS indicators. Note. Adapted from Reference [6].

Section A:	Destination Management
A.1	**Sustainable Tourism Public Policy**
A.1.1	Percentage of the destination with a sustainable tourism strategy/action plan, with agreed monitoring, development control and evaluation arrangement
A.1.1.1	Percentage of residents satisfied with their involvement and their influence in the planning and development of tourism
A.1.1.2	Percentage of the destination represented by a destination management organization
A.2	**Sustainable Tourism Management in Tourism Enterprises**
A.2.1	Percentage of tourism enterprises/establishments in the destination using a voluntary verified certification/labelling for environmental/quality/sustainability and/or Corporate Social Responsibility (CSR) measures
A.2.2.1	Number of tourism enterprises/establishments with sustainability reports in accordance with the Global Reporting Initiative (GRI)
A.3	**Customer Satisfaction**
A.3.1	Percentage of visitors that are satisfied with their overall experience in the destination
A.3.1.1	Percentage of repeat/return visitors (within 5 years)
A.4	**Information and Communication**
A.4.1	The percentage of visitors who note that they are aware of destination sustainability efforts
A.4.1.1	The percentage of businesses that communicate their sustainability efforts to visitors in their products, marketing, or branding

Table A1. *Cont.*

Section B:	Economic Value
B.1	**Tourism Flow (volume and value) at Destination**
B.1.1	Number of tourist nights per month
B.1.1.1	Relative contribution of tourism to the destination's economy (% GDP)
B.1.1.2	Number of 'same day' visitors in high season and low season
B.1.1.3	Daily spending per same day visitor
B.1.2	Daily spending per tourist (accommodation, food and drinks, other services)
B.2	**Tourism Enterprise(s) Performance**
B.2.1	Average length of stay of tourists (nights)
B.2.1.1	Average length of stay of same day visitors (hours)
B.2.1.2	Percentage of ten largest tourism enterprises involved in destination management/cooperative marketing
B.2.2	Occupancy rate in commercial accommodation per month and average for the year
B.2.2.1	Average price per room in the destination
B.3	**Quantity and Quality of Employment**
B.3.1	Direct tourism employment as percentage of total employment in the destination
B.3.1.1	Percentage of jobs in tourism that are seasonal
B.3.1.2	Percentage of tourism enterprises providing student internships
B.4	**Safety and Health**
B.4.1	Percentage of tourism enterprises inspected for fire safety in the last year
B.4.1.1	Percentage of tourists who register a complaint with the police
B.5	**Tourism Supply Chain**
B.5.1	Percentage of tourism enterprises actively taking steps to source local, sustainable, and fair trade goods and services
B.5.1.1	Percentage of the destination covered by a policy promoting local, sustainable and/or fair trade products and services
B.5.1.2	Percentage of tourism enterprises sourcing a minimum of 25% of food and drink from local/regional producers
Section C:	Social and Cultural Impact
C.1	**Community/Social Impact**
C.1.1	Number of tourists/visitors per 100 residents
C.1.1.1	Percentage of residents who are satisfied with tourism in the destination (per month/season)
C.1.1.2	Number of beds available in commercial visitor accommodation per 100 residents
C.1.1.3	Number of second/rental homes per 100 homes
C.2	**Gender Equality**
C.2.1	Percentage of men and women employed in the tourism sector
C.2.1.1	Percentage of tourism enterprises where the general manager position is held by a woman
C.2.1.2	Average wage in tourism for women compared to average wage for men (sorted by tourism job type)
C.3	**Equality/Accessibility**
C.3.1	Percentage of commercial accommodation with rooms accessible to people with disabilities and/or participating in recognized accessibility schemes
C.3.1.1	Percentage of destination served by public transport that is accessible to people with disabilities and people with specific access requirements
C.3.2	Percentage of visitor attractions that are accessible to people with disabilities and/or participating in recognized accessibility schemes
C.3.2.1	Percentage of visitors satisfied with the accessibility of the destination for those with disabilities or specific access requirements
C.4	**Protecting and Enhancing Cultural Heritage, Local Identity and Assets**
C.4.1	Percentage of the destination covered by a policy or plan that protects cultural heritage
C.4.1.1	Percentage of residents who have positive or negative views on the impact of tourism on destination identity
C.4.1.2	Percentage of the destination's biggest events that are focused on traditional/local culture and assets

Table A1. *Cont.*

Section D:	Environmental Impact
D.1	**Reducing Transport Impact**
D.1.1	Percentage of tourists and same day visitors using different modes of transport to arrive at the destination (public/private and type)
D.1.1.1	Percentage of visitors using local/soft mobility/public transport services to get around the destination
D.1.2	Average travel (km) by tourists to and from home or average travel (km) from the previous destination to the current destination
D.1.2.1	Average travel (km) by same day visitors from and to destination
D.2	**Climate Change**
D.2.1	Percentage of tourism enterprises involved in climate change mitigation schemes—such as: CO_2 offset, low energy systems, etc.—and "adaptation" responses and actions
D.2.1.1	Percentage of the destination included in climate change adaptation strategy or planning
D.2.1.2	Percentage of tourism accommodation and attraction infrastructure located in "vulnerable zones."
D.3	**Solid Waste Management**
D.3.1	Waste volume produced by destination (tonnes per resident per year or per month)
D.3.1.1	Percentage of tourism enterprises separating different types of waste
D.3.2	Volume of waste recycled (percent or per resident per year)
D.4	**Sewage Treatment**
D.4.1	Percentage of sewage from the destination treated to at least secondary level prior to discharge
D.4.1.1	Percentage of commercial accommodation connected to central sewage system and/or employing tertiary sewage treatment
D.5	**Water Management**
D.5.1	Fresh water consumption per tourist night compared to general population water consumption per person night
D.5.1.1	Percentage of tourism enterprises with low-flow shower heads and taps and/or dual flush toilets/waterless urinals
D.5.1.2	Percentage of tourism enterprises using recycled water
D.5.1.3	Percentage of water use derived from recycled water in the destination
D.6	**Energy Usage**
D.6.1	Energy consumption per tourist night compared to general population energy consumption per person night
D.6.1.1	Percentage of tourism enterprises that have switched to low-energy lighting
D.6.1.2	Annual amount of energy consumed from renewable sources (Mwh) as a percentage of overall energy consumption
D.7	**Landscape and Biodiversity Protection**
D.7.1	Percentage of destination (area in km^2) that is designated for protection
D.7.1.1	Percentage of local enterprises in the tourism sector actively supporting protection, conservation, and management of local biodiversity and landscapes.
D.7.1.2	Percentage of destination covered by a biodiversity management and monitoring plan
D.8	**Light and Noise Management**
D.8.1	The destination has policies in place that require tourism enterprises to minimize light and noise pollution
D.8.1.1	Percentage of the destination and percentage of population covered by local strategy and/or plans to reduce noise and light pollution
D.9	**Bathing Water Quality**
D.9.1	Level of contamination per 100 mL (fecal coliforms, campylobacter)
D.9.1.1	Number of days beach/shore closed due to contamination

References

1. Bramwell, B.; Higham, J.; Lane, B.; Miller, G. Twenty-five years of sustainable tourism and the Journal of Sustainable Tourism: Looking back and moving forward. *J. Sustain. Tour.* **2017**, *25*, 1–9. [CrossRef]

2.	Hall, C.M. Framing behavioural approaches to understanding and governing sustainable tourism consumption: Beyond neoliberalism, "nudging" and "green growth"? *J. Sustain. Tour.* **2013**, *21*, 1091–1109. [CrossRef]

3.	Miller, G. The development of indicators for sustainable tourism: Results of a Delphi survey of tourism researchers. *Tour. Manag.* **2001**, *22*, 351–362. [CrossRef]

4.	Torres-Delgado, A.; Lopez Palomeque, F. Measuring Sustainable Tourism at the Municipal Level. *Ann. Tour. Res.* **2014**, *49*, 122–137. [CrossRef]

5.	Torres-Delgado, A.; Saarinen, J. Using indicators to assess sustainable tourism development: A review. *Tour. Geogr.* **2014**, *16*, 31–47. [CrossRef]

6.	European Commission. *European Tourism Indicator System for Sustainable Destinations—Detailed Indicator Reference Sheets*; European Union: Brussels, Belgium, 2013.

7.	European Commission. *Communication Europe, the World's No 1 Tourist Destination—A New Political Framework for Tourism in Europe*; European Union: Bruxels, Belgium, 2010.

8.	Sistema Informativo di Raccolta ed Elaborazione Dati SIRED. 2018. Available online: http://osservatorio. sardegnaturismo.it/sites/default/files/2018-06/OsservatorioTurismoreport2017online_20180517_0.pdf (accessed on 4 June 2018).

9.	European Commission. *European Tourism Indicator System for Sustainable Destinations*; European Union: Bruxels, Belgium, 2016.

10.	Hunter, C. Sustainable tourism as an adaptive paradigm. *Ann. Tour. Res.* **1997**, *24*, 850–867. [CrossRef]

11.	Daly, H.; Cobb, J.B. *For the Common Good: Restructuring the Economy toward Community, the Environment and a Sustainable Future*; Beacon Press: Boston, MA, USA, 1989.

12.	Pepper, D. *The Roots of Modern Environmentalism*; Croom Helm: London, UK, 1984.

13.	Trainer, T. A Rejection of the Brundtland Report. *IFAD Dossier* **1990**, *77*, 71–84.

14.	Butler, R.W. Sustainable tourism—A state of the art review. *Tour. Geogr.* **1999**, *1*, 7–25. [CrossRef]

15.	Sinclair, D.; Jayawardena, C. The development of sustainable tourism in the Guianas. *Int. J. Contemp. Hosp. Manag.* **2003**, *15*, 402–407. [CrossRef]

16.	Butler, R.W. Tourism, environment, and sustainable development. *Environ. Conserv.* **1991**, *18*, 201–209. [CrossRef]

17.	Dowling, R. An Environmentally-Based Planning Model for Regional Tourism Development. *J. Sustain. Plan. Model Reg. Tour. Dev. Tour.* **1993**, *1*, 17–37. [CrossRef]

18.	Eagles, P.F.J. Understanding the market for sustainable tourism. In *Linking Tourism, the Environment and Sustainability*; McCool, S.F., Watson, A.E., Eds.; General Technical Report INT-GTR-323; USDA Service Center: Ogden, UT, USA, 1994; pp. 23–33.

19.	Farrel, B. Tourism as an Element in Sustainable Development: Hana, Maui. In *Tourism Alternatives*; Smith, V., Eadington, W., Eds.; University of Pennsylvania Press: Philadelphia, PA, USA, 1992.

20.	Forsyth, T. *Sustainable Tourism: Moving from Theory to Practice*; World Wildlife Fund/Tourism Concern: Godalming, UK, 1996.

21.	Hunter, C. Environmental impact assessment and tourism Development. In *Tourism and the Environment: A Sustainable Relationship?* Hunter, C., Green, H., Eds.; Routledge: London, UK, 1995.

22.	Lane, B. Sustainable Rural Tourism strategies: A Tool for Development and Conservation. *J. Sustain. Tour.* **1994**, *2*, 102–111. [CrossRef]

23.	McCool, S.F. Linking tourism, the environment, and concepts of sustainability: Setting the stage. In *Linking Tourism, the Environment and Sustainability*; McCool, S.F., Watson, A.E., Eds.; General Technical Report INT-GTR-323; USDA Service Center: Ogden, UT, USA, 1994; pp. 3–7.

24.	McKercher, B. Some fundamental truths about tourism: Understanding tourism's social and environmental impacts. *J. Sustain. Tour.* **1993**, *1*, 6–16. [CrossRef]

25.	Sanson, L. An Ecotourism Case Study in Sub-Antarctic Island. *Ann. Tour. Res.* **1994**, *21*, 344–354. [CrossRef]

26.	Wheeller, B. Sustaining the ego. *J. Sustain. Tour.* **1993**, *1*, 121–129. [CrossRef]

27.	Morgan, M. Dressing up to survive: Marketing Majorca Anew. *Tour. Manag.* **1991**, *12*, 15–20. [CrossRef]

28.	Owen, R.E.; Witt, S.; Gammon, S. Sustainable Tourism Development in Wales: From Theory to Practice. *Tour. Manag.* **1993**, *14*, 463–474. [CrossRef]

29.	Sanchez, C.I.; Jaramillo-Hurtado, M.E. Policies for enhancing sustainability and competitiveness in tourism in Colombia. *Worldw. Hosp. Tour. Themes* **2010**, *2*, 153–162. [CrossRef]

30. May, V. Tourism, environment and development—Values, sustainability and stewardship. *Tour. Manag.* **1991**, *12*, 112–118. [CrossRef]

31. Stocking, M.; Perkin, S. Conservation-with-Development: An application of the concept in the Usambara Mountains, Tanzania. *Trans. Inst. Br. Geogr.* **1992**, *17*, 337–349. [CrossRef]

32. Pretty, J.; Pimbert, M. Beyond Conservation Ideology and the Wilderness Myth. *Nat. Resour.* **1995**, *19*, 5–14.

33. Oreja Rodriguez, J.R.; Yanes-Estevez, V.; Parra Lopez, E. The sustainability of island destinations: Tourism area life cycle and teleological perspectives. The Case of Tenerife. *Tour. Manag.* **2008**, *29*, 53–65. [CrossRef]

34. Spenceley, A. Requirements for Sustainable Nature-based Tourism in Transfrontier Conservation Areas: A Southern African Delphi Consultation. *Tour. Geogr.* **2008**, *10*, 285–311. [CrossRef]

35. Woodside, G.; Dubelaar, C. A General Theory of Tourism Consumption Systems: A Conceptual Framework and an Empirical Exploration. *J. Travel Res.* **2002**, *41*, 120–132. [CrossRef]

36. Twining-Ward, L.; Butler, R. Implementing STD on a Small Island: Development and Use of Sustainable Tourism Development Indicators in Samoa. *J. Sustain. Tour.* **2002**, *10*, 363–387. [CrossRef]

37. Nijkamp, P.; Van der Bergh, C.J.M.; Soeteman, F.J. Regional Sustainable Development and Natural Resource Use. In Proceedings of the World Bank Annual Conference on Development Economics, Washington, DC, USA, 26–27 April 1990.

38. Swarbrooke, J. *Sustainable Tourism Management*; CABI Publishing: Wallingford, UK, 1999.

39. Carley, M. *Social Measurement and Social Indicators: Issues of Policy and Theory*; George Allen and Unwin: London, UK, 1981.

40. Hart, S. Beyond Greening: Strategies for a Sustainable World. *Harvard Business Review.* January–February 1997, pp. 67–76. Available online: https://hbr.org/1997/01/beyond-greening-strategies-for-a-sustainable-world (accessed on 2 September 2018).

41. Van Esch, S. Indicators for the Environment Programme in the Netherlands. In *Sustainability Indicators: Report of the Project on Indicators of Sustainable Development*; Moldan, B., Bilharz, S., Eds.; Wiley & Sons: Chichester, UK, 1997.

42. Bramwell, B.; Henry, I.; Jackson, G.; Prat, A.G.; Richards, G.; Van der Straaten, J. (Eds.) *Sustainable Tourism Management: Principles and Practice*; Tilburg University Press: Tilburg, The Netherlands, 1996.

43. Eber, S. *Beyond the Green Horizon: A Discussion Paper on Principles for Sustainable Tourism*; Worldwide Fund for Nature: Godalming, UK, 1992.

44. Gerken, G. *Die Geburt der Neuen Kultur—Vom Industrialismus zum Light-Age*; ECON Verlag: Dusseldorf, Germany; Wien, Austria; New York, NY, USA, 1988.

45. McIntyre, G. *Sustainable Tourism Development: Guide for Local Planners*; World Tourism Organization (WTO): Madrid, Spain, 1993.

46. World Travel & Tourism Council (WTTC); World Tourism Organization (WTO); Earth Council. *Agenda 21 for the Travel & Tourism Industry*; World Travel & Tourism Council: London, UK, 1996.

47. Dymond, S.J. Indicators of sustainable tourism in New Zealand: A local government perspective. *J. Sustain. Tour.* **1997**, *5*, 279–293. [CrossRef]

48. Goodall, B.; Stabler, M.J. Principles Influencing the Determination of Environmental Standards for Sustainable Tourism. In *Tourism & Sustainability: Principles to Practice*; Stabler, M.J., Ed.; CAB International: Wallingford, UK, 1997.

49. Gunn, C.A. *Tourism Planning*, 2nd ed.; Taylor and Frances: Washington, DC, USA, 1988.

50. Moisey, R.N.; McCool, S.F. Sustainable tourism in the 21st century: Lessons from the past: Challenges to address. In *Tourism Recreation and Sustainability*; McCool, S.F., Moisey, R.N., Eds.; CAB International: Oxford, UK, 2001; pp. 343–352.

51. Mowforth, A.; Munt, I. *Tourism and Sustainability: New Tourism in the Third World*; Routledge: London, UK, 1998.

52. Weaver, D.B. Introduction to ecotourism. In *Ecotourism in the Less Developed World*; Weaver, D.B., Ed.; CAB International: Wallingford, UK, 1998; pp. 1–33.

53. Buckley, R. Sustainable tourism: Research and reality. *Ann. Tour. Res.* **2012**, *39*, 528–546. [CrossRef]

54. Spangenberg, J.H. Environmental space and the prism of sustainability: Frameworks for indicators measuring sustainable development. *Ecol. Indic.* **2002**, *2*, 295–309. [CrossRef]

55. Liu, Z. Sustainable Tourism Development: A critique. *J. Sustain. Tour.* **2003**, *11*, 459–475. [CrossRef]

56. Tudorache, D.M.; Simon, T.; Frent, C.; Musteață-Pavel, M. Difficulties and Challenges in Applying the European Tourism Indicators System (ETIS) for Sustainable Tourist Destinations: The Case of Brașov County in the Romanian Carpathians. *Sustainability* **2017**, *9*, 1879. [CrossRef]
57. Zamfir, A.; Corbos, R.A. Towards Sustainable Tourism Development in Urban Areas: Case Study on Bucharest as Tourist Destination. *Sustainability* **2015**, *7*, 12709–12722. [CrossRef]
58. Zabetta, M.C.; Sacerdotti, S.L.; Mauro, S. Community-based monitoring in tourism sector: An application of the European Tourism Indicators System, in the "A.T.L. del Cuneese". In *Leadership and Governance for Sustainable Tourism: Proceeding of Summer School 2014*; Keskinarkaus, S., Matilainen, A., Barbone, S., Makela, A.-M., Eds.; University of Helsinki, Ruralia Insitute: Helsinki, Finland, 2014.
59. Cannas, R.; Theuma, N. Strategies and tools for sustainable tourism destination management: Applying the European Tourism Indicator System in Malta. In Proceedings of the International Conference on Tourism (ICOT 2013)—Trends, Impacts and Policies on Sustainable Tourism Development, Limassol, Cyprus, 5–8 June 2013; Andriotis, K., Ed.; International Association for Tourism Policy: Patras, Greece, 2013.
60. Iunius, R.; Cismaru, L.; Foris, D. Raising Competitiveness for Tourist Destinations through Information Technologies within the Newest Tourism Action Framework Proposed by the European Commission. *Sustainability* **2015**, *7*, 12891–12909. [CrossRef]
61. Byrd, E.T.; Cárdenes, D.A.; Greenwood, J.B. Factors of stakeholder understanding of tourism: The case of Eastern North Carolina. *Tour. Hosp. Res.* **2008**, *8*, 192–204. [CrossRef]
62. European Commission. *The European Tourism Indicator System—ETIS Toolkit for Sustainable Destination Management*; Publications Office of the European Union: Luxembourg, 2013.
63. Kalsbeek, W.D. Sampling minority groups in health surveys. *Stat. Med.* **2003**, *22*, 1527–1549. [CrossRef] [PubMed]

MDPI

St. Alban-Anlage 66

4052 Basel

Switzerland

Tel. +41 61 683 77 34

Fax +41 61 302 89 18

www.mdpi.com

Sustainability Editorial Office

E-mail: sustainability@mdpi.com

www.mdpi.com/journal/sustainability

www.ingramcontent.com/pod-product-compliance
Lightning Source LLC
Chambersburg PA
CBHW051857210326
41597CB00033B/5937